DO NOT REMOVE
CARDS FROM POCKET

ALLEN COUNTY PUBLIC LIBRARY

FORT WAYNE, INDIANA 46802

You may return this book to any agency, branch,
or bookmobile of the Allen County Public Library.

Rx for Recovery

The Medical and Health Guide
for Alcoholics, Addicts
and Their Families

JEFFREY WEISBERG, M.D.
and
GENE HAWES

FRANKLIN WATTS
New York □ Toronto □ 1989

Notice to the Reader: This book presents guidance not otherwise available in print on crucial questions for men and women recovering from alcohol or drug abuse, and for their families. Findings and recommendations in it are drawn from extensive clinical experience and many case histories and are presented here as general information both for the reader and for interested medical practitioners. Obviously, the content of the book cannot possibly serve as medical treatment. On any questions of medical care, readers should consult thoroughly informed and competent physicians.

All names of medications presented throughout the book with the initial letter or letters of their names capitalized are trade names or registered trade marks of their producers and/or distributors.

Library of Congress Number: 88-51593
ISBN 0-531-15096-8

Printed in the United States of America

6 5 4 3 2 1

Dedicated
to
Alcoholics Anonymous
the fellowship that, as we have learned,
invented recovery
and recreates it every day

. . . and dedicated also
to
John Wylie
and
Jeffrey Foxx

Acknowledgments

RESEARCH IN RELEVANT LITERATURE, SURVEYS, AND ESPECIALLY A great many interviews with individuals recovering from alcoholism or drug addiction were used to develop the material presented in this book. Many interviews were carried out with members of Alcoholics Anonymous (AA) and of such related recovery programs as Narcotics Anonymous and Cocaine Anonymous. Material in the book is also extensively based on case histories of individuals treated by Dr. Weisberg in the course of his medical practice.

The identities of individuals involved in the case histories or interviewed as alcoholics/addicts have been altered in the book to render them unrecognizable. We have done this both to protect the confidentiality of the physician-patient relationship, and to support the principle of anonymity in AA and other recovery programs. To each individual whose experience contributes so invaluably to the book, we feel immensely grateful. We're sure each individual in turn appreciates our respect for her or his anonymity.

Selected treatment centers for alcoholism/addiction throughout the United States and Canada generously responded to the original survey we made especially for the book. Information they supplied appears in the directory of treatment centers in Appendix 2. We very much appreciate their public-spirited cooperation.

Certain individuals who can be identified helped us in special ways. Barbara Stanton, a credentialed alcoholism counselor with the National Council on Alcoholism and Other Drug Addictions/Westchester, Inc., was wonderfully generous in providing much essential advice and interview material. Geri Franklin, an accomplished writer, assisted with the research and drafting of Chapter 7, "Women in Recovery and Their Special Needs." Harry Evarts similarly aided with the research and drafting of Chapter 6, "Avoiding Special Hazards with Medicines." To each of them, heartfelt thanks.

Individuals on the staffs of several treatment centers aided by generously advising us on the directory of treatment centers. These individuals are Charles L. Beem of The Caron Foundation in Wernersville, Pennsylvania; Dori J. Dysland of the Alcohol and Drug Recovery Center at Sequoia Hospital in Redwood City, California; Gerald Horowitz of the Smithers Alcoholism Treatment and Training Center in New York, New York; and Susan Stevens of the Betty Ford Center at Eisenhower Medical Center, Rancho Mirage, California.

Organizations and agencies were also most cooperative in providing information. Those that furnished generous assistance include Alcoholics Anonymous World Services office; the National Council on Alcoholism central office; Al-Anon Family Groups Headquarters; the American Medical Society on Alcoholism and Other Drug Dependencies; the Center of Alcohol Studies at Rutgers, the State University of New Jersey; the National Institute on Alcohol Abuse and Alcoholism; and the National Institute on Drug Abuse.

To all these and others who helped, we express most grateful appreciation.

—J. A. W., G. R.

Contents

Introduction

IT WAS YEARS AGO THAT I FIRST BECAME AWARE OF AN UNDERGROUND epidemic. As an emergency medicine specialist in the 1970s, I treated acute intoxication, drug overdoses, drug-induced psychiatric catastrophes, alcohol withdrawal, convulsions, delirium tremens, drug-related trauma, cocaine psychosis, alcoholic cardiac and liver disease, narcotic-induced respiratory arrest, drug-related family crises, acute esophageal hemorrhage, and on and on. I was constantly faced with desperate people locked in their addiction. Some pretended to have physical ailments in order to obtain prescription drugs; others became victims of tragic disability and death as the result of untethered drug and alcohol abuse.

There seemed to be little awareness of or focus on the source of all this human chaos. The medical world saw hepatitis, broken bones, and drug withdrawal symptoms. More socially oriented professionals saw placement problems, family disorder, and domestic abuse. Cultural critics discussed the reasons for increased "recreational" drug use—and the suffering continued.

As my career progressed, I at one point had the opportunity to participate in organizing an alcohol and drug rehabilitation program. This gave me my first insight into alcoholism and drug addiction as primary pathology. My clinical interest was awakened, and over the years since that time, I have observed and treated alcoholics and drug addicts with ever-increasing interest and understanding.

I have worked with alcoholism and drug counselors, consulted with recovering alcoholics and addicts, and explored the literature. But more than any of this, the clinical arena has been where my ideas, understanding, and positions have taken form. I have formulated my views of alcoholism and drug addiction from observing patients and others over the years, and from listening carefully to their stories.

It is clinical evidence which convinces me that this affliction is a disease. It is clinical evidence which tells me that the alcoholic or addict is never cured and can only arrest the disease. It is clinical evidence which has shown me that the recovering alcoholic/addict can never again take a mood-altering substance without risk to his or her sobriety. And it is clinical experience which has taught me that the recovering alcoholic/addict must interact with the medical world in a way designed to protect sobriety.

In my private practice I am continually faced with questions regarding medical aspects of recovery. Often, these inquiries center around the safety of taking certain medications; often, the questions involve more subtle issues. I have paid close attention to these questions, as I have to the clinical course of active addiction and recovery.

I have come to believe that a general reference is needed to address certain of these issues. The ever-expanding recovering community needs more accessible answers regarding matters of vital interest. Mr. Hawes and I agreed that such information would be valuable, not only to recovering people themselves, but to their families, their physicians, and everyone with any involvement in alcoholism or drug addiction. What follows, then, is a personal and clinical assessment. Alcohol and drug addiction is an epidemic that is no longer underground.

—Jeffrey A. Weisberg

Chappaqua, New York
January 1989

More than three decades and thirty books ago, I started writing books that readers could use to improve their lives and themselves. I like to do books which help with especially important personal problems of the times. Many of my early books guided people through the remarkable opportunities opened to them by an amazing social invention that was then rapidly expanding and improving—college education in America.

Many later books helped people find their way with optimum personal fulfillment within one of the most dynamic and intricate social organizations of all time—the American economy. These were books on careers: career choice and career change.

Now, in the 1980s, my books more often help people make the most lifesaving—and life-giving—decisions for themselves. These are books in one of the most personal and revolutionary areas of all, health and medicine. A recent example, written with Dr. Ruth Watson Lubic, is *Childbearing: A Book of Choices*.

Lifesaving and life giving are truly the ultimate aims here. Nothing less than continued survival is at stake for those who need the many observations that the book puts into print for the first time. This is the survival of yourself, if you are among the two million or more Americans recovering from alcoholism or drug addiction. This is the survival of someone you love, if you are among the members of the *one in every four* American families found in surveys to have heart-rending troubles due to alcohol or drug abuse.

Knowing what is in this book can spell survival because, once developed, alcoholism or drug addiction proves fatal in most cases unless the victim begins recovery by absolute abstinence. Alcoholism and drug addiction are also incurable because, if the recovering victim fails to continue absolute abstinence, addiction resumes.

Indeed, unguarded intake of any mood-altering substance can reactivate addiction. And when it resumes it is usually worse than before—with acceleration of irresistible and ultimately fatal self-poisoning.

The essentials for survival given in the book are primarily the answers to all the major medical and health problems that can threaten and destroy recovery. In addition, the book answers all main questions that bear on how best to promote recovery and the restoration of good health. The book also explains the most effective ways to begin recovery or to help an alcoholic/addict to begin.

Appendix 1 guides you to sources of help and information, providing the names, addresses, phone numbers, and help of the main recovery organizations throughout the country, such as Alcoholics Anonymous, Narcotics Anonymous, Al-Anon Family Groups, Alateen, Cocaine Anonymous, and the National Council on Alcoholism. It also identifies other books and publications to consult for further knowledge. Appendix 2 is a directory of leading treatment centers from which you can get help to begin recovery in any part of the United States and Canada.

For what help it might bring to alcoholics or addicts and their families, I've personally found great satisfaction in coauthoring the book. I'm especially glad to have been able to write it with the indispensable and superb collaboration of my neighbor and friend, Dr. Weisberg.

—Gene R. Hawes

January 1989
Chappaqua, New York

CHAPTER 1

Reaching for Recovery: A Medical Perspective

ALCOHOLISM, AS A PHENOMENON, HAS ALWAYS HAD A HIGH PROFILE IN OUR culture. Whether it involved the tragic hero or the town drunk in our cinema, a literary or political celebrity in our current affairs, or, more recently, unique athletic talent gone to ruin, the phenomenon of alcoholism has been a major presence in society.

What is this phenomenon? Is it merely a random selection of people who consume too much alcohol? True, everyone would agree that alcohol plays a major role in defining alcoholism, but doesn't it seem that there must be something more involved here? Why are these particular people afflicted? They are so different from one another in most respects. Do they simply lack willpower? Is that what First Lady Betty Ford, actor Jason Robards, Congressman Wilbur Mills, guitarist/singer Pete Townshend of The Who rock group, actresses Elizabeth Taylor and Liza Minelli, and Dodgers pitcher Don Newcombe have in common? When we look at these people, we see they often have considerable discipline and willpower in other areas of their lives.

What, then, is going on? Is it that this group of people represents a selection of individuals who lack willpower only when it comes to alcohol? Does this simple, common characteristic account for the tragedy of alcoholism and the massive impact alcoholism has had on the society, the family, and the workplace in our culture?

The authors think not. It is our clinical judgment that alcoholism is a complex disease, one not characterized by a lack of willpower, but by interrelating physiologic and emotional factors that create a destructive compulsion. We are aware that there may be some controversy about this position, but the American Medical Association has accepted alcoholism as a disease since 1956—and, for all practical purposes, we feel solid in the position that alcoholism or drug addiction is a disease.

Extensive clinical evidence supports this position. In medical practice, alcoholism is seen frequently. Once recognized, the dynamics and prognosis of the disease are very predictable. It is chronic, progressive, and, in the end, fatal. Indeed, other diseases (which are easily accepted as such) are often less predictable.

For example, I recall a patient, Phil W., who came to me with a swollen knee. As part of his evaluation, blood tests were performed, and he had positive test results that indicated rheumatoid arthritis. His father had had the same disease. The diagnosis was clear. When Phil asked what he could expect as time went on, I told him that usually symmetrical joints become involved with pain and swelling of varying degrees. There are medicines and physical measures to help, I said, but often deformity results. I did say that every situation is different, however, and we'd just have to wait and see. The swelling in Phil's knee went down within two weeks, and he has had no symptoms of rheumatoid arthritis since. That was eight years ago.

The point here is that had Phil come to me instead with a deteriorating marriage and depression related to drinking too much, I would have been able to predict his future much more accurately. "If you continue to drink," I would have said, "your marriage will become unsalvageable. You'll become isolated and lonely, filled with self-disgust and fear. You will begin to drink every night until you pass out, and there will be nothing in your life besides work and drinking. You won't have any fun in life; you'll be beseiged by problems that seem insurmountable, and soon you'll have trouble at work. Your liver tests will show alcoholic hepatitis; you'll develop gastritis or ulcers, and then more serious consequences. Finally, if you keep drinking, in time there will be a critical or fatal event, either a medical catastrophe or a fatal accident."

This clinical predictability is uncannily accurate. We invariably see a complex pattern of emotional and physical circumstances that leads to a compulsion to drink a toxic chemical which then sets up a cascade of events that, without fail, result in the deterioration of one's physical, social, and emotional health.

The hereditary character of alcoholism is clear, supporting the definition of alcoholism as a disease. A classic forty-five-year long-itudinal study of alcoholism found that more than three times as many men with relatives who abuse alcohol developed alcohol dependence, compared to men with no relatives who abuse alcohol. (This was reported in *The Natural History of Alcoholism*, by George E. Vaillant in 1983.) Another classic study of careful design analyzed alcoholism among two groups of Danish men who had been adopted in early infancy by nonrelatives. One group consisted of men with at least one alcoholic biological parent. The second, matched group consisted of men with biological parents who were not alcoholics. Four times as many men with an alcoholic biological parent became alcoholics. In addition, there was no consistent relationship between alcoholism in adoptive parents and alcoholism in the adopted sons—suggesting that environmental factors were inconsequential compared to hereditary factors. (Goodwin, Donald W., F. Schul-singer, L. Hermansen, S. B. Guze, and G. Winokur, "Alcohol Problems in Adoptees Raised Apart from Biological Parents," *Archives of General Psychiatry*, 1973, 28:238–243.) In all, more than one hundred scientific studies on the genetic character of alcoholism have been made. More currently under way include research projects finding characteristic patterns of brain-wave output and hormonal production that distinguish sons and daughters of alcoholics from the children of nonalcoholics.

Most diseases are first detected as a collection of observations that describe their clinical picture. These clinical patterns are usually first recognized in their most severe or pronounced form. Later more subtle and less severe forms of the disease are recognized, and soon the disease has a much broader definition. Eventually, scientific research establishes diagnostic parameters for a given disease (laboratory tests, x-ray findings, and the like), and then, when possible, a cause, or *etiology*, is uncovered. A treatment or cure may be found during this development.

An example of this development might be imagined with diabetes mellitus. The description of the disease originally might have out-lined a person who progressively lost weight and had periods of confusion and dehydration, and eventually entered a coma. Soon after this stage, death ensued.

Scientific work might then have found that this disease was characterized by sugar in the urine and elevated sugar in the blood. Subsequently, people with elevated blood sugar of lesser degrees might have been found. These people would not yet have reached the stage of coma and would be able to be treated simply by avoiding sugar in their diet. Eventually the disease was found to be marked by a relative lack of insulin, and therefore insulin became the treatment for diabetes. There are still many mysteries in diabetes, and its actual cause is still unknown.

This process, whereby we first discover and then learn successively more and more about a disease, is happening with alcoholism. At first it was only the hopeless, extreme cases who were recognized as alcoholics. In the 1930s, when Alcoholics Anonymous (AA) was established, it emerged and developed with these extreme cases serving as the model of the disease. The founders of AA thought the disease to be an allergy to a substance for which the afflicted had a compulsive desire.

Since then, less extreme cases with varying patterns of drinking have broadened the concept of the disease of alcoholism. The American Medical Association first officially defined alcoholism as a disease in 1956, as noted before. A recent revision of the official diagnostic manual of the American Psychiatric Association specified three main criteria for the diagnoses of alcohol or drug dependency: (1) the suffering of withdrawal symptoms after intake is stopped; (2) the need for ingesting constantly increased quantities in order to realize the desired effect; and (3) obsession with alcohol or drugs so severe that it leads to taking risks to obtain them and to serious interference with the individual's work and social life. Other organizations that define alcoholism as a disease include the American College of Physicians, the American Hospital Association, the American Public Health Association, the American Psychological Association, the National Association of Social Workers, and the World Health Organization.

Thus, there are several ways to view alcoholism, but, as a clinical disease, it can be described as a maladaptive and self-destructive behavior pattern involving the compulsive consumption of alcohol leading to personal, emotional, and physical deterioration. This behavior pattern is associated with an inappropriate excess of fear, depression, and anxiety, and a resulting difficulty in coping with the normal stresses of life.

Whether the abnormal reaction to alcohol and the associated personality pattern are both grounded in a physical phenomenon is as yet unclear. However, there is recent scientific information that uncovers some interesting biologic relationships which suggest at least some physiologic basis for alcoholism/addiction. The development of scientific findings in reaching a true understanding of a disease process is slow and complex. Having an infinite number of roads to follow, researchers find only some roads enlightening. Various patterns develop as more and more work is done and gradually the relationships come into focus. This process is still in an early phase with respect to the physiology of addiction, but attention recently has been drawn to the chemistry of the brain and its neurotransmitters as well as to certain findings with respect to hepatic physiology.

One interesting line of research begins with the first breakdown product of alclohol in the body, acetaldehyde. This is produced in an oxidation reaction chemically carried out by the action of nicotinamide adenine dinucleotide (NAD). Normally, acetaldehyde is next converted to acetate in the liver by the action of acetaldehyde dehydrogenase, and eventually the acetate is excreted by the body as carbon dioxide and water.

Acetaldehyde is far more toxic than alcohol, so these breakdown reactions that metabolize acetaldehyde are therefore very critical in averting painfully severe reactions. An example of a painful buildup of acetaldehyde results from the reaction of alcohol and the medicine, Antabuse (disulfiram). This medicine is sometimes used to help alcoholics avoid alcohol. Drinking alcohol while on Antabuse causes nausea, pain, and a feeling of being deathly ill. Antabuse blocks the enzyme that breaks down acetaldehyde; acetaldehyde then builds up in the blood and its toxic properties create severe illness.

Acetaldehyde, then, is the primary breakdown product of alcohol and seems to play a role in alcoholism. Dr. Charles Lieber has shown that alcoholics produce a new form of an enzyme, cytochrome P-450, that increases acetaldehyde levels in the liver. There have also been reports that acetaldehyde dehydrogenase activity in liver biopsy specimens is significantly lower in alcoholics than in nonalcoholics. Therefore alcoholics may have two factors that result in increased levels of acetaldehyde concentration in the body.

These findings became even more interesting when acetaldehyde was shown to react with the neurotransmitters of the brain. The *neurotransmitters* are chemicals released from neurons in the brain to serve in the process of carrying messages from one neuron to another. These substances also play a role in certain diseases such as Parkinson's disease and have been shown to influence mood and mental illness.

Acetaldehyde reacts with the neurotransmitters to form chemical products called *tetrahydroisoquinolines* (TIQs). Interestingly, when these TIQs are infused into the brain of monkeys, the monkeys develop a liking for alcohol. These same monkeys in the wild avoid alcohol. But when treated with TIQs, they drink huge amounts of it. These monkeys continue to imbibe large quantities of alcohol in preference to water for long periods of time, much as their alcoholic human counterparts do. In fact, once TIQs have been infused and a stable drinking pattern established, the animals' high level of alcohol consumption appears to be irreversible.

The assumption might be made that alcoholics first produce excess acetaldehyde through hepatic reactions and then, because of neurochemical reactions, produce TIQs, which seem to be associated with addictlike behavior. It has been postulated that this is so because of a chemical similarity between certain TIQs and morphine. We know now, for instance, that one of the TIQs binds to the same sites in the brain as beta-endorphin and morphine do. So, in effect, many of the TIQs, which are products of alcohol consumption, act as narcotics in the brain.

Beta-endorphin is a natural morphinelike substance. It is one of a group of narcoticlike substances produced in the brain. One recent theory is that alcoholics/addicts are either born with or develop a deficiency in the brain's supply of these natural morphinelike substances. Studies have actually shown deficiencies in beta-endorphin levels in alcoholics. Since the body can construct its own narcoticlike substances—TIQs—from alcohol, perhaps this is one factor in the compulsive drive to drink or take drugs.

Not everyone would agree that these findings indicate an underlying physiologic mechanism of alcoholism or drug addiction. However, the relationships we have outlined seem to be strong evidence that alcoholism and addiction are diseases whose physical component lies in the complexities of the biochemical processes of the liver and brain.

The disease of alcoholism is also characterized by varying degrees of toxic damage brought on by excessive consumption. Alcohol is of course toxic to the nonalcoholic as well as to the alcoholic. As a drug, it is absorbed directly through the stomach wall or walls of the small intestine and passes quickly into the bloodstream. It then moves into every part of the body that contains water. Five percent of it is eliminated through the breath, urine, or sweat, but the remaining 95 percent must be broken down by the liver. The liver processes alcohol at the rate of about one-third ounce of ethanol (pure, 200-proof alcohol) per hour. Any more than this continues to circulate in the blood and the cells.

Within a few minutes alcohol reaches the brain, where it initially stimulates and agitates but eventually acts as a depressant. First the functions of inhibition and judgment are depressed and this accounts for the release of normal restraint. Sexual inhibitions, for example, may initially be relaxed, but alcohol actually impairs sexual function, performance, and eventually desire. Mood changes are severe with intoxication, and some people suffer Jekyll-and-Hyde personality changes.

Alcohol then affects motor ability, reaction time, eyesight, and other functions, and if there is continued intake, vital functions can be affected and death can occur. Usually the body rejects the alcohol by vomiting first; later it may enter a comatose state before a fatal dose can be consumed.

Disabling levels of alcohol intake are widely defined in terms of percentages specifying *blood alcohol concentration* (BAC). For example, highway police in New York State have given cards on BAC levels to motorists they stop at roadblocks set up to apprehend drunk drivers. Cards define *driving while intoxicated* (DWI) as having a BAC of ".10% & UP" (0.10 percent or greater). For such levels of blood alcohol concentration they advise, "Do Not Drive." These levels make drivers subject to arrest with heavy fines or prison sentences. Charts on the cards also show that a 100-pound person can reach that DWI level of 0.10 percent BAC with about three drinks in two hours; a 180-pound person can attain that level with five drinks in two hours (with a drink defined as 1.5 ounces of liquor or 12 ounces of beer). Breath analyzer instruments are commonly used to measure BAC. It can also be measured by laboratory tests of urine or blood samples.

Mathematically, BAC definitions used throughout the United States express the percentage of alcohol in the blood. The DWI level of 0.10 percent BAC means 0.1 part alcohol per 100 parts of blood.

Disability rises as an individual's BAC level increases. Not only New York but many states of the U.S. define 0.10 percent BAC as the minimum level for criminal inability to drive. Increasing BAC levels interfere with consciousness, respiration, and heartbeat. A BAC of 0.30 or 0.40 percent can cause the drinker to fall into a coma. Heartbeat and breathing can slow down dangerously with a BAC of around 0.50 percent. Death is certain for most persons at a BAC of 0.60 percent. Death due to excessive alcohol ingestion has actually occurred in recent years in some celebrated cases involving college fraternity hazing parties.

Excessive drinking produces the well-known hangover with headache, upset stomach, and dehydration. During this state the body is actually in withdrawal, for which time and drinking of liquids are the only cure.

Since alcohol reaches every cell and organ of the body, its physical effects are wide-ranging. When chronic alcohol intake persists, the result is metabolic damage everywhere: in the liver, the central nervous system, the gastrointestinal system, and the heart. Other effects include impaired vision, impaired sexual function, circulation problems, malnutrition, water retention, pancreatitis, skin disorders (such as acne and dilation of blood vessels), muscle atrophy, and decreased resistance to infection.

The liver is the most common site of alcohol toxicity. The direct toxic effect on cellular function in the liver causes, first, "fatty liver," an infiltration of the liver with abnormal fatty cells producing general liver enlargement. Next comes alcoholic hepatitis, in which the cells are injured and some die. Further alcohol exposure eventually causes cirrhosis, the irreversible destruction of liver cells and fibrous scarring of the entire liver architecture. Obstruction of the flow of blood through the liver and deterioration of liver function result. Many bodily functions are disturbed by each of these liver diseases and, even with alcoholic hepatitis, death results in from 10 to 30 percent of cases.

Alcohol reduces the amount of oxygen reaching the brain and destroys brain cells directly. With chronic abuse, destruction reaches the point of causing seizures and certain neurologic disorders characterized by dementia, known in one form as *Korsakoff's syndrome*. Symptoms include amnesia, disorientation, hallucinations, emotional disturbances, and loss of muscle control.

The digestive system suffers various injuries, both directly and indirectly, when alcohol abuse is chronic. Direct inflammation of the esophagus and stomach (esophagitis and gastritis) and increased incidence of ulcers result. Indirectly there is dilation of the blood vessels in the esophagus due to obstruction of blood flow in the portal system of the liver. This can lead to fatal hemorrhage.

There is also an increased frequency of cancer both in the liver and in upper gastrointestinal organs (such as the esophagus).

The heart is affected directly by a disease of the heart muscle called a *cardiomyopathy*, and indirectly by high blood pressure and arrhythmias.

So now we see alcoholism as a disease with a compulsive drive to consume a toxic substance (perhaps driven by the biochemical relationships discussed earlier), with varying physical pathology due to the toxicity of the drug itself, and with an emotional and psychologic pattern laced with fear, anxiety, and depression.

As a disease, alcoholism is relentlessly *progressive*. That is, as long as drinking continues, all parameters steadily worsen. There are no spontaneous cures of any symptoms if drinking continues. The rate of the destructive progression varies, often with long periods of slow decline and then sudden periods of much more rapid deterioration. As with other diseases, every case is somewhat different from the next.

Some alcoholics begin drinking abnormally from their first drink, behaving from the beginning in ways destructive to their health. For others, there is a period of acceptable social drinking. Perhaps there are a few "drunks" and related hangovers, but, on looking back, it would be difficult to distinguish the early alcoholic from the social drinker. Indeed, most alcoholics have had an early period when there was still some fun in their drinking.

Sooner or later, however, the alcoholic begins inappropriately to use alcohol or drugs for their mood-altering qualities. In the early stages, perhaps the drinking is limited to recreational (reward) periods. That is, he still is working well and handling his life adequately, but weekends are characterized by needing some form of escaping or decreasing tension. Drinking or drugging becomes the chief activity of nonworking recreational time. Activities are chosen subconsciously because they involve drinking or drugging. Gradually the alcoholic will socialize mainly or only with others who drink; he'll plan dinners and events that involve drinking—such as visits to restaurants suited to several cocktails and wine with dinner, family outings to pizza parlors where having a pitcher of beer is appropriate, or trips to sports events where beer is plentiful.

In time all recreational activity probably has some relationship to drinking and the alcoholic comes to depend more and more on the mood-altering qualities of the drug. A drink is needed to relax, to celebrate, to mourn, to welcome the weekend. Soon the special occasion is any occasion.

At this stage, the alcoholic begins to feel anxious and uncomfortable with many of life's normal activities. He may tend to need a few quick drinks to get ready for a party or social engagement. He may even avoid social activities in favor of staying home and drinking in front of the TV or going to his favorite bar.

Some alcoholics may consciously control the number of drinks they allow themselves (for instance, "no more than two before dinner"). As time goes on, however, alcoholics find their drinking time to be increasingly important. They may make it through the workday without drinking, but they begin to get tense toward afternoon and sometimes even become obsessed with the idea of getting home, where they are able to drink. The compulsion to get the first drink of the day increases. The first drink may move into the workday and to an earlier hour on the weekends.

Although his tolerance for alcohol may become high, the alcoholic begins to have more periods of drunkenness and soon has blackouts (periods of memory-loss). For example, it was in this phase that Terry C. drove from San Francisco, California, to Reno, Nevada, and got married, never remembering any of it afterward. Some alcoholics won't be aware of blackouts for they don't have people around to describe the forgotten events.

By this time, there are usually significant problems as a result of alcoholism. The alcoholic may feel depressed and may think he drinks because of depression. During this phase, many alcoholics try psychotherapy, and because they deny their drinking problem, they usually get little help. They usually know something is wrong, but their drinking seems secondary, a response to anxiety and depression. They can't see drinking as the primary problem.

Marital problems, social problems, and health problems may now be part of the picture. The alcoholic at this stage is having no fun. He is desperately trying to avoid the pain he doesn't understand. Only drinking does the trick briefly. But the pain returns daily. Anxiety, fearfulness, difficulty making it through each day, and a sense of doom and failure characterize his life.

The drink or drug now sets up a craving for more, and matters are totally out of control. Awful things sometimes happen at this point—a spouse may leave; a serious accident may occur; a job may be lost. Something can easily happen that can be identified as bringing on "the bottom." The alcoholic's bottom is that point of such hopelessness and desperation that he will do anything to change and will even consider that the drinking itself may be the problem. There is now a crack, however small, in the alcoholic's denial.

This progression is a general description. Many alcoholics go through long periods of trying to control their drinking or even attempting to stop somewhere during the process. Without recovery programs, however, this rarely helps. The emotional part of the disease persists during self-imposed attempts at control or abstinence, and eventually the progression picks up steam again. Active alcoholics attempt to control their progression in varying ways. Many switch from liquor to beer or to wine or even to other drugs, convincing themselves that this may solve their problem. Sometimes an alcoholic gives up drinking to prove himself not to be an alcoholic, but takes Valium or other drugs instead, and the disease presses on. Others try a "geographic cure," moving to a new state or job to start over. These are desperate moves to treat the confusing, painful turmoil in the alcoholic's life. He still can't see alcohol or drugs as the primary problem. Denial is an extremely strong mechanism in addiction.

Denial tells the alcoholic that alcohol is not his problem. Although he is caught in a tumultous array of troubles all linked to his drinking, denial allows the alcoholic to blame everything but drinking for them. Drinking is rationalized to be the result of his problems, not the cause. The alcoholic thinks he gets drunk because of stress, depression, situations at work, unfairness, and the like.

Toward the end, everyone suffers. The alcoholic blames everyone around him and spreads his self-centered misery to each family member—even though he may not wish to.

At the end, there is an alcoholic who loathes himself, who is constantly miserable and crawling out of his skin with trembling anxiety, who is isolated from the world and profoundly depressed. Suicide may enter his mind. He is obsessed with alcohol and will keep drinking, possibly around the clock, despite the pleading of those close to him. Health problems, lost job, lost family, and even legal problems may be part of the picture. Often alcoholics reach the state of being too sick to drink and too sick not to drink. Withdrawal symptoms surface when alcohol cannot be absorbed, ranging from shakes to delirium to convulsions. The alcoholic is a physical wreck, and if he does not begin recovery at this point he will end up hospitalized or dead.

The concept of "the bottom" is important to alcoholic recovery. For some reason, it seems that a bottom must be reached for recovery to begin. It is important to realize, however, that one's bottom need not be the absolute end of the road as described here. Many alcoholics hit bottom long before they have serious disruptions in their health or careers. To some, the bottom may come when they are confronted by their boss; to others it may be the acting out of their children. "High-bottom" and "low-bottom" drunks are terms that refer to two differing levels of alcoholic progression needed for denial to be pierced and recovery to begin.

Let us remember too that there are many alcoholics who never find recovery. They die, or become permanently brain-injured psychiatric hospital inmates, or go on living at a bottom. These are all horrifying tragedies.

We have referred to the compulsive drive to drink as being one of the benchmarks in understanding alcoholism. The alcoholic does reach a stage where one drink creates a craving for another, and consequently the typical alcoholic pattern eventually includes daily drinking. There is another pattern, however, which deserves mention, that of the *periodic alcoholic,* who does not drink daily but has drinking bouts of varying frequency. He may drink once a month or just a few times a year. Each bout, however, usually produces drunkenness and demonstrates the person's "powerlessness" over the drink. The periodic alcoholic is often just as sick as the daily drinker. The denial may be even stronger here since there are long periods of abstinence to convince the drinker that he doesn't have a problem.

Alcoholism, thus far, has been presented as a disease with many dimensions: the compulsion and its possible physiologic basis, the physical damage resulting from toxicity, the psychologic and emotional manifestations, and the inevitable progression.

Progression is another characteristic of alcoholism that makes the disease concept even more compelling. From a physical perspective, progression is the clinical fact that an alcoholic seems to have an internal mechanism that drives his disease at a rate independent of external factors. In other words, when an alcoholic begins drinking, his tolerance for alcohol and the strength of his compulsion are both low. As his drinking goes on through the years, both the tolerance and the compulsion increase. In late stages, the tolerance falls but the compulsion remains strong. Therefore a very late-stage alcoholic may have an irrepressible compulsion to drink but may have blackouts and become quite sick from just a few drinks. Years earlier he could typically have held a fifth of vodka without any problem. The fascinating and repeatedly demonstrated feature of this progression is that it continues even if the alcoholic stops drinking. Clinically, this is manifested by the many stories of alcoholics who had stopped drinking for years, but who had started again to find their tolerance and compulsion progressed even further than they had been previously.

Carl C. was an example. Carl had started drinking in college, where he was one of those who could down tremendous quantities of beer. He later became a journalist, and his alcoholism progressed through the years. At first his drinking was limited to evenings at home, but eventually he was having several drinks at lunch, and, in time, he was hiding bottles in his office and at home, and drinking up to one-and-a-half fifths of vodka per day. As his disease progressed, he lost his family and was hospitalized several times with painful pancreatitis. Finally, after twenty years of abuse, Carl would get sick and black out after drinking only half a pint. Sometimes he couldn't even drink that without getting sick. He was in a constant state of illness and withdrawal when he was visited by an old friend who convinced him to go to a detoxification and rehabilitation program.

Carl became sober and stayed with an AA recovery program. Things went well after a while. He established a rather normal life. Eight years later he became extremely angry over something that happened at work. He became obsessed by it and one night went to a local restaurant and, before dinner, had a drink. Feeling that the drink had caused him no problem, he had two more—and didn't remember anything that occurred after that. Apparently, Carl went into a blackout with his second drink, was taken home by a friend, and proceeded to pass out for the night. The next day he had an awful hangover, but, by afternoon, he drank again, only to have the same scenario repeat itself. After two weeks of torture, Carl suffered a convulsion and was taken to a hospital detoxification program, where he stayed five days before being transferred to a rehabilitation program. Carl then proceeded to commit himself to his AA recovery program with new intensity, realizing the inevitable horror of returning to alcohol.

This is not a unique story. Many such clinical examples illustrate the mysterious fact that the progression of the disease, as measured by physical tolerance, marches on even during periods of abstinence. Carl's experience also points out that the compulsion is triggered by the first exposure to alcohol, even after years of abstention. These dynamics certainly suggest a definite physiologic basis for at least these elements of the disease of alcoholism/addiction.

Carl's example and thousands like his also point out the most basic and most important principle of therapy and recovery: that this disease can be arrested only with complete abstinence. There are no cures, and let no one forget the wise AA observation that it's the first drink that makes the alcoholic drunk, not the tenth.

When alcoholics/addicts reach such desperation that their denial begins to weaken, there is a chance they will accept some form of help. Sometimes it is a severe health problem that prompts this acceptance; sometimes it is a formal intervention (see Chapter 2); sometimes it is the urging of a relative or friend; and sometimes the addict seeks help on his own. At this point, recovery may begin, but the road ahead is not necessarily smooth. Recovery rates are difficult to estimate because of the lack of record keeping of many programs, such as AA. Rehabilitation centers have some idea of their success rates, as the following table indicates:

Recovery-Rate Summary of Treatment Centers Surveyed for Appendix 2: Percentage Ranges of Those in Recovery (with Continued Abstinence) 1 Year after In-Patient Treatment

Percentage of Centers	1-Year Recovery-Rate Range Reported by Centers
15%	80%–90%
42%	70%–79%
35%	60%–69%
8%	under 60%

On accepting the need to stop drinking, the alcoholic begins the journey into recovery by first undergoing detoxification. At this point most alcoholics are not aware that their disease involves much more than drinking. If they continue into recovery, they will be surprised to learn that it includes an attitude and mood disorder creating psychologic and social dysfunction. The alcoholic/addict will slowly become aware of how comprehensive his recovery must be.

First, however, is *detoxification:* acute withdrawal, as the body is forced to acclimate to a new environment and find a physiologic balance in the absence of the drug that has bathed every tissue for so long. Although bodily changes continue for long periods after the alcoholic stops drinking, the acute "detox" period lasts from three to seven days after complete alcohol abstinence begins.

Acute symptoms of withdrawal are usually significant and can be life-threatening. Common withdrawal symptoms include disorientation, acute anxiety and fear, auditory and visual hallucinations, insomnia, shakiness, agitation, profuse perspiration, rapid pulse, abdominal cramps, diarrhea, and sometimes vomiting. A feeling of internal tremors is often described. More dangerous symptoms include fever, delirium tremens, and convulsions or epileptic seizures.

After the detoxification period, physical and emotional discomforts continue through many weeks or even many months for quite a few individuals recovering from alcoholism and/or addiction. Physical difficulties may include insomnia, headaches, and minor but nagging aches and pains in various parts of the body. Among emotional troubles may be extreme mood swings, anxiety, nervous tension, continuing depression, restlessness, and boredom. Health professionals who work with recovering alcoholics and addicts are beginning to term such discomforts early in recovery, "protracted withdrawal syndrome."

The other drugs of abuse (such as cocaine, narcotics, tranquilizers, and barbiturates) all have varying acute withdrawal or detoxification intervals, depending somewhat on the amount of chronic intake and the duration of the addiction. Symptoms for all drugs are not identical. Narcotics withdrawal, for instance, involves long periods of marked general discomfort, depression, abdominal and muscle cramps, and periods of extreme agitation, whereas barbiturate withdrawal can include dangerous seizure activity. Valium withdrawal entails long-lasting and profound mood swings.

This stressful period of detoxification is preferably spent under medical supervision. The hospital (and specifically its "detox ward") is the most common site for such supervision. Some hospital detox programs are integrated with treatment programs or rehabilitation centers, and some operate independently.

More recently, some drug and alcohol counselors, in cooperation with experienced physicians, have been able to design "ambulatory" detoxification programs for appropriate individuals. This, of course, must be done carefully and on a selective basis, but it is an option available in many parts of the country. In such cases, the alcoholic/addict is seen by the counselor and the doctor as an outpatient. He is usually observed daily for the acute period of withdrawal, and less frequently thereafter until he is safely involved in a recovery program such as AA or NA.

The detoxification period is indeed the first step in recovery from alcoholism. During this time mental functions are cloudy and concentration is difficult. It is after "detox" that the alcoholic/addict must begin to focus on the principles of recovery. His success will depend on his commitment to those principles from that time on.

The alcoholic/addict will learn that he will always be in the process of recovery. He will hear that his disease can only be arrested and held in remission. It cannot, at least with present knowledge, be cured. Nevertheless, with the disease in remission, the alcoholic/addict can live a full life, normal in every respect except that he can never take one drink or mood-altering substance again, except under specially supervised medical circumstances. These exceptions are discussed in later chapters.

Two diagrams on accompanying pages summarize in visual form the downward swing marking the progression of the disease of alcoholism/addiction, the bottom, and the upward swing in recovery of those victims fortunate enough to recover. The first diagram depicts the progression for the alcoholic/addict, and is titled, "Chemical Dependency & Its Progression." The second diagram depicts the progression for family members or others close to the alcoholic/addict, and is titled, "Co-Dependency & Its Progression." Permission to reprint the diagrams was generously granted by Seabrook House, Seabrook, New Jersey (a treatment center which holds the copyright on the diagrams in this form; an entry for Seabrook House appears in Appendix 2).

The diagram for the alcoholic/addict is widely used in alcoholism/addiction treatment programs, and in some programs is called "the Jellinek chart." Others call it "the Max Glatt chart." Its downward swing to a bottom was developed by E. M. Jellinek, whose definition of alcoholism as a disease in the 1940s was later adopted by the World Health Organization. Its upward swing in recovery was developed by M. M. Glatt and introduced in "Group Therapy in Alcoholism," *The British Journal of Addiction*, Vol. 54, No. 2, 1957–1959 (according to the Library of the Center for Alcohol Studies at Rutgers, the State University of New Jersey).

At this point, the concept of cross-addiction or dual addiction must be clarified. This aspect of addiction necessitates that the recovering alcoholic/addict exercise care and knowledge where health issues and medical treatment are concerned.

Cross-Addiction or Dual Addiction

In this book, we often refer to the alcoholic and to the drug addict interchangeably. Indeed, many alcoholics in our present culture also use other drugs, and many drug addicts abuse alcohol as well. In fact, as indicated by our survey of rehabilitation centers (Appendix 2), a majority of persons entering treatment today are addicted to more than one substance. The ability of alcoholics/addicts to change their addictive use from one drug to another is seen in many settings. When drug addicts or alcoholics begin to worry about their depen-

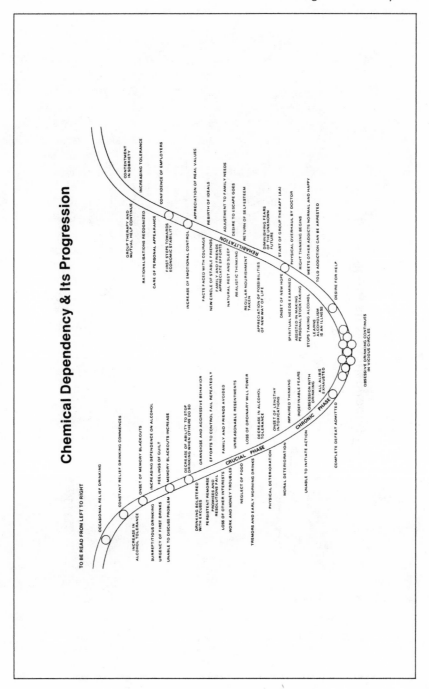

Chemical Dependency & Its Progression

TO BE READ FROM LEFT TO RIGHT

OCCASIONAL RELIEF DRINKING

INCREASE IN ALCOHOL TOLERANCE

CONSTANT RELIEF DRINKING COMMENCES

ONSET OF MEMORY BLACKOUTS

SURREPTITIOUS DRINKING

INCREASING DEPENDENCE ON ALCOHOL

URGENCY OF FIRST DRINKS

FEELINGS OF GUILT

UNABLE TO DISCUSS PROBLEM

MEMORY BLACKOUTS INCREASE

DRINKING BOLSTERED WITH EXCUSES

DECREASE OF ABILITY TO STOP DRINKING WHEN OTHERS DO SO

GRANDIOSE AND AGGRESSIVE BEHAVIOR

PERSISTENT REMORSE

PROMISES AND RESOLUTIONS FAIL

EFFORTS TO CONTROL FAIL REPEATEDLY

LOSS OF OTHER INTERESTS

FAMILY AND FRIENDS AVOIDED

WORK AND MONEY TROUBLES

UNREASONABLE RESENTMENTS

NEGLECT OF FOOD

LOSS OF ORDINARY WILL POWER

TREMORS AND EARLY MORNING DRINKS

DECREASE IN ALCOHOL TOLERANCE

PHYSICAL DETERIORATION

ONSET OF LENGTHY INTOXICATIONS

MORAL DETERIORATION

IMPAIRED THINKING

INDEFINABLE FEARS

UNABLE TO INITIATE ACTION

OBSESSION WITH DRINKING

ALL ALIBIS EXHAUSTED

COMPLETE DEFEAT ADMITTED

CRUCIAL PHASE

CHRONIC PHASE

OBSESSIVE DRINKING CONTINUES IN VICIOUS CIRCLES

LEARNS ALCOHOLISM IS AN ILLNESS

STOPS TAKING ALCOHOL

ASSISTED IN MAKING PERSONAL STOCKTAKING

SPIRITUAL NEEDS EXAMINED

ONSET OF NEW HOPE

APPRECIATION OF POSSIBILITIES OF NEW WAY OF LIFE

REGULAR NOURISHMENT TAKEN

REALISTIC THINKING

NATURAL REST AND SLEEP

FAMILY AND FRIENDS APPRECIATE EFFORTS

NEW CIRCLE OF STABLE FRIENDS

FACTS FACED WITH COURAGE

INCREASE OF EMOTIONAL CONTROL

FIRST STEPS TOWARDS ECONOMIC STABILITY

CARE OF PERSONAL APPEARANCE

RATIONALISATIONS RECOGNIZED

GROUP THERAPY AND MUTUAL HELP CONTINUE

DESIRE FOR HELP

TOLD ADDICTION CAN BE ARRESTED

MEETS OTHER ADDICTS NORMAL AND HAPPY

RIGHT THINKING BEGINS

PHYSICAL OVERHAUL BY DOCTOR

START OF GROUP THERAPY (AA)

DIMINISHING FEARS OF THE UNKNOWN FUTURE

RETURN OF SELFESTEEM

DESIRE TO ESCAPE GOES

ADJUSTMENT TO FAMILY NEEDS

REBIRTH OF IDEALS

APPRECIATION OF REAL VALUES

CONFIDENCE OF EMPLOYERS

INCREASING TOLERANCE

CONTENTMENT IN SOBRIETY

REHABILITATION

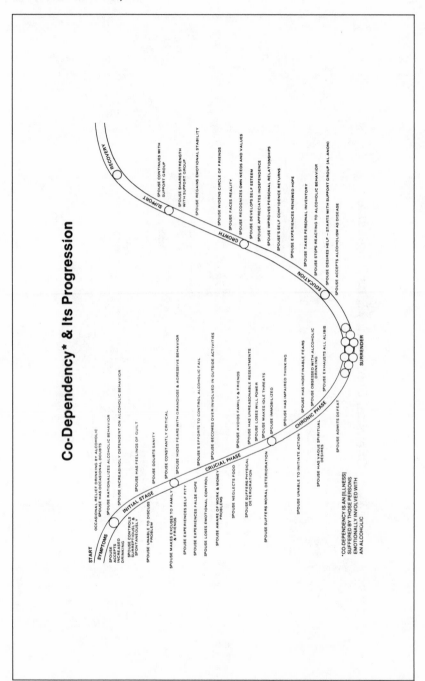

Co-Dependency* & Its Progression

START

SYMPTOMS

OCCASIONAL RELIEF DRINKING BY ALCOHOLIC
SPOUSE HAS OCCASIONAL DOUBTS

SPOUSE ACCEPTS INCREASED DRINKING

SPOUSE RATIONALIZES ALCOHOLIC BEHAVIOR

SPOUSE INCREASINGLY DEPENDENT ON ALCOHOLIC BEHAVIOR

SPOUSE CONTROLS SURREPTITIOUSLY & SPONTANEOUSLY

SPOUSE HAS FEELINGS OF GUILT

SPOUSE UNABLE TO DISCUSS PROBLEM

SPOUSE DOUBTS SANITY

INITIAL STAGE

SPOUSE CONSTANTLY CRITICAL

SPOUSE MAKES EXCUSES TO FAMILY & FRIENDS

SPOUSE HIDES FEARS WITH GRANDIOSE & AGGRESSIVE BEHAVIOR

SPOUSE EXPERIENCES SELF PITY

SPOUSE'S EFFORTS TO CONTROL ALCOHOLIC FAIL

SPOUSE EXPERIENCES FALSE HOPE

SPOUSE LOSES EMOTIONAL CONTROL

SPOUSE BECOMES OVER-INVOLVED IN OUTSIDE ACTIVITIES

SPOUSE AWARE OF WORK & MONEY PROBLEMS

SPOUSE AVOIDS FAMILY & FRIENDS

CRUCIAL PHASE

SPOUSE NEGLECTS FOOD

SPOUSE HAS UNREASONABLE RESENTMENTS

SPOUSE SUFFERS PHYSICAL DETERIORATION

SPOUSE LOSES WILL POWER

SPOUSE MAKES IDLE THREATS

SPOUSE SUFFERS MORAL DETERIORATION

SPOUSE IMMOBILIZED

SPOUSE HAS IMPAIRED THINKING

SPOUSE UNABLE TO INITIATE ACTION

SPOUSE HAS INDEFINABLE FEARS

SPOUSE OBSESSED WITH ALCOHOLIC DRINKING

CHRONIC PHASE

SPOUSE HAS VAGUE SPIRITUAL DESIRES

SPOUSE EXHAUSTS ALL ALIBIS

SPOUSE ADMITS DEFEAT

SURRENDER

*CO-DEPENDENCY IS AN [ILLNESS] SUFFERED BY THOSE PERSONS EMOTIONALLY INVOLVED WITH AN ALCOHOLIC

EDUCATION

SPOUSE ACCEPTS ALCOHOLISM AS DISEASE

SPOUSE DESIRES HELP — STARTS WITH SUPPORT GROUP (AL-ANON)

SPOUSE STOPS REACTING TO ALCOHOLIC BEHAVIOR

SPOUSE TAKES PERSONAL INVENTORY

GROWTH

SPOUSE EXPERIENCES RENEWED HOPE

SPOUSE'S SELF CONFIDENCE RETURNS

SPOUSE IMPROVES PERSONAL RELATIONSHIPS

SPOUSE APPRECIATES INDEPENDENCE

SPOUSE DEVELOPS SELF ESTEEM

SPOUSE RECOGNIZES OWN NEEDS AND VALUES

SPOUSE FACES REALITY

SPOUSE WIDENS CIRCLE OF FRIENDS

SUPPORT

SPOUSE REGAINS EMOTIONAL STABILITY

SPOUSE SHARES STRENGTH WITH SUPPORT GROUP

SPOUSE CONTINUES WITH SUPPORT GROUP

RECOVERY

dence on a particular substance, they often switch to another drug, trying to convince themselves that they really aren't "hooked."

Alan S., for example, had been a "recreational" drug user in his early twenties. He smoked marijuana, drank "socially," experienced hallucinogens such as lysergic acid diethylamide (LSD), and tried cocaine several times at parties. His life was stable, however, as he was developing a professional career and a new marital relationship. He only used alcohol and drugs at parties and with friends. He certainly didn't think he had a problem.

Alan was always restless and intermittently depressed, but he put on a good act and most people he knew regarded him as a successful young man. One day he sustained a back injury that caused severe pain. His doctor prescribed rest at home and Percodan for pain. Alan found the Percodan not only relieved the discomfort but also gave him a delightful feeling. He looked forward to each dose and took the pills for a general sense of well-being even after the pain had subsided. When the prescription ran out, he didn't seek more pills immediately, but he remembered the effect of the Percodan.

One night, weeks later, Alan didn't sleep well and the following day he was anxious and uncomfortable. He thought that Percodan would certainly help relieve this discomfort, so he called his doctor, told him his back was acting up, and got a prescription for Percodan. The pills really did the trick.

For five years after that, Alan used Percodan periodically. At times he would become physically addicted and would put himself through painful and disruptive days of withdrawal. He felt anxious about being addicted, but thought he had just gone a bit too far. Each time he stopped the pills, a certain tension would build, and within a few weeks he'd start using it again.

During this time, Alan continued his recreational drug use as well. He smoked marijuana, used more and more cocaine, and began to take Valium and other prescription drugs. He felt he was just someone who liked to have a good time more than others, but periodically he worried that he was taking too many drugs. When he really thought about it, Alan felt that he had certain anxieties and depressions that made him use drugs and alcohol. Most of the time, he avoided thinking about it.

As he became more worried about his dependence on drugs and as the effort to obtain drugs became more stressful, Alan turned more and more to alcohol. Daily vodka intake during that time approached a fifth a day. He couldn't drink at work, however, and the days became intolerably stressful. There was an internal, irritable tension he could barely stand. Soon he was back to a mixture of drugs (usually Percodan and Valium) during the day, and alcohol at night.

Alan went on for several years trying to control alcohol, only to see his drug intake increase, and then trying to control drugs only to find his alcohol consumption increase. His life, finally, consisted of periods of horrible tension and discomfort interspersed with periods of drug- or alcohol-induced oblivion. He ended up in a treatment center.

Many alcoholics/addicts have stories resembling his. Their disease is addiction, and any mood-altering substance will serve to keep it alive.

Cocaine addicts may feel that alcohol is not their problem, but case after case shows that the cocaine addict cannot drink alcohol if he wants to arrest his disease and recover. Similarly, the alcoholic who never abused other drugs cannot, in recovery, smoke marijuana, take Valium, or snort cocaine. When recovering alcoholics/addicts try to give up their drug of choice but still use another, they stop their growth in recovery and begin an inevitable course back to their drug of choice or into uncontrollable use of the secondary substance. Interviews with members indicate that occasional cases like this occur in many an AA group—cases in which a member smokes marijuana or abuses prescription narcotics while attending AA meetings, eventually relapsing into runaway addiction with alcohol or drugs.

Quite a few similar examples were also seen in addicts who had been through a number of the early heroin recovery programs in the 1960s and 1970s. Cross-addiction was little understood at the time, and recovering heroin addicts often left recovery programs without having been warned against alcohol. Years later many of these same people developed alcoholism and entered treatment centers, having learned the hard way that any mood-altering substance can take hold of the reins of their disease.

Dually addicted alcoholics/addicts (those who abuse two drugs) usually realize the need for total abstinence in recovery. The alcoholics/addicts who have the most trouble understanding the need to avoid all mood-altering drugs are those who abused only one substance. The pure alcoholic finds it hard to accept the danger of his taking codeine or Valium. Drugs, he often feels, were not his problem. Recovering cocaine-only addicts often similarly find it hard to accept that they can never drink.

Nevertheless, as more and more experience with recovering alcoholics/addicts accumulates, the principle becomes clear:

A recovering alcoholic/addict must forever avoid all mood-altering substances for the rest of his or her life.

If he does not, he runs a very high risk of becoming an active alcoholic/addict once again. This road back to the drug of choice is not always direct, but once a mood-changing drug is allowed to trigger the disease of addiction, eventually the alcoholic/addict will reactivate uncontrollable substance abuse.

Tony M., for example, was a narcotic addict who hit bottom after developing a life-threatening infection from an unsterile injection. Tony, a lawyer, finally realized the depths to which his life had fallen. He began a drug rehabilitation program in earnest. He was deeply dedicated to recovering and, with difficulty, made solid progress. He spent three and a half years in this outpatient program before leaving treatment. After this he did well for three more years, when a "little voice" told him he was all right again and could have a little wine with dinner. That one glass of wine led within weeks to considerably more wine, and soon Tony was drinking the way he had formerly used heroin. After another year, he began using a prescription narcotic, and only a few weeks later he was in a detoxification ward, having lost his family and his career.

Basic Recovery Program Terms Explained

Some of the case histories in this chapter and various passages in later chapters refer to "recovery programs" and key features of such programs. Terms applying to these programs and brief explanations of them follow.

RECOVERY PROGRAM

Recovery programs include the following major voluntary associations for recovering alcoholics/addicts: Alcoholics Anonymous (AA), Narcotics Anonymous (NA), and Cocaine Anonymous (CA). The term *recovery program* also refers to the course of actions typically recommended in these organizations to assure ongoing recovery by continued abstinence. (Such meaning is clear from the context.)

Related recovery programs are also available for the family members of active or recovering alcoholics/addicts. They include Al-Anon Family Groups, Alateen, and Adult Children of Alcoholics (ACOA). Occasionally we refer to these related organizations and their recommended course of action in the context of discussions of family members of alcoholics/addicts.

Appendix 1 gives names, addresses, and telephone numbers for the main offices of these recovery programs.

SPONSOR IN ONE'S RECOVERY PROGRAM

Customary practice in a recovery program is that each recoveree has a more experienced member serve as his or her "sponsor." Sponsorship arrangements are made informally and mutually by the two persons involved. A sponsor by custom guides the person sponsored in the most effective actions to take in order to protect and promote sobriety. A sponsor brings the principles of recovery as well as personal support to the relationship.

PRINCIPLES OF ONE'S RECOVERY PROGRAM

Each recovery program has developed a body of precepts and practices that have been found by trial and error to promote recovery. Continued abstinence is the primary principle. As examples, well-known basic principles of AA include the following: don't drink one day at a time; it's the first drink that gets you drunk (in other words, complete abstinence is necessary); stay away from people, places, and things connected with your former active addiction; and keep in daily communication with other recovering members by attending regular program meetings and/or by phoning them.

CHAPTER 2

How Family Members Can Help an Alcoholic or Addict in the Family—and Greatly Help Themselves

FAMILY MEMBERS LIVING WITH AN ALCOHOLIC OR ADDICT—ONE YOUNG OR old, male or female—can play crucial roles in helping that person. Moreover, while helping the alcoholic/addict in the family, you can also be helping yourself in very important ways. For alcoholism or addiction of another person in the family takes a terrible toll on you, too. This toll is inescapable if you live in the same home as the active alcoholic/addict. But you can learn proven ways to minimize the

27

damage that his or her addictive disease wreaks on you. You can learn to recover from the effects of the disease on you.

ONE IN EVERY FOUR FAMILIES IN THE UNITED STATES HAS AN ALCOHOL PROBLEM

There's a good chance you're right if you strongly suspect that someone in your family—your husband, your wife, your child, or your parent—has a problem with alcohol. A 1987 Gallup Poll found that 24 percent of all U.S. families said that drinking had caused family problems. Adding to that one-in-four chance is the fact that both families and individuals very strongly tend to deny that excessive drinking (or drug use) is causing serious trouble. Among common denial reactions are:

—It went too far this time for some plausible reason other than alcohol or drug abuse.
—It certainly won't happen again.
—It's really not all that bad.

But neither these nor many more denials are actually true, you know deep down after out-of-control drinking or drug use brings on painful trouble time and time again.

Such doubts about denial have led one in every five Americans over age seventeen to seek medical or other professional help with his or her own drinking problem or that of a family member, another 1987 Gallup Poll indicated.

Before Recovery—First Main Point: For Troubles, What Help to Get— and Where to Get It

Your most urgent need in a family with someone who may be becoming an impaired alcoholic/addict may well be help with troubles, serious troubles. Troubles explode more and more often as the disease of alcoholism/addiction intensifies.

You've probably already begun suffering such troubles if you're reading this chapter. And once your family starts having the tragically common problems like those that are described next, you'll very likely see ever more and worse troubles as a "codependent." (*Codependent* is a term used for a person with a family member who is addictively dependent on alcohol or drugs.)

Typical troubles with which you may badly need help as a codependent include:

—Worry over disappearances of the alcoholic/addict family member from home and the family, without any advance warning before or reasonable explanation (or any explanation) after.

—Concern over increasing neglect of the family and of normal family responsibilities and enjoyments.

—Disgrace through repeated episodes of drunken or drugged behavior before friends and neighbors.

—Heartbreak over frequent drunken or drugged behavior at special family occasions such as celebrations of birthdays, graduations, or anniversaries, and at social gatherings.

—Terror over drunken or drugged condition while driving, especially with you or other family members riding in the car.

—Anxiety over possible or actual loss of a job and family income due to frequent episodes of drunken or drugged behavior followed by disablement from intense hangovers.

—Anguish over terrible arguments often started by the family member when drunk or drugged, possibly with physical violence to people and possessions.

—Disgust with uncontrolled vomiting, defecation, and other filthiness by the family member when drunk or drugged.

—Fear of terrifying changes in the personality of the family member when drunk or drugged.

—Incapacitation for everyday activities and dereliction of responsibilities due to drunken or drugged condition, on some or many occasions.

—Arrests and jailings due to behavior after alcohol or drug use.

—Desperate visits to hospital emergency rooms due to frequent serious injuries and illnesses brought on by drunken or drugged condition.

Help with Any of These Troubles— What Help to Get and Where

You don't have to have experienced most of these troubles in order to be justified in getting help with them. Suffering only a few or even just one can be deeply disturbing. Here's how to get help with facing and handling one or more of such problems.

FOR DANGEROUS BEHAVIOR, CALL THE POLICE

Don't stand helpless and paralyzed when the alcoholic/addict in your family acts in truly dangerous ways at home or in public. It really doesn't help anyone for you to ignore or dismiss dangerous or destructive behavior.

Find out in advance how to call the police. Then, when necessary for the protection of yourself and of others, call them in for safety.

FOR ACCIDENTS AND INJURIES, BE READY WITH AMBULANCE SERVICES AND HOSPITAL EMERGENCY ROOMS

A family member who repeatedly abuses alcohol or drugs runs high risks of serious accidents and injuries. Find out how to call ambulances and how to get to the nearest hospital emergency rooms at all hours. You'll then know what to do when such an emergency does arise.

FOR WORRIES ABOUT LOSING THE JOB, FIND OUT WHETHER THE EMPLOYER HAS AN EMPLOYEE ASSISTANCE PROGRAM

So widespread is the epidemic of alcoholism/addiction today that many companies have Employee Assistance Programs (EAPs) to aid employees impaired by substance abuse. These programs provide impaired employees with special help in recovering from their disease.

Typically, alcoholics/addicts try desperately to hide their abuse from their employers. But if the employer has an EAP, the impaired employee often benefits enormously from finally acknowledging his or her disease and accepting EAP help. Help like this typically includes a leave-of-absence from work for inpatient treatment of addiction at a treatment center (with treatment paid for by the employee's health-insurance plan). Impaired employees entering EAPs also often have the high motivation of being guaranteed their jobs if they continue in recovery but being told they'll be fired if they go back to drinking or drugs.

To pursue this possibility, you can phone the personnel director or department of your impaired relative's employer to inquire whether they have an EAP. If so, you might arrange to go in and talk confidentially with an EAP adviser about possible help.

FOR HELP WITH YOUR OVERALL SHOCK AND HORROR ABOUT THE ALCOHOLIC/ADDICT IN YOUR FAMILY

You can also get help of a particularly important kind with all the alarming and disturbing experiences you're having with your possibly addicted family member. This is help freely given by others who also face problems with apparently addicted family members.

These individuals have learned how to cope effectively with troubles like those in your family life. They can help you learn ways to relieve your own feelings and problems caused by your difficult family member. And they can help you learn ways that may influence the sick family member to stop substance abuse and start recovery—ways that succeed in many cases, but also may never succeed in others.

Such help is available through two voluntary associations related to Alcoholics Anonymous. Their names are: Al-Anon Family Groups (usually called just "Al-Anon") and Alateen.

Al-Anon is for adults who are relatives or friends of alcoholics; Alateen is for young people twelve to twenty years old. Anyone who wants help in dealing with a family member possibly suffering from alcoholism/addiction can join and attend meetings of either group. Both are nonprofit and absolutely noncommercial. You pay only what you care to contribute in voluntary collections made by passing baskets around at meetings.

Thousands of Al-Anon and Alateen groups operate throughout the

United States and in more than eighty-two other countries. You should certainly be able to locate one or more groups whose meetings you can attend. To find the whereabouts of an Al-Anon or Alateen group in your vicinity, first check in your local telephone directory—under "Al-Anon" or "Al-Anon Family Groups"—either in the white pages or in the classified-directory yellow pages under a heading such as "Alcoholism Information & Treatment Centers." If you find no phone book listing, write to or phone the central office (for both Al-Anon and Alateen):

Al-Anon Family Group Headquarters
P.O. Box 862
Midtown Station
New York, NY 10018-0862
Phone: 212-302-7240

Al-Anon members can usually tell you where to find Alateen meetings and groups, since it's common for Alateen groups to meet in their own Alateen rooms but at the same times and in the same buildings as Al-Anon groups.

You're likely to begin feeling relief at your very first Al-Anon or Alateen meeting. One of the hardest parts of being a codependent is the sense that you're the only person in the world who's going through such torments—that it may really be all your fault in some crazy way, or that maybe you're blowing it up all out of proportion.

But finding other people who have problems and troubles that are very much like yours often brings an immense relief. You begin to see that these problems and troubles are real, and that they're caused by the disease of your alcoholic/addict family member. You can hear about and talk over ways to deal with these troubles that will work better for you than the old ways of perhaps mostly brushing them aside and hoping they'll just go away.

Before Recovery—Second Main Point: How Do You Know for Sure Whether Your Family Member Has the Disease of Alcoholism/ Addiction?

It's not important for you to be absolutely certain that your family member has the disease of alcoholism/addiction. You should continue to attend Al-Anon (or Alateen) meetings and actively listen, talk, and read the program's literature as long as doing so helps you deal with the drinking or drug taking of your family member. In addition, being active and learning in Al-Anon will give you an increasingly vivid and practical understanding of the disease. Of course, reading this book will help you to recognize the major signs and symptoms of the disease—including the amazingly devious and persuasive ways in which it can lead the alcoholic/addict to deny having it.

If you like, you might try to answer one of the standard sets of diagnostic questions for self-use by a person who wonders whether he or she is an alcoholic—answering them for your family member who may have a problem. One of the most widely used sets consists of the twelve questions given in the short Alcoholics Anonymous publication *Is AA for You?* (You can get a free copy at an Al-Anon or related AA group meeting or by requesting a copy—and enclosing a stamped, self-addressed return envelope—from AA General Services Office, Box 459, Grand Central Station, New York, NY 10163.)

That booklet's yes-or-no questions range from the first—"Have you ever decided to stop drinking for a week or so, but only lasted for a couple of days?"—through queries on drink's causing trouble at home or days missed from work (or from school) or "blackouts," and on to a last question on whether you've ever thought your life would be better if you didn't drink. Honestly answering yes to four of the questions indicates probable trouble with alcohol.

For your purposes as a codependent, though, the question can be much simpler. The key one about your possibly addicted family member is, Does he or she go on drinking and/or using drugs even though troubles and hurts due to drunken/drugged behavior keep on happening, and possibly getting worse?

The simple fact is that nonaddicted individuals stop overusing and stop using completely in order to keep their jobs, or avoid drunk-driving arrests, or make family members stop complaining.

Individuals whose disease has advanced to a fairly severe level do not stop in spite of what happens to them, in most cases. Some do manage to cut down or even to stop altogether for a certain period of time—sometimes a few hours, a week, six months, or maybe even a year—after they've been terrified by some incident or threat. They do so without entering any recovery program. Indeed, they may force themselves to cut down or stop so that they won't have to enter a recovery program.

These cases are especially tormenting for codependents. On the one hand, the addicted persons will be full of anger, frustration, depression, and hostility from suffering the cravings of addiction without having done anything to recover from it. They make life very difficult for their codependents. And on the other hand, most who cut down or stop like this do, in time, go back to alcohol and/or drugs with worse results than ever before. As a result, codependents whose hopes have been raised are both bitterly disappointed and ago-nizingly confused.

So, if you're helped by going to Al-Anon or Alateen and by working with the Al Anon/Alateen program, keep it up.

Before Recovery—Third Main Point:
Reacting to the Disease in the Healthiest Way for You and for Your Alcoholic/Addict Relative

Through actively learning in Al-Anon/Alateen, you can also de-velop the most healthy reactions to a family member's possible disease of alcoholism/addiction. Meetings, members, and literature of these codependent groups help with this process in a great many ways. Two of the most important principles may illustrate the power of the help you can get.

"Stop enabling" is one of these especially powerful principles that

Al-Anon teaches. In this view, *enabling* is anything the codependent does to shield the active alcoholic/addict from the consequences of the addictive disease, or to help the alcoholic/addict continue practicing the addiction.

Normal family life induces family members to help each other with illness, accidents, setbacks, and misfortunes. But the disease of alcoholism/addiction perverts these normally generous and loving reactions to tighten the grip of the fatal disease, and to consume anything or anyone in the life of the alcoholic/addict in order to continue ravaging its victim.

Al-Anon's "stop enabling" strategy is based on recognizing this perverting force of the disease. It is also based on the insight that only hitting a bottom (as explained in Chapter 1) can break the hideous grip of denial in the alcoholic/addict and open the road to recovery. Shielding the alcoholic/addict from the results of addiction only postpones the time when the alcoholic/addict realizes the ghastly consequences of the disease.

Enabling is done in countless large and small ways. Among examples are:

—The child or spouse who lies on the phone to cover up for the addictive family member, saying things like "Mom didn't make it to work today because she's sick" (she's drunk) or "Dad can't explain why the bill isn't paid because he's out" (he's standing nearby telling his child what to say).

—The working wife who supports the alcoholic/addict husband after his disease has made him unemployable and who provides him with a home, money for his liquor and drugs, and nursing care when he vomits, passes out, and has injuries and hangovers (or vice versa for the alcoholic wife).

—The daughter who forgives mom or dad for being disgracefully drunk or drugged at parent's night at school.

—The son who cooks dinner night after night with no complaint because the mother gets drunk and passes out without getting dinner for the family.

—The spouse or child who lies on the phone to the friends of an alcoholic/addict family member, saying that the family member can't join them as planned because "he's sick" though actually he has passed out or is hung over.

—The parents who don't carry out their threats to make the adult son or daughter leave their home after the child has gone on using more and more alcohol and/or drugs after a series of car wrecks, job firings, jailings, and serious injuries.

—The spouse or parent who bails the alcoholic/addict out of jail and pays lawyers to smooth over the whole escapade in which drink and/or drugs led the alcoholic/addict to break the law and be arrested.

By contrast, Al-Anon veterans urge new members to practice a new and true variety of kindness and love for their diseased family members. If the alcoholic/addict passes out on the living-room floor, they urge, let him lie there all night; do not put him to bed. Let the alcoholic/addict whose addiction has led to his arrest stay in jail and see just where his disease has brought him. Force the alcoholic/addict out of the home—with police enforcement through a court order of protection, if necessary—when his or her drunken/drugged behavior in the home has become intolerable.

These are truly caring reactions, Al-Anon veterans explain, because they hasten recovery. Reacting differently only enables the addiction to continue torturing the alcoholic/addict and to bring on grave physical sickness and death.

"Detach with love" sums up a second powerful way in which Al-Anon can help you react in a healthy manner to your addicted family member. In applying it, you practice the first step in the Al-Anon program—a step in which you understand that you are powerless over the alcoholic, and that your life has become unmanageable (through the disruptions of alcoholism).

Using this Al-Anon precept makes it possible for you to stop enabling while still caring deeply for your addicted family member. Hate is all too tempting a reaction for you as a codependent, after the alcoholic/addict endlessly uses your money, affection, belongings, concern, and caring only to go on abusing alcohol/drugs. And with hate can come severe internal conflict for you—especially since you know that your addicted family member is driven to these destructive acts by a fatal disease over which he or she has no control.

In detaching with love, you can accept your inability to influence the disease and still go on caring about your family member. In fact, you can care in a way that has some real chance of getting him or her into recovery. Going on in helpless enabling or cutting off in hate instead tends only to let the disease rage on to destroy your family member. Detaching with love is also healthy for you, for it grounds you in reality and in constructive action and emotion. It helps free you from the insane denial and stunned agony of life as an impotent codependent.

Before Recovery—Fourth Main Point: Try an "Intervention" If You Possibly Can

Once you conclude that your family member does have the disease, by all means consider trying an approach that may save him/her, you, and the family years of further damage and torment due to alcoholism/addiction. This approach is intervention.

Intervention is a highly developed method for letting the alcoholic/addict hit bottom and begin recovery as early as possible. Counselors specially qualified for it by experience and training typically lead the process. Among them are clergy, physicians, Certified Alcoholism Counselors, social workers, psychotherapists, and other health-care professionals.

Intervention is carefully prepared for and planned over a number of weeks. It is carried out with the alcoholic/addict, insofar as possible, at a time when he or she is experiencing intense crisis and difficulty with the disease. Close family members or friends or work associates usually initiate the intervention.

Intervention culminates in a conference timed to surprise the alcoholic/addict. All the most significant and authoritative individuals for the alcoholic/addict generally attend—spouse or lover, children, parents, closest brothers or sisters, closest friend, boss, perhaps priest and doctor, and the intervention counselor.

In a typical conference, all these individuals try to break through the denial of the alcoholic/addict to persuade him or her to agree to enter an inpatient treatment center for detoxification and rehabilitation. Usually, all individuals in turn assure the alcoholic/addict of how much they care for him or her. The individual then very calmly and directly recites the facts of one especially bad incident of drunken/drugged behavior which terribly hurt that individual. The individual then tries to tell how much it hurt and how much the individual wants the alcoholic/addict to begin recovering from the disease and enter treatment. The individual last tells what protective action the individual will have to take if the alcoholic/addict does not enter treatment—such as cutting off financial support, forcing the alcoholic/addict out of the home, firing the alcoholic/addict from the job, or never seeing the alcoholic/addict again until embarked on recovery.

Guiding the process is the intervention counselor, who at the end is ready with the treatment admissions arrangements and an agreement for the alcoholic/addict to sign to start treatment. Treatment should start immediately, experts stress.

Intervention does succeed in persuading the alcoholic/addict to enter treatment in numbers of cases. What proportion hardly matters, for two reasons. First, if it should succeed in the case of your family member, the proportion of other cases in which it doesn't work has no importance for you. Second, some positive results develop even when the alcoholic/addict refuses to enter treatment. Those closest to the person know that they have made the greatest possible effort to end his or her suffering. And the alcoholic/addict learns precisely what the consequences of continued substance abuse will be from those closest to him or her. The alcoholic/addict may therefore hit bottom and be willing to enter treatment sooner than he or she would have without the intervention.

For help with intervention, you may telephone one of the treatment centers in your vicinity that are listed in Appendix 2 or find out the names of qualified intervention counselors nearby by writing or phoning: National Council on Alcoholism, Seventh Floor, 12 W. 21st St., New York, NY 10010, 212-206-6770.

Before Recovery—Fifth Main Point: What to Do If Your Alcoholic/ Addict Relative Hits Bottom Without Intervention

Before you can (or do) plan an intervention, your alcoholic/addict family member may hit bottom and want to start recovery. Count yourself terribly lucky if this happens. Be ready to act on that possibility if it should occur. What you do at this turning point can prove crucial. It may even save the life of your family member.

Follow a two-prong preparation, and have your arrangements ready for use at any time. First, have one or two phone numbers at which you can reach members of AA at any hour of the day or night to make a so-called twelfth-step call on your family member. These numbers are to be used right away if the family member finally feels so desperately sick and terrified that he or she wants to stop alcohol/drug abuse.

In a twelfth-step call, members of AA help an active alcoholic/addict who is hitting his or her bottom and is possibly ready for the first steps of recovery. People in AA are often unusually effective in helping other alcoholics/addicts stop. They draw on their own experiences of addiction and recovery to prove to still-active addicts that they know exactly what it feels like and that recovery can be achieved. They also selflessly and patiently help an active alcoholic/addict who is trying to stop—in large part because they learn in their AA program that only by doing so can they maintain their own sobriety and continuing recovery.

You can try several sources of phone numbers for AA members available for twelfth-step calls. Among them are senior members of your Al-Anon group, senior members of AA groups in your locale (fellow Al-Anon members can very probably tell you where and when such groups meet), and Alcoholics Anonymous information sources listed in your local phone book. One further source to try if needed is the main AA office (Alcoholics Anonymous, General Service Office, P.O. Box 459, Grand Central Station, New York, NY 10163, 212-686-1100).

Also as this first part of your two-prong preparation, you might attend some "open" AA meetings. These are meetings open to the public (that is, to nonalcoholics). At them, two or three members typically tell their stories—how their active alcohol/drug abuse originated and went on to devastate their lives, how they hit bottom and began recovery, and what they did and are doing to achieve an ongoing recovery from their disease. The time-honored, basic purpose of such talks is to help others who are struggling to begin and continue recovery—to show them and persons close to them what the disease is and does, that recovery works, and how recovery can be achieved.

In the second part of your two-prong preparation, get initial details about one or more nearby detoxification and rehabilitation treatment centers (referred to as "detox" and "rehab" at Al-Anon and AA meetings). The ones you select should be centers to which your addicted family member could go for treatment if needed right after hitting a bottom naturally. Check Appendix 2 for a listing of such centers throughout the United States and Canada.

If you don't find a center listed there that meets your needs, phone a center in your general locale for help. Request a referral to a center that can provide what you need in features such as location and services.

From a center that does meet your needs, get answers to basic questions such as hours and procedures for admission, health-insurance or other payment arrangements to be made, and any other helpful information for the family of a prospective entering patient. Since you are also inquiring in advance, you might also ask about possible intervention counseling and planning services available from the treatment center. This could be helpful for future use if your addicted family member does not soon hit a bottom naturally.

If possible, try to select a potential treatment center providing both detoxification and rehabilitation services, instead of rehabilitation services alone. Your family member may benefit from having detoxifying services at the outset of treatment. And it can be advantageous to have detoxification lead continuously at the same center right on into rehabilitation. In addition, inpatient treatment programs (those in which the patients reside at the center offering the program) are considered in many cases to be more effective than centers with outpatient programs, especially for the most severe cases.

Armed with these two types of preparations, you're in a strong position to mobilize vital aid when and if your alcoholic/addict relative hits bottom spontaneously. That background can also prove valuable should your family member start recovery through intervention.

In Early Recovery—First Main Point:
What to Do If Your Alcoholic/ Addict Relative Enters a Treatment Center

You're certainly justified in feeling great hope and great relief if your alcoholic/addict family member enters a treatment center.

You'll be informed by center staff members about what to expect and how to cooperate in the treatment. It may be helpful to know about some especially important matters that typically arise, though. Detoxification usually lasts five to seven days, and inpatient rehabilitation treatment typically takes some twenty-eight days (though it can last as long as three to six months for some centers or patients). Often, through the first week or more, patients are not allowed to talk on the phone with anyone outside the center and are not allowed to have visitors. Such a separation frees the patient from outside concerns to focus without distraction on the disease of alcoholism/addiction.

Typical rehabilitation offerings include a "family program" through which the closest relatives spend several days or a week or more at the center. It is very important for you to join in this part of the treatment with all the cooperation you can muster.

You will be given full instructions and explanations for the family program by a center counselor. In sum, though, it consists largely of sessions between codependents and the counselor, and between you, codependents in other families also attending the center, and counselors. These sessions generally seek to provide a clear understanding of the truth of the disease. They aim at helping codependents see how the disease has forced family members to form mutually destructive relationships with the sick family member and with each other—relationships based on dishonesty, deceit, and denial of the disease.

Efforts are made first to expose and then to eradicate these fallacies and all the hurt and pain underlying them. Insofar as possible, they are replaced with new perceptions of the true events and feelings of pivotal past situations. In addition, at least one session is held between your sick family member, you codependents in the family, and the counselor. At such a session, codependents talk to the sick family member in much the same way as they would in an intervention—that is, each codependent tells of one or more incidents in which the alcoholic/addict hurt him or her. The main purpose of such a session is to help break through the denial of the alcoholic/addict and of the codependent, and thereby help open the way to recovery from the disease.

Of great importance near the end of the treatment period is the determination to support your family member's resolve to join an AA (or NA) group and start being very active in it as soon as he or she gets home. Seasoned counselors usually recommend that the patients completing treatment and going home should attend a meeting every night (or day) for at least ninety days. Not drinking (or taking drugs) and going to a meeting a day reinforces continued recovery after leaving the treatment center for that important three-month period.

In Early Recovery—Second Main Point: What to Do If Your Alcoholic/Addict Relative Starts Recovery by Joining AA or NA

Perhaps one out of every four or five individuals recovering in AA didn't first go to an inpatient treatment center. Instead, this person started attending nightly AA meetings after hitting bottom. Some went through alcohol/addiction withdrawal under a doctor's care on an outpatient basis, a wise precaution for protection against possible withdrawal reactions such as convulsions.

Your alcoholic/addict family member may decide to try getting sober and straight this way in AA (or NA). If so, follow the recommendations often made by experienced members of AA and Al-Anon in situations like this. They typically advise that by all means you encourage your family member not only to go to meetings every night (or day) but to join a group and become as active as possible. In addition, they recommend carrying out all the following actions to give solid backing to your family member in trying to get sober through the AA program:

—Remove all liquor, wine, beer, and drugs (including mood-altering medicines in your bathroom medicine chest) from the home (or move them out of sight and under lock and key with only you holding the key).

—Don't serve any liquor or alcoholic beverages in the home.

—Do all you can to have your family member stay away from people or places associated with past or present drinking or drugging.

—If necessary, remind the family member to go to the daily meeting early, arriving ahead of time in order to chat and staying after to chat some more. Expect that he or she may probably go out for coffee and a snack with fellow members after the meeting.

—Go often to any open meetings of his or her home group (held once a week by many groups).

They usually also advise that, after your family member has attended ninety meetings in ninety days, you should support his or her practice of going daily or almost daily to meetings. Your relative may need meetings almost every day for a year or more in order to stay sober. An occasional night without a meeting for another important reason shouldn't cause a problem. But meeting attendance should be cut down only slowly and with great care. Some AA members drink or take drugs again, having relapses, or so-called slips. Most of those who do have slips find that they slipped after they had cut down on their meetings.

In Ongoing Recovery—First Main Point: Helping Your Alcoholic/ Addict Relative Stay Abstinent and Find a New Life

You can very substantially help your family member who becomes a recovering alcoholic/addict to continue in ongoing recovery through the months and years in a number of ways.

First, always remember, act on, and remind him or her as needed of the basic things you've learned about the disease of alcoholism/ addiction:

—It's incurable, progressive, and fatal if not arrested by complete abstinence.

—Stay away from the first drink or drug, for any use whatever might reactivate the latent addiction in its most extreme and destructive form.

—Continued active participation in AA or NA provides the best protection against a relapse.

Second, with health and health care, cooperate with the family member on important actions recommended throughout this book.

For example, help him or her guard against medicines that might trigger the addiction (as described and identified in Chapter 6).

Third, be interested and cooperative about what your family member is doing and learning in the AA or NA program. You'll very probably find that his or her general mental health improves steadily—and, in time, enormously—through participation in the program. Of course, the old compulsions and fears and lies and frenzies that had developed with the addiction need continued attention through the principles of the AA recovery program. Increasingly in evidence, however, will be new qualities of calm, warmth, confidence, helpfulness, and good humor.

If the process succeeds, your family member has found a new and healthy life. This comes about for understandable reasons. The old life had been ever more and more driven by the addiction. By contrast, the new life becomes more and more driven by recovery.

In Ongoing Recovery—Second Main Point: Helping Yourself Recover as a Codependent and Find a New Life

Increasingly, too, you should find that the deep emotional scars of the old life of terror and lies in a family with a critically ill alcoholic/addict have started to heal. Give yourself time for the old emotional reactions to change. Perhaps continued membership in Al-Anon will help promote such change, particularly as you work to help new members struggling with the hellish problems that have been resolved for your family. Al-Anon participation is often recommended to help a codependent like you recover from the traumas of living for years in a family made dysfunctional by alcoholism/addiction. Psychotherapy is also suggested to help your recovery, if severe old anxieties or depressions persist.

In time, you too should find yourself pursuing a whole new life—a life free from all that old sick fear, hate, anger, and shame. Recovery should feel very good and very healthy for you, too.

CHAPTER 3

How to Choose and Work with Doctors

SOME AREAS OF EVERYDAY LIVING REQUIRE SPECIAL CONSIDERATION IN terms of their potential impact on sobriety. These special areas are relatively few, but deserve attention and forethought.

Each recovering alcoholic or addict encounters the need for medical care. Sometimes the need is minor, such as treatment of a respiratory infection. Sometimes there are more significant problems requiring medical procedures or treatment; sometimes surgery is needed, and anesthesia and pain must be considered. How do you approach these emotionally difficult situations while maximally protecting sobriety?

As stated previously, it is better to anticipate the problems presented by these situations than to find yourself plunged into the center of an anxiety-ridden medical problem without having considered the special needs of a recovering alcoholic or addict.

How do you choose a doctor? What specifics do you tell your physician? What pitfalls exist in these areas? When undergoing surgery, why must you alert an anesthesiologist to your disease and its idiosyncrasies? How much true understanding and knowledge can you expect from the medical world? These are questions that are better considered before the needs arise.

Generally speaking, proceeding carefully in these areas is crucial for several reasons—some obvious, and some more subtle. It is obvious that, because drugs are prescribed by doctors, it is essential that both you and the doctor clearly understand the potential dangers carried by mind-altering or affect-changing medications.

It is less obvious that sobriety is more vulnerable when pain overtakes the recovering alcoholic or addict, as well as when the anxiety and fear of health-threatening conditions must be faced. Should you bear physical pain without the usual help provided by analgesic medications? Which threatens sobriety more—debilitating pain or narcotic medication? These are complex questions. There aren't always answers that are obviously right or wrong. However, the best choices can only be made by a knowledgeable physician and by the patient who has taken sobriety into account and is aware of the dangers inherent in these medical situations.

In considering all these issues, you must discuss your options with your close associates in AA. The importance of open decision making cannot be overemphasized. A recovering alcoholic or addict learns that it's essential to share decisions highly charged with emotion. The disease of alcoholism is always present to distort reasoning. Thus, it is vitally important for you NOT to plan in secret when the issues at hand can directly threaten sobriety.

How to Find Out Whether a Doctor Understands Alcoholism or Addiction

Now, how do you choose a doctor who will safeguard rather than imperil sobriety? As a first possibility, some persons will have a physician when they begin recovery, one with whom they have established a good relationship.

If you have such a physician with whom you'd like to continue, it is important to know what understanding your doctor has about the disease of alcoholism. This assessment is not easy to make, but it is probably best to make an appointment with your physician and to do your best to discuss the issue openly.

Remember, your doctor has many other things to take into consideration. He or she may or may not give the issue the same importance that you do.

When meeting with the doctor, tell him or her that you have realized you are an alcoholic (or an addict) and that you have begun your recovery. Remind the doctor that you have a disease, and say that you have been warned about taking certain medications. If your physician is well versed in these areas, it should soon be apparent. If he or she is not fully aware of these concepts, it is understandable. Medical training has improved through recent years in teaching about the disease of alcoholism, but there is still a general lack of clinical experience with alcoholism. If your doctor is open to the entire issue and your relationship is comfortable, you can build on this basic understanding on future occasions.

On the other hand, if your doctor resists the disease concept or doesn't fully accept the dangers of mind-altering medications (pain relievers, tranquilizers, sleep medications, and so on), you should seriously consider finding another physician. An alcoholic or addict cannot take the chance of receiving medical care from a doctor who won't accept certain basic principles about recovery from addiction. First, the physician must understand that alcoholism or addiction is a disease that is never cured, but only arrested on a daily basis.

Second, the physician must also understand how experience has shown that drugs which affect mood (that is, drugs that sedate, drugs that are euphoric, drugs that are "uppers") are potentially fatal to the recovering alcoholic or addict. An alcoholic or addict most often has a drug of choice. Recovery lifts the compulsive behavior of using this drug. However, any mind-altering substance can either directly trigger the old compulsive behavior or indirectly weaken the state of abstinence, eventually allowing the compulsive disorder to re-establish itself. Thus it is critical for the recovering person to find a physician who understands these principles.

How to Get Referrals to Doctors Who Understand Alcoholism or Addiction

As a second possibility, you may not have a physician you visit for your basic medical care. If so, how can you find an appropriate doctor? Word of mouth can often help. You can use friends in AA (or a similar recovery program) as a resource or call a nearby alcoholism/ addiction treatment center for referrals. You can also check the local office of the National Council on Alcoholism or of a local or state government council or bureau on alcoholism or drug abuse. (You can usually get the phone numbers and addresses of such offices from telephone directories or public libraries.)

Remember, you should not simply assume that a doctor has an adequate understanding of alcoholism. An alcoholic or addict must be protected by being sure of the right choice. However, in discussing the matter with any potential physician, take care not to mount a crusade to educate that professional. Simply assess whether the doctor at hand understands the basic concepts necessary to protect sobriety.

Doctors with Special Certification in Alcoholism and Drug Dependence Are Available in Increasing Numbers

Starting in 1986, licensed medical doctors (M.D.s) or doctors of osteopathy (O.D.s) could earn special certification in alcoholism and drug dependence. Some 650 physicians qualified for such certification on the basis of the first offering of written professional examinations given that year by the American Medical Society on Alcoholism and Other Drug Dependencies (AMSAODD).

AMSAODD is an organization of more than two thousand physicians "interested in the causes and consequences of alcoholism, alcohol-related problems, and other mood-changing drugs of dependency." It encourages "research, teaching, and the delivery of better care to the chemically dependent persons and their families," according to an official statement.

Additional offerings of the examinations in late 1987 and 1988 brought to well over one thousand the numbers of doctors holding the certification. No certification examinations were planned for 1989, but the Society expects to offer them periodically in future years. Any M.D. or O.D. recommended by a member may join AM-

SAODD, and only members are eligible to register for the examinations.

Is it important that a recovering alcoholic/addict seek a physician holding such certification? No. Many doctors who are competent in general or family practice and are well informed about alcoholism/addiction can quite satisfactorily promote continued recovery and abstinence while providing primary medical and health care.

Moreover, doctors with such certification may not be available for primary medical care. To a large extent, the certification is designed for doctors who concentrate much or all of their practice in alcoholism and other drug dependencies. And the numbers of doctors with such certification are as yet so relatively small that none may be accessible in your locale.

Of course, for the treatment of alcoholism/addiction itself, doctors with AMSAODD certification are particularly appropriate. AMSAODD members, and members with certification, are identified in the Society's directory. Inquiries may be addressed to the Society's office at 12 W. 21st St., New York, NY 10010, phone 212-206-6770.

Which Areas of Medical Treatment Are Most Dangerous

The areas of medical treatment most fraught with danger for recovering alcoholics/addicts are the use of anesthesia and the treatment of pain.

Mild pain, caused by most headaches, muscle and joint sprains, and the like, can be handled easily. Don't even consider taking dangerous drugs (that is, possibly habit-forming or addictive ones as identified in Chapter 6). Perhaps no drugs should be used at all for mild pain, since it might be best to resist the reflex to take a drug in any uncomfortable situation. Try heat or ice packs (whichever is suitable), hot showers, massages, or other mechanical measures to ease minor pain. However, when such mechanical measures may not be enough, try aspirin, acetaminophen (as in Tylenol), or ibuprofen to relieve minor pain. (These and other safe *analgesics*, or pain-relievers, are listed in Chapter 6.)

Moderate and severe pain, particularly postoperative pain, requires more serious consideration. Alcoholics are often told that when medically indicated, narcotic drugs and the like can be used.

However, this is not a simple matter. Everyone's pain threshhold differs, and "medically indicated" is not an absolute. It is the authors' belief that if pain is severe, a recovering alcoholic or addict can justifiably use narcotic analgesic medications that are habit-forming (and hence normally dangerous for recovering alcoholics or addicts). But this should be done only with certain precautions.

First of all, if you are anticipating pain from a surgical procedure, you should plan the situation long before the operation. You should first discuss your plans for postoperative pain medication with your sponsor in AA (or similar recovery program) and with other friends in the program. It is dangerous for you to make these decisions alone. If you keep your plans secret, your addiction-prone mind will almost surely find rationalizations to take drugs inappropriately or will fall into one of numerous traps that the compulsive disease will offer.

The only safe way to plan for appropriate use of pain medication is first to discuss it with fellow recovering alcoholics or addicts and then with the doctor, so that everyone understands the problem and the plan. Any alcoholic or addict who goes into an operating room takes a dangerous disease along—and must therefore plan carefully to protect his or her sobriety. The potential danger cannot be combatted effectively in the state of mind that exists postoperatively, when pain and the effects of anesthesia distort thinking. Advance planning is essential. Moreover, if narcotic medications were among the alcoholic's/addict's drugs of choice, then he or she is all the more vulnerable. It is impossible to be too careful in adhering to a well-devised plan.

Essential Actions for Coping with Severe Pain

The authors consider the following suggestions essential in getting through postoperative or other severe pain with maximum safety:

1. Discuss the situation and design a plan before surgery, as described directly above.
2. Discuss the plan with the doctor beforehand.
3. Keep a written log of all pain medications and sedatives taken. Doing this prevents distortions and self-deception about the

amount of medication actually used. Review this log with your sponsor or friends in AA (or similar program).

4. Stop using the pain medication as soon as possible. First discontinue injections at the earliest feasible time, and then discontinue pills—preferably, before going home from the hospital. Some pain endurance may be the price that has to be paid.

5. If treatment includes continued use of pain pills at home, maintain a written log of the number and frequency of pills taken, and—

6. Preferably, give the pills to a close friend in the recovery program to administer when they are needed. Having to ask for them will keep you honest.

7. Discard all unused medications immediately.

Essential Actions for Coping with Major Surgery and Anesthesia

An alcoholic or addict who faces surgery must take special care with regard to the use of anesthesia. This mandates discussing your individual situation with the anesthesiologist as well as the surgeon. The *anesthesiologist* is the physician who will choose the drugs used to induce sleep or to act as sedation during surgery, as well as pre- and postoperatively.

There are several relevant areas of concern here. Tell the doctor which classes or types of drugs you had abused. First, be clear about your drugs of choice. If tranquilizers, sedatives, or narcotics must be used during your hospitalization, then discuss whether the drugs used could be of a different class from your drugs of choice. This is important for, although any mood-changing substance carries a certain risk, the authors believe that using a drug of choice carries a special danger in triggering as yet unexplained physiologic or psychologic reflexes of addiction. If nothing else, the experience of "getting high" with a drug of choice will bring with it all the feelings and memories of your days of abuse. However, don't forget that, if alcohol was your only drug of choice, the basic principle still holds—any mood-changing medication (sedatives, narcotics, and so on) is dangerous for you.

For all alcoholics or addicts, another concern should be discussed with the anesthesiologist and the surgeon. In interviewing numerous recovering persons, the authors have found that many medications elicit unexpected or idiosyncratic responses in the alcoholic or addict. Whether you have abused only alcohol, only other drugs, or both, you need to anticipate possible unpredictable responses to pain relievers, anesthetics, sedatives, and even everyday drugs such as decongestants.

For example, many alcoholics report requiring much-heavier-than-normal doses of pain medication postoperatively or in other painful circumstances (such as dental pain or bone fractures). On the other hand, many alcoholics or addicts who have used narcotics as a drug of choice report being overly reactive to pain medications—that is, they require lower-than-normal doses, and have actually overdosed on normal amounts. The exact response to a medication cannot be predicted, but some unusual reaction should be anticipated.

Discuss these principles with your doctors. Your anesthesiologist in particular should understand that he or she can expect unusual reactions to medication. This forewarning can be invaluable information for optimal and safe anesthetic administration and care.

In summary, before any major surgery, as an alcoholic or addict, you must reach an understanding with your doctor and anesthesiologist by clearly conveying and emphasizing the following points:

1. That your former drug or drugs of choice should be avoided, if at all possible.

2. That any mood-changing substances carry cross-addiction potential for you and generally have a risk of triggering dangerous mechanisms of addiction.

3. That you may exhibit unusual reactions to various medications.

CHAPTER 4

Building Good Health in Recovery from Alcoholism/ Addiction

ACTIVE ALCOHOLISM/ADDICTION IN ITS ADVANCED STAGES WREAKS HAVOC with one's general health. You may recall from Chapter 1 that virtually all systems are adversely affected by chronic alcohol/drug abuse. When hitting bottom, the alcoholic/addict often shows the results of incredibly neglected nutrition. He or she may suffer with blotched and puffy skin, lost muscle mass and tone, little or no physical endurance, and various gastrointestinal disorders. He or she probably has atrocious health habits, neglecting regular sleep as well as personal cleanliness or dental care.

Rebuilding physical health in all these directions accordingly represents a major priority for most alcoholics/addicts through early recovery. It can also serve as a safeguard to continued recovery, for the sense of well-being it brings.

Actions to Meet Your Nutritional Needs Can Range from Lifesaving Measures to Minor Improvements

Nutritional needs vary widely among alcoholics/addicts in early recovery. Those needing detoxification from alcohol or drugs in some cases require relatively large amounts of certaiin vitamins and minerals to help correct gross nutritional deficiencies, if their substance abuse had led them to forego nutritious meals—or almost any meals—for many months or even years. Extreme substance abuse can give rise to maladies of the nervous system such as chronically numb and tingling extremeties (*polyneuropathy*), or more serious conditions marked by such symptoms as severe mental confusion, agitation, and loss of memory (*Wernicke's encephalopathy* and *Korsakoff's syndrome*). Symptoms of these maladies are often relieved during detoxification by large infusions of B vitamins. Among other vitamins and minerals that might well be given in large doses during detoxification are vitamin C, calcium, magnesium, and such specific B vitamins as thiamine, folic acid, and pantothenic acid.

And for other major nutritional therapy, the widespread twenty-eight day inpatient rehabilitation programs usually provide meals and snacks designed by dieticians to be therapeutically nutritious for persons typically malnourished and poisoned through years of substance abuse.

For some individuals in early and ongoing recovery, meeting nutritional needs may be almost a matter of life and death. As extreme examples, alcoholics who have suffered toxic damage to the pancreas leading to diabetes must control the amount of sugar in their diet (and have daily insulin injections) in order to survive.

Some recovering alcoholics have *hypoglycemia* (chronically low blood-sugar level) and consequently need to follow hypoglycemic diets. If they don't, they can in some cases suffer bouts of nearly unbearable worry, irritability, depression, headaches, and physical weakness. Such reactions can greatly strain their sobriety and at times help bring on a relapse into uncontrollable alcohol abuse.

Other individuals in recovery may have had comparatively high bottoms and, as part of their denial, may have made sure to practice good nutrition. Recovering alcoholics/addicts like these do not show the extent of damage from nutritional neglect that is typical of many persons starting to recover. Those who thus assure fairly sound nutrition during substance abuse may need to make only minor improvements in their nutrition to promote good health in recovery. Increasingly large proportions of young persons in their early twenties and younger begin recovery and enter recovery programs like AA. Among them, evidence of severe nutritional neglect at the start of recovery is relatively rare.

How to Determine Your Nutritional Needs in Recovery

The following guidelines will assist the recovering alcoholic/addict in regaining his or her health by satisfying nutritional requirements.

DETERMINING WHETHER YOU'RE A DIABETIC

If you have developed diabetes mellitus, the symptoms probably have already led you to see a doctor. First signs of the disease that usually prompt persons to seek treatment are thirst for far larger quantities of liquids than customary and passing of far larger quantities of urine than customary. Other signs are unaccustomed weakness and substantial weight loss due to no apparent cause.

Tests for determining whether a patient has the disease and assessing its severity measure the amount of sugar in the urine or blood. These reveal the consequences of its underlying cause—the failure of the pancreas to continue producing enough *insulin*, a hormone that regulates the amount of sugar in the blood. Too little insulin results in too much sugar in the blood, a condition called *hyperglycemia*.

Waste no time in seeing a doctor and being tested for diabetes if you think you've developed the symptoms. Persons who have it but do not get treatment can suffer needless complications.

MEETING YOUR NUTRITIONAL NEEDS AS A DIABETIC

Rely on your doctor for not only treatment but nutritional instructions if you have diabetes. Treatment usually includes daily insulin injections or oral medications monitored closely and adjusted by a doctor. It also often includes diet instructions providing for limited and uniform amounts of sugar in the foods eaten daily.

DETERMINING WHETHER YOU HAVE HYPOGLYCEMIA

Some authorities on recovery from alcoholism maintain that large proportions of alcoholics suffer from *hypoglycemia* (a condition of low levels of sugar in the blood, the opposite of diabetes, which is characterized by high levels of blood sugar). For instance, hypoglycemia "is prevalent among both early- and late-state alcoholics," declare Dr. James R. Milam and Katherine Ketchum in *Under the Influence* (New York: Bantam, 1981); Dr. Milam is cofounder of the Milam Recovery Centers near Seattle, Washington).

Hypoglycemia unquestionably does afflict some recovering alcoholics, even though research on its extent among alcoholics seems somewhat inconclusive thus far. Its effects can be serious enough to justify checking further if signs indicate you might have it.

Characteristic signs of hypoglycemia might appear in the way you feel. Having too low a level of *glucose* (a form of sugar) in the blood brings on sensations that typically include:

—Irritability
—Depression
—Lack of energy, tiredness, drowsiness
—Sweating, worry, anxiety
—Headaches (in some cases)
—Difficulty in concentrating
—Hunger
—Tremors, dizziness

Someone having such feelings due to the hypoglycemic condition of low blood sugar would find those feelings relieved quite soon after eating a high-sugar food such as a candy bar, pastry, or ice cream. The food would result in a sudden jump in blood-sugar level. But that jump and its relief would shortly be followed by a sharp drop both in blood-sugar level and in mood. All the former uncomfortable sensations would set in again, stronger than before. And the condition tends to steadily worsen with this kind of jolting, up-and-down experience of fluctuating blood-sugar levels.

If you think you have hypoglycemia because of such signs or for other reasons, arrange with your physician to get the standard medical test for this condition, the *glucose tolerance test*. In taking it, you first have nothing to eat or drink after about 9 or 10 P.M. on the night before the test. The next morning you report for the test at a doctor's office or clinic and have a blood sample taken. The sample is analyzed for a baseline sugar content. You are then given a high-sugar liquid to drink. After each of the first two half-hours and at each successive hour, your blood-sugar level is similarly measured over a period of five to six hours. Your doctor interprets the test results.

  Should you thereby find that you have hypoglycemia, you can probably obtain ongoing relief by following a diet given you by your doctor or a physician who specializes in nutritional problems.

Hypoglycemia has been used by many to explain symptoms that may not be related to nutritional problems. You should not be tempted to seize upon hypoglycemia as an explanation for problems that may have their basis in emotional disorders or other psychological mechanisms. If you need to clarify these issues, seek help from both medical and psychiatric professionals.

DETERMINING WHETHER YOU'RE FREE OF ANY OTHER SPECIFIC NUTRITIONAL PROBLEMS

Should you find yourself free of any serious signs of either diabetes or hypoglycemia, you may possibly still be concerned about some other nutritional deficiency. If you're chronically underweight or bothered about your eating habits, you may find the Chapter 8 section "Eating Disorders" particularly helpful. For this or any other nutritional concern, however, it is best to have a medical evaluation. As with any other medical condition, get help from a doctor well informed about alcoholism/addiction. (A special warning concerns taking any amphetamine medications for weight loss—these can put alcoholics/addicts at high risk for reactivating their addictions.)

On the other hand, you may have no special nutritional problems. If so, a normally sound diet (outlined later) should assure the nutrition you need for good health in early recovery.

Meeting Your Nutritional Needs in Early Recovery If You're Free of Specific Nutritional Problems

Use a diet like the following to meet your nutritional needs in early recovery from alcoholism/addiction if you have no special nutritional needs. (Special nutritional needs might stem from your having diabetes or hypoglycemia, or another special medical problem, such as a heart condition necessitating a low-salt diet.) Eating foods like the ones recommended in this diet should rebuild cells and tissues damaged by neglectful eating habits during acute substance abuse. This diet parallels those recommended for pregnant women, who obviously need sound nutrition for building new tissues.

YOUR NORMAL EARLY RECOVERY DIET— WHAT TO EAT AND DRINK IN YOUR MEALS AND SNACKS EVERY DAY

1. 4 *servings* (a *serving* is a normal family-meal portion of moderate size) *of meat, fish, eggs, or other high-protein foods:* Choose lean meats or preferably poultry; avoid processed meats such as hot dogs and cold cuts because of their high fat content and chemicals; vegetarian high-protein foods include soybeans; nuts; sunflower or sesame or pumpkin seeds; beans; and alfalfa sprouts.
2. 4 *to 5 servings of vegetables and fruits:* Try to eat 1 or 2 servings of citrus fruits, and 1 or 2 servings of green leafy vegetables; pure vegetables or fruit juices can substitute for vegetables and fruits; avoid canned fruit with added sugar syrup and frozen fruit with added sugar.
3. 4 *to 5 servings of grains:* such as whole-grain bread or cereal, brown rice, spaghetti, noodles, or cornmeal.
4. 4 *servings of milk or milk products:* representing one serving are an 8-ounce glass of whole or skim milk; a cup of yogurt, ice milk, or ice cream; a half-cup of cottage cheese; or 2 or 3 slices of cheese.

5. *2 tablespoons of fats and oils:* butter or margarine, mayonnaise, peanut butter, or vegetable oil, as in salad dressing.
6. *4 glasses or more of water:* a quart or more a day.

These are minimum daily amounts for women and men with a usual body weight of up to about 120 to 150 pounds. Eat more if you're unusually tall or large-boned.

For attaining best nutrition—and avoiding excess fat—eat little or none of common snack foods and beverages, which typically provide mainly "empty calories" and chemical food additives (which serve no nutritional needs and may prove harmful).

Among these are:

—Various chips and crackers (potato chips and cheese chips)
—Carbonated soda and cola drinks
—Candy
—Pastries that are highly sweetened (cookies, pies, and cakes)
—Sugar-coated cold cereals

Concerning such sweets as candy and pastries, it's traditionally been common in AA for newcomers struggling not to take the first drink to be told to eat something sweet whenever the craving is intense. Doing this in the first few weeks or months of sobriety should not be very harmful nutritionally if it really does help prevent taking a drink. It certainly is infinitely less harmful than drinking. But for the most desirable nutrition, cut down in time on the sweets to very few or none.

However, if you're hypoglycemic, begin a hypoglycemic diet as early as possible and ignore the advice about eating candy or a pastry to quell urges to drink. With hypoglycemia, the urge to drink can get stronger and stronger if you combat it by eating sweets. A sweet can at first reduce the urge, but as the sugar's effect wears off, the urge to drink can return stronger than before—and so on.

The foods and liquids outlined should provide all the vitamins and minerals normally needed for sound nutrition. However, while the exact nutritional needs of early recovery have not been fully clarified, some physicians will prescribe supplementary vitamins in the early weeks of recovery. It would be advisable to discuss this when consulting a physician on your health needs in early recovery.

Follow your doctor's recommendations on such viatmin and mineral supplements. As a general guide, an accompanying table presents the *recommended dietary allowances* (RDA) as recently defined by

RDA Values for Vitamins and Minerals for Typical Mid-life Adults

Vitamin or Mineral	RDA Amount
Vitamin A	1000 mg RE* (5000 IU)
Vitamin D	10 mcg (400 IU)
Vitamin E	10 mg
Vitamin C	80 mg
Thiamin	1.4 mg
Riboflavin	1.6 mg
Niacin	18 mg
Vitamin B_6	2.6 mg
Folic acid	800 mcg
Vitamin B_{12}	4 mcg
Calcium	1200 mg
Phosphorus	1200 mg
Magnesium	450 mg
Iron	60 mg
Zinc	20 mg
Iodine	175 mcg

*retinol equivalents
Source: National Academy of Science, National Research Board

the federal government (through the National Academy of Science-National Research Board). Those daily RDA values are approximately as shown in the following table. (The table lists the approximate RDA values for a man in his thirties weighing about 155 pounds or for a pregnant woman in her thirties with a normal nonpregnant weight of about 120 pounds. The daily amount of iron shown is the maximum value recommended during pregnancy and can be attained only by iron tablets rather than from the foods you eat; 10 to 18 milligrams is the amount recommended for a person who is not pregnant.)

Meeting Your Nutritional Needs in Recovery If You Have Hypoglycemia

If you find that you do have hypoglycemia, the success with which you manage your nutrition may prove decisive for continuing in recovery from alcoholism/addiction. Some authorities on recovery hold that hypoglycemic reactions not prevented by special diets can inflict distress so severe that some recovering alcoholics/addicts with the condition find it impossible not to resume drinking for relief.

Fortunately, following a special diet for hypoglycemia prevents the painful sensations resulting from a hypoglycemic reaction (including intense depression, irritability, weakness, tremors, dizziness, and nausea). You can obtain such a special diet from a doctor who specializes in nutritional problems.

An Illustrative Case: An Alcoholic with Severe Hypoglycemia

The difficulty of diagnosing and starting to recover from both a severe case of hypoglycemia and alcoholism is illustrated by Gloria B., a health-club fitness consultant-teacher and mother now in her late thirties. Staying thin was a major obsession for Gloria throughout her teens in an affluent suburb of a large midwestern city, she recounts.

"I drank coffee all day, and at night I drank wine," she says. "As a result, I could go without eating almost anything at all. Although I didn't realize it, I used alcohol as a way of controlling my diet."

Gloria had developed a regular dietary regimen for slimness by her early twenties. She measured all her food and could thus make sure that every morning she had exactly four ounces of orange juice. She also had two hardboiled eggs and two cups of coffee. She ate no lunch. Around midafternoon she ate one banana or one apple and drank "lots of coffee."

By late afternoon, Gloria would have done her four hours a day of aerobic workouts, some in classes she taught and the rest in classes she was taking. At dinner she typically had meat, vegetables, a salad, and "a lot of wine." Her total intake of calories would thus run less than one thousand calories a day—not including the wine.

For more than a year, at one point, Gloria had no menstrual periods. This didn't bother her once she found that a suspension of periods is fairly common in women athletes and women dancers. It probably results from a lack of body fat, she learned.

Gloria was troubled, though, by often feeling unwell and tired. And she had an almost constant craving for sweet, sugary foods, such as ice cream and especially hot fudge sundaes. Most of the time she could resist this craving by stirring up her fears of getting fat. But periodically the craving became just overwhelming. She'd break down and, in actions like those of the bar-hopping active alcoholic, she'd go from one restaurant to the next gorging herself on hot fudge sundaes.

To her horror, she also had irresistible urges to binge on sweets at dinner parties. The special hunger would come over her. She would steal extra desserts, go to the bathroom with them, lock herself in, and then gorge herself.

Gloria grew expert at spotting the special hunger as it came on. As hunger impulses grew she asked herself, "Is it head hunger? Or is it stomach hunger?"

"I could ignore stomach hunger," she says. "That was just normal hunger."

But her "head hunger" would go on getting worse. It would make her eyes blur; make her feel dizzy, driven to eat, enormously irritated, and finally frenzied, crazy—"crazy hungry," she says. After that point she couldn't prevent herself from having a binge on sweets.

This kind of out-of-control hunger was later found to result from a hypoglycemic reaction she was having. But for years she had no inkling whatever of the cause.

One day a friend happened to tell Gloria how a doctor in the area had helped her get over problems with hypoglycemia. Gloria went to see him. He gave her the glucose tolerance test, and the results proved that Gloria did indeed have hypoglycemia. He gave her a hypoglycemia diet to follow.

"At first, I gained quite a bit of weight," Gloria says. She explains that some of the high-protein foods in the diet also had high calories, among them nuts, red meats, cheese, and eggs. She also gave up wine and coffee for a month after starting on the diet. After she'd been on the diet for about a year, she stopped drinking wine and stopped having binges on high-sugar foods.

About that time she went with her family to a large wedding celebration of friends in a major eastern city. The first night there she drank a cocktail. It triggered her alcoholism. For the next three days of the wedding functions, she continued drinking heavily. In addition, on the third day, she went on an ice cream binge.

Once they'd returned home, she says, "I had horrible headaches, muscle spasms, and a backache—a very bad backache. I couldn't straighten up. My back was frozen. I knew it was a reaction—a reaction to all that liquor and ice cream."

Terrified, Gloria at once got help by entering Overeaters Anonymous (OA), a mutual-help fellowship closely patterned on Alcoholics Anonymous, but seeking to help those addicted to overeating instead of alcohol. In OA Gloria had a food sponsor (an experienced member to help her learn and use the OA program) and worked out a food plan or diet. Her diet generally paralleled a hypoglycemia diet, Gloria says, and had a high-protein, low-carbohydrate content consisting largely of vegetables, fruits, and high-protein foods.

Gloria asked her food sponsor when she might be able to include a glass of wine in her OA food plan. Her sponsor replied that maybe wine was one of Gloria's binge foods. Binge foods are of course those that an individual in OA can't stop eating. Ice cream and hot fudge sundaes were clearly binge foods for Gloria.

But Gloria was furious when her food sponsor said that wine might be a binge food for her. She fired that sponsor and got a second sponsor, who told her that it would be all right to have one glass of wine with dinner. That night she had the first glass of wine—but right afterward went on to have many more glasses. This gave her so bad a hangover that she went for several weeks without having any wine at all.

After those weeks Gloria felt again that she might be safe in having only that one glass of wine which her sponsor had said would be all right. So at dinner one night she tried having one glass again. "Even before I finished that single glassful," Gloria says, "I felt sick, terribly dizzy, nauseous. I had a three-day hangover from that one glass of wine."

Deeply alarmed, Gloria concluded she was also an alcoholic and joined AA. Since then she has been completely abstinent from alcohol and has had no food binges.

Today, Gloria follows a diet that is basically a hypoglycemia diet, she says. She also takes a carefully worked-out and extensive array of vitamins and minerals that she believes to be essential to her continued recovery from hypoglycemia and alcoholism. In addition, exercise plays an important part in helping keep hypoglycemia inn check, she says.

Of fellow recovering AA members, she notes, "So many people have what look to me to be hypoglycemic reactions after they get in the program. As I did, they feel unwell after they drink too much coffee, or have too many doughnuts, or binge on cakes, pies, or cookies. It makes their blood sugar and their mood shoot up for a while, but then comes the drop."

Exercise to Build Good Health in Recovery

Gradually developing a regular routine of appropriate exercise represents another way of building your health in recovery. Active alcohol or drug abuse produces inactivity and isolation for most, with such results as atrophy of the muscular system, severe decline in fitness of the circulatory and respiratory systems, and pallid and puffy skin. Exercising sensibly and enjoyably in recovery can help reverse such physical deterioration and may help relieve depression and chronic fatigue. For many in recovery, exercise can very substantially reinforce their defenses against a possible renewed outbreak of their disease.

GUIDELINES FOR EXERCISE IN RECOVERY

Major guidelines for beneficial exercise in recovery include the following:

1. *Refrain from taxing exercise during detoxification.* Your system is undergoing massive strains of rapid physical change while it is detoxifying in recovery. This is particularly true during the first five to seven days of abstinence, but it holds true as well for several weeks thereafter. It is accordingly advisable to avoid any taxing exercise during the early weeks of your abstinence. This will prevent musculo-skeletal damage, as well as untoward physiologic reactions (such as dehydration or seizures).

2. *Base your exercise on a medical examination and advice.* To be safe, have a comprehensive medical examination early in recovery. Its results should guide your plans to restore adequate health practices including exercise. Medical guidance can inform you of your general physical condition and determine the exercise appropriate for it. Specific needs can then be safely addressed.

3. *As feasible, carry out three kinds of exercise. Include strengthening, or isometric; cardiovascular conditioning, or aerobic; and stretching, or flexibility building.* General fitness recommendations by many exercise physiologists call for carrying out a weekly exercise routine that includes three types of exercise adapted to your physical condition. All three can be practiced in appropriate forms for almost any age or physical status. Detailed instructions for thus adapting and carrying out all three types of exercise are available to health-club members, in widespread adult education fitness or exercise classes, and in books and videocassette tapes on fitness and exercise at libraries and stores carrying books or tapes.

Strengthening Exercises

In strengthening exercise, you develop muscular strength either by time-honored workout routines (such as push-ups or chin-ups, deep knee bends, and hand clenches), by weight-lifting, or by health-club activities like those on Nautilus apparatus. Such strengthening or isometric exercises help to rebuild your muscle mass and restore your muscle tone in recovery. Heavy strengthening workouts should be done every other day, physical conditioning experts usually advise, to allow the muscle tissue time to recover and develop.

Aerobic Exercise

Jogging is the most familiar widespread example of the aerobic or cardiovascular conditioning type of exercise. However, by no means do you need to go jogging for your exercise of this type unless it appeals to you. Any exercise sustained without a break for at least twenty minutes a day at a specified level of moderate exertion is considered aerobic. It can consist of such activities as workout routines (at home or a health club), bicycling, swimming, cross-country skiing, rowing, sessions on a stationary exercise bicycle or other exercise apparatus, or even just rapid walking.

You should work up gradually—on the basis of medical advice and over a period of weeks—to the full twenty-minute duration of full aerobic sessions. Some authorities advise that you do your aerobic exercise sessions only every other day, in order to give your heart muscles and the muscles involved with your lungs and the rest of your circulatory system time to recover. Others advise daily aerobics instead. Ask your medical adviser which would be better for you.

Experts advise using a simple method for gauging the specified level of exertion to attain to make your exercise session aerobic. Through the twenty or more minutes of your aerobic exercise session, your correct pulse rate (in beats per minute) can be determined by the following equation:

(220 minus your age to the nearest year) × 70 percent = minimum pulse rate (in beats per minute)

For age 25, the formula yields 136 pulse beats per minute as an appropriate pulse rate. For age 65, that minimum pulse rate would be

109. In addition, do not exceed a maximum pulse rate calculated by a similar formula, 220 minus your age times 80 percent (yielding, for age 25, a maximum pulse rate of 156; for age 65, a maximum of 124). You might find it easiest to take your pulse by counting it for 15 seconds and then multiplying by 4 to obtain the pulse beats per minute.

Be especially careful to use medical advice to guide your aerobic exercise. As you're aware, recovering alcoholics/addicts have compulsive tendencies, and these can be focused on wholesome as well as destructive activities. And aerobic exercise can be dangerously overdone.

Nevertheless, you should realize substantial values from safely practiced aerobic exercise. Such exercise strengthens and conditions your entire cardiovascular system and lungs and thereby lowers your blood pressure, possibly warding off cardiovascular disease (and is thought by advocates to add years to your life). Also, aerobic exercise seems to be beneficial as a way of maintaining glucose utilization (and thereby possibly contributing to a sense of energy due to adequate blood-sugar levels).

Stretching Exercises

Stretching, or flexibility-building, exercises represent a third type to include in your weekly routine. These stretch your joints and muscles to preserve and extend maximum freedom of movement. They also help maintain good posture. Exercises that stretch are included in most workout routines. They're also the warm-up exercises used by athletes and joggers to limber up for their major efforts. As a further example, yoga exercises incorporate stretching to an unusually healthful extent.

4. *Make your exercising as enjoyable as possible.* To the extent that you can, combine recreation and socializing with exercise to make it enjoyable and not just drudgery. Hiking, swimming, canoeing or rowing, tennis, baseball, basketball, and golf are all good forms of exercise that are also fun. Getting your exercise enjoyably helps assure that you'll carry out an activity important for full recovery and health.

Building Other Sound Health Habits in Recovery

Other habits to cultivate to promote sound health in recovery from alcoholism/addiction include sleep, regular health care, and relaxation with avoidance of stress.

HEALTHFUL SLEEP HABITS

Disturbed and troubled sleep patterns are common among alcoholics/addicts both before and after starting recovery. Establish regular habits for getting sufficient sleep—or trying to get it—as early as possible in recovery. Hold to regular times for going to bed at night and for getting up in the morning insofar as you can, and allow enough hours for sleep or rest—generally eight hours a night. (It has been noted that brain-wave patterns are also physiologically disturbed for some time after recovery begins, in a number of cases.)

Even if you cannot sleep, do your best to stay relaxed and continue resting. Your system gets almost as much benefit from rest as it does when you are actually asleep.

One rule is vitally important: *Take no pills of any kind for sleeplessness.* Sleeping pills are one of the major causes of relapses among alcoholics/addicts who have started recovery. Moreover, they tend to prolong and perhaps even intensify the causes of sleeplessness. Doing without them generally relieves the condition of sleeplessness sooner.

For sleeplessness, the following measures are often advised by alcoholics/addicts long experienced in recovery programs:

1. Exercise to get physically tired. Do this, though, perhaps two hours before trying to sleep, to let the effect of adrenalin released by the exercise wear off.

2. Drink some warm milk.

3. Take a warm, relaxing bath.

4. Read some of the literature of your recovery program (AA or NA, for example).

5. Just lie there and repeat silently to yourself, over and over, favorite slogans of your recovery program or the "serenity prayer" recommended in the program.

ADEQUATE HEALTH CARE

Make it a habit in recovery to obtain adequate health care. Too often, active alcoholics/addicts neglect getting care for their teeth or their vision or their injuries. First, make a plan for correcting old areas of long neglect—for instance, by getting long-deferred dental care or having your eyes examined for eyeglasses or contact lenses.

Then, as illnesses or health problems arise, make it a habit to get health care for them promptly. Doing so will clear up health difficulties more quickly and easily and will reinforce good feelings about yourself.

RELAXATION AND STRESS AVOIDANCE

Take time to relax in your life, with days off, vacations, or just intervals of enjoyable idleness. Many alcoholics/addicts are also workaholics—and what might be called "stressaholics." Times for relaxation should optimally be what normal people typically allow—a couple of evenings a week, at least a half-day and evening on a weekend, and at least two weeks a year of vacation. If relaxed times of those lengths would be a problem, make yours shorter as needed, but be sure to provide for them.

Second, as anyone should, try to avoid unnecessary stress. For example, don't commit yourself to unreasonably heavy responsibilities or unreasonably short deadlines. Make it a habit to watch for high-stress situations you can avoid or modify. Use that familiar AA slogan, "Easy Does It."

CHAPTER 5

Avoiding Special Hazards with Common Health Problems

CERTAIN EVERYDAY HEALTH PROBLEMS OR CONCERNS CAN POSE POTEN-
tially grave dangers to continued abstinence for the recovering
alcoholic or addict. These threats and ways of avoiding them are
explained in this chapter for the following common health problems:

Pain
Dental care
Sleeplessness
Home hygiene (mouthwashes, breath deodorizers, toothpastes)
Home treatment of minor illnesses and injuries

Pain

Dealing with pain as a recovering alcoholic/addict requires special efforts and, on occasion, courage. Pain, of course, comes in many forms and in varying degrees, and every individual has a different threshhold for tolerating it.

Alcoholics/addicts seem to focus more than others on physical discomfort. There is often an element of panic in the way recovering addicts react to mild or moderate pain. Severe pain, however, is often tolerated relatively well by them. Mild to moderate pain often provokes a desperate instinct in the alcoholic/addict to seek medication for relief without thinking clearly about the problem at hand.

First, it is necessary to emphasize the concept of cross-addiction. A recovering alcoholic whose only drug of choice was alcohol still is in danger of activating the disease by using other mood-altering substances. He could either become addicted to the pain-relieving substance itself or be led back to his drug of choice (that is, alcohol). Or, at the very least, the individual could develop a dangerous behavior pattern of associating substances with a sense of physical or psychological relief.

Stan T., for instance, was sober for five years when he developed a pattern of headaches. He had taken a drug called Fiorinal for headaches before he stopped drinking, and he asked his doctor to renew the prescription after the headaches developed during sobriety. The doctor complied, and Stan began using Fiorinal tablets for his headaches.

Soon the headaches and the pill use increased. In time, it was difficult for Stan to know which was the prime problem—the headaches or the pills. Matters got worse and Stan finally had to enter a hospital for detoxification.

Why did his tragic relapse occur? The pills he was taking contain a barbiturate (a sedative) that, for Stan, had become addicting. They also contain considerable amounts of caffeine, and many of his headaches could well have resulted from what might be termed between-dose caffeine-withdrawal symptoms as his Fiornal abuse had accelerated. Thus, Stan had felt he needed more pills and the situation deteriorated.

Of course, his disease was activated, and denial reared its ugly head. Stan wouldn't accept the possibility that the pills could be a problem. He insisted that his only problem was "terrible headaches." That was his only focus.

These situations are extremely complicated. They often confuse everybody for long periods of time. The disease of addiction will latch onto anything to nourish itself—and physical pain is one of those things. Then lies, deception, and denial can thrust a sober person into a costly, humiliating, and perhaps even fatal, reactivation of the disease.

Caution therefore must accompany any type of pain treatment. Back problems, headaches, dental work, and minor injuries are some of the often minor ailments which may have major complications.

Kathy M. comes to mind as another example. Kathy had been sober for three years when an old back problem was aggravated. The pain became quite severe, and, at first, Kathy talked about it with her AA friends and merely rested and used heat treatments.

Soon, however, she grew quite depressed. She could do nothing but focus on the pain. She saw a doctor, who gave her a prescription for Tylenol with Codeine. She took the pills without discussing the move with her AA sponsor. Soon she was using them daily and, because of the pain, stopped going to her AA meetings. In several weeks she couldn't stop the pills and was still in pain. She was very depressed and began drinking.

Trials like these are very hard for the recovering alcoholic/addict. Pain, after all, is very real. In such situations, pain ruins the quality of life. It interferes with the positive process of recovery. And significant pain leaves few alternatives to the use of mood-altering substances. What can a recovering alcoholic/addict do to safeguard continued abstinence? He or she can't be expected to suffer unbearably. Here are some suggestions.

First, have any symptoms of pain evaluated medically. Learn as much about the physical problem and therapeutic alternatives as you can. Next, before taking any steps, discuss the situation fully with your AA sponsor and others in the AA group. See what the experience of other persons has been. If medication is necessary make a plan with your sponsor.

We suggest that such a plan include the following actions:

1. Keep a written record of every dose of pain medication taken.

2. Call your sponsor before taking the medication.

3. Go to as many meetings as possible during this time and talk about the situation there.

4. Obviously, discontinue the use of the medication as soon as possible.

A further technique might be to ask one's sponsor to keep the medicine so that a phone call would be necessary to receive each dose. This, of course, is not always practical, but we know of situations where people went this far to protect their sobriety.

For people whose active addiction involved drugs, the management of pain is even more difficult. Although the same principles apply, for these addicts, exposure to pain-relieving narcotics has an even greater chance of triggering cravings and potential relapses.

Valerie M. lived in California and had used cocaine and Valium as well as alcohol. She hit a horrible bottom, losing her family and her job. She joined AA in terrible health and may not have survived much longer had she kept on drinking and drugging.

Valerie got sober with difficulty, but after a year and a half she was doing very well. She was working again. She had a cordial relationship with her former husband and her daughter, and she worked hard at her AA program. For the next four years, her recovery progressed. She helped many other recovering women and life improved in all areas.

After six years of sobriety, severe headaches brought her to a doctor. Darvocet was prescribed and Valerie took the pills without any special precautions, even though the doctor had told her that they contained a narcotic. She went on using them for several weeks and the headaches ceased. She kept the pills in her medicine chest but didn't use them until a second siege of headaches occurred a month of so later.

A fellow AA member who saw Valerie take the pills registered surprise. Valerie said, "My doctor prescribed the medicine for my headache, and this kind of pill was never my thing anyhow." She went on periodically renewing the prescription and taking the pills for headaches every month or so.

About a year later she developed back pain, a flare-up of a sciatica that she had had after a horseback-riding accident twelve years before.

She again began taking the Darvocet, but the back pain was very strong. The medicine didn't bring relief. Valerie didn't talk to people in AA about her distress. She went to several doctors and got a prescription from one of them for Percodan. She knew this was a drug with a high potential for abuse, but she rationalized taking it, saying that narcotics were never "her thing" and besides the pain was so severe she had to take the Percodan.

She tended to talk only to people who condoned her using the pills. When AA friends expressed concern, Valerie avoided meetings.

Soon she was taking pills every day and became obsessed with her "pain problem." After many months of desperation, she was admitted to a hospital and a long detoxification began. When Valerie left the hospital, she avoided AA meetings, began drinking, and is now in worse shape than when she first joined AA.

Valerie's case illustrates several principles. First, she used the initial medication without appropriate concern and safeguards. She took control of the medication herself and underplayed the danger. She began ignoring the reality of what she was doing and wouldn't listen to the warnings of her AA friends.

Next, Valerie escalated to one of the most addictive euphoric narcotics, Percodan. Whether or not her back pain was severe, a red flag should have been raised at this point. Certain pain medications seem to be more addictive than others. Percodan is one. Dilaudid is another. Demerol is a third. All narcotics are addicting and dangerous to abstinence for the recovering alcoholic/addict, but these three seem to be in a class by themselves—in being favored by active addicts and in being treacherous therapy for alcoholics/addicts in recovery.

Another dimension to Valerie's case was her avoidance of meetings and AA friends who were disturbed by her drug use. When pain and drugs enter the life of a recovering alcoholic/addict, their disease gains incredible momentum. Denial and rationalization take over, and often the person begins manipulating everyone—AA friends, doctors, work colleagues, and family. They start to receive only the messages that condone taking drugs very selectively. They remember that people say it's OK to take prescribed medications for a medical condition. They don't remember the cautions and restraints.

Again, these situations are very complex but point out vividly the need for the recovering alcoholic/addict to put decisions regarding pain treatment into the hands of AA colleagues and knowledgeable professionals. Use of pain-relieving drugs should *never* be left to the sole judgment of the recovering person. For normal people, the pain prescription often reads: "One or two tablets every four hours as needed for pain." For alcoholics/addicts, it should read:

> One dosage if absolutely necessary after fully discussing the need for the medicine with your sponsor, and fully disclosing and recording how many pills you have taken for this problem, and seriously considering whether you can do without the pill, and being aware and concerned about all properties, dangers, and warnings with respect to this medication and your health.

Pain and drugs are a combination that any recovering alcoholic/ addict can never take too seriously or handle too carefully.

We've been discussing situations in which pain leads to the use of narcotics or related mood-altering drugs. We must emphasize that other means of pain control should be considered and used instead of narcotics wherever possible. Among alternatives are physical therapies, acupuncture, biofeedback, and other techniques offered by specialized pain clinics or doctors found in many parts of the country. Although the recovering alcoholic/addict should evaluate such differing modalities carefully as to their applicability to his condition, he should not overlook them. It is always preferable that a recovering alcoholic/addict avoid mood-altering medications wherever possible. For example, if you have a chronic pain problem, be sure to investigate local pain clinics or centers. Some of them may well offer techniques that you can substitute for medications, such as biofeedback.

You shouldn't forget there are nonnarcotic medications that are safe for recovering alcoholics/addicts. These generally are in the category of anti-inflammatory drugs such as Motrin, Advil, Naprosyn, and Indocin. It is true that these medications are rarely effective in completely relieving moderate to severe pain. However, for a recovering individual looking for safe alternatives to narcotics, these medications in conjunction with physical techniques can often be used to manage even severe pain.

Pain management is a difficult challenge for a recovering alcoholic/addict. But when faced with pain, you should carefully consider the principles summarized here rather than resort to careless use of prescription medications—use that could lead to a tragic loss of your sobriety.

Dental Care

Dental work is often undertaken during the early stages of sobriety. Recovering alcoholics/addicts seem to want to take care of neglected teeth once their self-improvement program gets rolling. Many report having had a lot of dental problems during active substance abuse. Perhaps years of abuse have a direct effect on dental condition, possibly compounded by the ravages of nutritional deficiencies. In any event, recovering alcoholics/addicts very commonly need dental care.

Special hazards to continued abstinence posed by dental work, of course, include how pain will be handled. There are also a few specific matters with regard to dentistry that should be understood.

For one, nitrous oxide as a dental anesthetic should be avoided because it is a mood-altering substance. "Laughing gas," as nitrous oxide has long been called, is used as a recreational drug by some persons. There are enough alternatives for anesthesia so that nitrous oxide should simply be rejected by recovering alcoholics/addicts whenever proposed.

Generally, dental work can be performed with local anesthesia. Such *local anesthetics* are injected by hypodermic needle to numb the area being worked on. The anesthetic agents used in this way (usually a liquid anesthetic named *Xylocaine*) are safe for persons in recovery. They are sometimes mixed with epinephrine to lengthen their effect. Injections with such added epinephrine give some persons in recovery an uncomfortable sensation of overstimulation. However, the feeling passes in a short time. In general, for recovering alcoholics/addicts, local anesthesia is the safe alternative for blocking pain caused by dental work.

Sleeplessness

Difficulty in falling asleep or staying asleep is often a problem early in sobriety. Certainly insomnia is a common feature of detoxification or withdrawal. A simple principle applies in case you should have this problem:

No drugs should be used to help you sleep.

Sleeplessness is surely an extremely uncomfortable state. But, as is often mentioned in recovery programs, "No one ever dies from lack of sleep." When your body gets tired enough, sleep will come.

During withdrawal, the body has to normalize. The effects of detoxification on the nervous system create an anxious, shaky, and often jittery state. Relaxation seems impossible. If not medically prohibited, mild exercise (such as a brisk walk) during the day and hot showers or baths at night often promote some degree of physical relaxation. However, if sleeplessness continues, you must simply bear it.

Once their early problems of insomnia pass, most recovering alcoholics/addicts have little difficulty with sleep. If there are periods of insomnia later in sobriety, again drugs cannot be used. All sleeping pills are mood-altering—and some are especially dangerous for individuals in recovery.

For example, Eddie P. had been sober for a year. He was doing well when a problem at work began to bother him. He became obsessed with something he considered unfair. Soon he couldn't sleep well at night, and he became irritable and more uncomfortable at work.

He talked about the work problem at his AA meetings and with his sponsor. But he never mentioned that he had seen his doctor about his insomnia, had obtained a prescription for a drug called Halcion, and had begun taking it at night. Soon he was using the pills almost every night and having difficulty sleeping when he didn't use them.

His work problem passed, but the sleep problem persisted. Eddie began feeling tired and often took a Halcion pill upon getting home from work. He slept through several AA meetings and soon was attending meetings only occasionally.

Months later, he was still using the pills daily and had completely withdrawn from his AA activities. He became severely depressed, lost his job, and, over a four-month period, lived isolated in his apartment. He then reached a bottom worse than the one that had originally brought him into AA.

Eventually Eddie's brother alerted his AA friends to the sleeping-pill problem. An intervention was arranged, and ultimately Eddie entered a hospital program for detoxification. That was followed by a twenty-eight-day rehab. He eventually became sober again, but it was a rough trip. Eddie experienced the long-lasting mood swings that are characteristic of withdrawal from the class of drugs that his sleeping pill represented. These drugs can cause depression for months after their use is discontinued.

Many cases of sleeping-pill addiction develop among addiction-prone individuals. In view of this, the principle for the recovering alcoholic/addict is rigid: Do not take any medications whatever for sleeplessness.

Home Hygiene (Mouthwashes, Breath Deodorizers, Toothpastes)

The major danger posed by products such as mouthwashes for personal or home hygiene is their alcohol content. Although seemingly trivial or obvious, the alcohol content of products such as Listerine has led to very serious problems for some individuals. Listerine, for example, has an alcohol content of 26.9 percent—greater than 50 proof, if calibrated in the system used for hard liquor.

Consider the case of Sarah M. Sarah was a nurse who had tremendous guilt feelings about her compulsion to drink. So great was her shame that she did stop drinking alcoholic beverages on her own. Every morning, though, she felt extremely anxious while getting ready for work. To ease her tension, she began swallowing more and more of the Listerine she used each morning to deodorize her breath. In time she found that drinking it down by gulps helped quite a bit with the morning anxiety.

Sarah's guilt about going into the liquor store was relieved by her Listerine habit, for she found she could buy a case of Listerine in the supermarket without embarrassment. Her consumption of the mouthwash steadily increased over a period of months. Then, one day she had a convulsion. Friends took her to a hospital emergency room. Attempts there to find the cause of her seizure disorder revealed her high blood-alcohol content. Her alcoholism was thus painfully exposed, and she had to confess her Listerine history. Her intake had risen to three bottles of Listerine a day by the time of her seizure.

The point is that alcohol is alcohol, whether in bourbon or in mouthwash. Vigilance is important when it comes to everyday home hygiene products.

This principle has general importance as well. A recovering alcoholic/addict does well to maintain extreme alertness on all fronts. There is no room for carelessness, and if reading every label seems too tedious to you, you're wrong. Any effort to stay out of trouble is more than worth it.

Home Treatment of Minor Illnesses and Injuries

In dealing with colds, infections, and other minor health problems, vigilance is again the key principle. There are multitudes of medications for lesser ailments such as colds, allergies, sore throats, and digestive-tract troubles—both over-the-counter and prescription drugs. It is advisable to consult Chapter 6 as a reference to verify the safety or danger of any drug proposed to you for these minor health problems. To repeat the very important theme of this chapter: A recovering alcoholic/addict cannot be too careful in protecting his or her sobriety. Prescription-drug abuse, ingestion of products containing alcohol, heedless use of habit-forming painkillers, and denial of the risk of cross-addiction have all led to tragic relapses.

Be careful!

CHAPTER 6

Avoiding Special Hazards with Medicines

MEDICATIONS PRESENT RECOVERING ALCOHOLICS/ADDICTS WITH SPECIAL and crucial risks. Many medications—among them, certain pain relievers, sedatives, and cough remedies—contain ingredients that may be habit-forming. Such substances are only possibly addictive for nonalcoholics/nonaddicts. But these substances have caused serious recurrences of active alcoholism or addiction in substantial numbers of recovering alcoholics/addicts.

That they do so gives compelling reason for an alcoholic/addict to know that any of these possibly addictive medications can be highly dangerous—possibly lethal. For maximum protection against their hazards, a recovering alcoholic/addict should carry out each of the following key actions absolutely without fail when considering or planning *any* use of—and when using—*any* medications:

1. Be completely honest and frank with your doctors and your sponsor.
2. Use as many alternatives to pills as possible to help break an old "pills habit."

3. Throw out any hazardous medications in your home as soon as their period of legitimate use ends.

4. Watch out for lies you tell to doctors in order to obtain medications.

5. Watch out for lies you tell yourself in order to justify getting medications.

This chapter tells why each of these five actions is vital and how to carry it out. It then gives a very extensive reference listing of medications; with it you can identify the dangers or safety of many hundreds of the most commonly used medications for recovering alcoholics/addicts.

Why Medications Can Fatally Endanger Recovering Alcoholics/ Addicts

Recovering alcoholics/addicts have crucial needs for special vigilance with medications for several reasons.

The principle of cross-addiction (see Chapter 1) demonstrates that exposure to any mood-altering substance can trigger the pathology of addiction. Alcohol or specifically abused drugs need not be the trigger. Rather, any substance with addictive or mood-altering properties or potential can lower resistance to compulsive use of alcohol or drugs. Such substances trigger in the recovering alcoholic/addict a typical cascade of events that often ends in the revival of addiction (usually in a more acute and terrifying form than ever before).

By no means does the alcoholic/addict evidence a simple reaction consisting merely of a euphoric "high" followed by the loss of willpower and control. Rather, ingestion of a potentially addictive substance sets off a whole series of events accompanied by lowered resistance to the latent disease of alcoholism/addiction. Individuals appear to vary in the extent to which their resistance is lowered, but risk develops with any drop in resistance.

How to Guard Against Dangers from Medicines

USE COMPLETE HONESTY, OPENNESS, AND SPONSOR GUIDANCE IN ANY POSSIBLE USE OF MEDICATIONS

First among important recommendations to follow is that the alcoholic/addict suspend his or her own judgment in these matters, instead relying completely on others who are more familiar with the disease of alcoholism/addiction. Such others include primarily one's "sponsor" or experienced guide in AA or a similar recovery program. They also include physicians experienced in the disease.

With such knowledgable advisers, the alcoholic/addict should be as truthful and frank as possible about every aspect of any need for medication—pain, distress, past reactions to medications, and the like.

USE AS MANY ALTERNATIVES TO PILLS AS POSSIBLE TO HELP BREAK AN OLD "PILLS HABIT"

Alcoholics/addicts starting in recovery programs often have an innate "pills habit" for dealing with any health condition. They are usually given sound advice to substitute different relief measures for conditions that had instead been occasions for pill-taking. For example, such individuals considering use of aspirin for a mild headache may be told to seek relief by taking a cold shower instead.

A summary of minor health problems and such ways to relieve them *without taking pills* are as follows (the individual's recovery-program sponsor and other friends in recovery can probably suggest many more, as needed).

If any of the symptoms are more than mildly incapacitating, consult your physician.

Health Problem	Way to Relieve Without Taking Pills
Headache	Have a shower (perhaps a cold shower)

Sleeplessness	Take a warm bath, drink warm milk; read recovery literature; get much daytime exercise to relax the body physically
Constipation	Eat prunes or drink prune juice; eat or drink other fruits or fruit juices; drink 8–10 large glasses of water daily
Anxiety; Tension	Breathe slowly, deeply for 5 minutes at a stretch; systematic relaxation techniques
Drowsiness	Stretch, exercise; drink tea or coffee; practice vigorous deep breathing; sleep as appropriate
Diarrhea	Drink fluids heavily; eat no fresh fruits; be patient; *especially* choose safe medications for the condition if drugs prove necessary
Drepression	Have enjoyable exercise; do useful manual tasks; phone or meet with sponsor or other recovery-program friend

DISCARD ANY HAZARDOUS MEDICATIONS IN THE HOME IMMEDIATELY AFTER THEIR PERIOD OF LEGITIMATE USE ENDS

Persons recovering from substance abuse are also commonly advised to dispose of any medications potentially dangerous for them immediately after the end of the time for which the medications were prescribed. Following this recommendation helps prevent later addictive abuse of the medication.

How important it is to take this precaution can be seen in the case of Tina M. A middle-aged attorney and homemaker, Tina had had a whiplash injury in an auto accident. She hadn't told her doctor that she was a recovering alcoholic/addict, nor taken any of the precautions with him of the types discussed earlier. As a result, the doctor prescribed Talwin, a potentially habit-forming analgesic, to relieve recurrent headaches caused by the injury. He told her to use the medication no longer than one week. Within four days her headaches ended, and Tina stopped taking the Talwin. But she left the bottle containing several unused tablets in her medicine chest.

Six months later, Tina lost an important case and her son broke a leg in an auto accident that wrecked the family's best car. She began to feel utterly hopeless, and one morning she noticed the Talwin bottle while putting on her makeup. Almost by reflex she reached out and took two tablets. She felt much better, she thought. That night she had a little cognac after dinner to help her unwind. In another three weeks she started on the worst binge of her life and a week later entered an alcoholism treatment center.

WATCH OUT FOR LIES TOLD TO THE DOCTOR IN ORDER TO OBTAIN MEDICATIONS

Their compulsions typically lead alcoholics/addicts to distort the truth with doctors in order to get medications that they consider imperative for relief. Any imaginable untruth may be told the doctor with a sense of complete justification by the alcoholic/addict. Deception may concern the intensity of pain or other discomfort felt or even alleged pain when none is actually present.

Recovering alcoholics/addicts sometimes engage in such "conning" of doctors just as unconsciously as those who are actively practicing their addictions. As a result, it is widely recommended that the recovering alcoholic/addict be completely informative in telling his or her sponsor about all plans and acts to obtain medications, and be on guard against a possible predisposition to mislead doctors in these ways. Of course, doctors are also widely urged to be on the alert for such tendencies and to avoid being taken in by them.

WATCH OUT FOR LIES TOLD TO ONESELF IN ORDER TO JUSTIFY GETTING MEDICATIONS

Conning doctors in order to obtain medications not really necessary or even hazardous is often done by alcoholics/addicts in all sincerity. In such instances, their disease of addiction first misleads them. They then need feel no restraint in saying whatever may work in fooling the doctor.

Accordingly, it is also widely recommended that recovering alcoholics/addicts understand that such self-deception is likely and discount their own convictions on questions of medications. Being completely honest and informative with one's sponsor and other advisers in recovery programs helps prevent such self-deception.

Hazards—or Safety—of Medications by Medication Types

This section provides a unique guide that identifies the dangers or safety of each one of hundreds of medications of the types that might include drugs potentially dangerous to sobriety. It also identifies the other commonly used types of medications that are safe with respect to sobriety. Quick access to such facts can often prove indispensable for continued abstinence and recovery from alcoholism/addiction.

The section covers both prescription and nonprescription medications. Types of medications are presented in alphabetical order of the type names.

Types that might include medications dangerous to the sobriety of recovering individuals are presented as follows: Under the type name heading appears essential information about the potential danger or safety for alcoholics/adults of medications of this type. After this information, each medication of that type is listed by trade name and generic name (in alphabetical order).

The term, "CAUTION," is used to indicate medications that pose potential danger (that is, high risk) to continued sobriety or abstinence for recovering alcoholics/addicts. The term, "WITHOUT RE-ACTIVATION RISK," is used to indicate medications that are safe (that is, without risk) with respect to continued abstinence.

Types of medications that are safe for recovering individuals with respect to continued sobriety are identified by type names (such as "Antihypertensives [High Blood Pressure Medications]," or "Hormones"). Text after the type name heading identifies drugs of this type as safe, briefly indicates their major uses, and names a few widely used drugs of this type as illustrative examples.

Use this section to find out about the potential dangers—or safety—of medication as follows:

1. Use the alphabetic index (at the back of the book) to locate the listing of the individual medication in this section. If you *do* find the medication in the index, proceed as follows:

2. Turn to the page number in this section given in the index for the medication, and find the listing for the medication on that page. In the listing, note any special advice which may be given right after the medication's name (if any is given there, as it is for a few drugs).

3. Then carefully move back to the information presented at the start of the group in which the medication is listed, and consult that information.

4. If you *do not* find the individual medication listed in the index at the back of the book, look up the name of the type of medication that it is in the index. (You can get the name of the type from your doctor or pharmacist, if you don't already know it.)

5. Turn to the page number in this section given for that type of medication, and read the information appearing after the type name heading.

6. If any medication—or type of medication—on which you seek advice happens not to be listed in this book, do not use any of the medication until after asking a doctor well informed on alcoholism/addiction about its possible hazards or safety for an alcoholic/addict.

The section covers the following major types of medications, in the following order:

A Few Medications That Call for Special Caution (lists individual medications)

Analgesics That Are Narcotics or Controlled Substances (lists individual medications)

Analgesics (Pain Relievers),–Antipyretics (Antifever Drugs), and Antimigraine Agents That Are not Narcotics or Addictive Controlled Substances (lists individual medications)

Anesthetics (lists individual medications)

Antiallergy Medications (Antihistamines/Antipruritics [anti-itching drugs]/Mast-Cell Stabilizers) (lists individual medications)

Antiarthritic Agents

Antiasthmatics (Bronchodilators)

Antibiotics

Anticancer Agents (Antineoplastics)

Anticoagulants

Anticonvulsants (lists individual medications)

Antidiabetics (Hypoglycemic Agents)

Antidyskinetics (relieve involuntary shaking or tremors) (Antiparkinsonism Agents)

Antifungal Agents; Antiviral Agents

Antigout Agents

Antihypertensive Agents (High Blood Pressure Medications)

Antiplatelet Agents (prevent blood clots)

Corticosteroids (hormones made by the adrenal glands) (lists individual medications)

Cough, Cold, or Other Upper Respiratory Medications (lists individual medications

Dental Preparations (lists individual medications)

Diagnostics

Diuretics ("Water Pills")

Gastrointestinal System Medications:

    Antacids, Antiflatulents, Digestants

    Antidiarrheal Agents; Oral Electrolyte Solutions (lists individual medications)

    Antinauseants (Antiemetics; Anti–Motion Sickness Agents) (lists individual medications)

    Antiulcer-Antisecretory Agents; Antispasmodics

    Laxatives; Stool Softeners (lists individual medications)

Geriatric Medications

Heart Disease Medications

Hemorrhoidal Medications

Hormones

Muscle Relaxants (lists individual medications)

Parasitic Disease Medications

Potassium Supplements

Psychoactive Agents (lists individual medications)

    Antianxiety Agents (Minor Tranquilizers)

    Antidepressants

    Major Tranquilizers (Antipsychotics)

    Central Nervous System (CNS) Stimulants

Sedatives/Hypnotics (lists individual medications)

Serum Cholesterol and Fat-Lowering Medications (Hypolipidemics) (used in treating heart conditions)

Urinary Tract Agents

Vitamin and Mineral Supplements; Nutritionals

Contraceptives

Important Note: "CAUTION" on the one hand, and "WITHOUT REACTIVATION RISK" on the other, when attributed to an individual medication or type of medication in this book, indicates only the following:

First, these terms apply only to use of the medication (or medication type) by men and women recovering from alcohol or drug abuse.

Second, these terms apply only to the possible effect of taking that medication (or medication type) on continued abstinence from substance abuse by such recovering persons. That is, the word *caution* is employed to indicate that taking the medication may tend to reactivate the person's substance abuse; the words *without reactivation risk* indicate that taking the medication will probably not tend to reactivate the person's substance abuse.

Attributions of these terms in these specific senses are based on information about the medications provided to the public by the producers of the medications, supplemented by widespread clinical experience and practice, as well as by the experience of those in the field of alcoholism and drug addiction. (That information about a medication provided to the public concerns such effects as action as a central nervous system depressant, tendency to be habit-forming, tendency to induce a mood of euphoria, tendency to relieve a mood of depression, and tendency to induce drowsiness or sleep.)

Third, characterization in this section of need for caution or without reactivation risk as defined here is provided only for general information. It is not set forth as either medical counseling or medical treatment. Readers should take (or should not take) any medications—including those referred to in this book—only as advised by their physicians.

In addition, all names of medications presented in this chapter (and throughout the book) with the initial letter (or letters) of their names capitalized are trade names or registered trademarks of their producers and/or distributors.

Essential Reference Listing of Each Medication's Dangers or Safety for Recovering Alcoholics

Names of medications most often shown in the listing are their brand names. Medications or drugs are also often shown in the listing by their *generic name* (scientific, chemical, or other established-usage name that is not a registered trademark). Medications in some cases are also shown in the listing by their *street names*, names given them in conversational usage such as "uppers," "downers," or "diet pills."

Typographic style used in the listing to indicate the type of name being given is as follows (such style parallels conventional practice):

Trade Name: given in initial capital (or uppercase) letters, for example, Bufferin Analgesic Tablets
generic name: given in lowercase letters, for example, codeine
street name: given in lowercase letters and enclosed in double quotation marks, for example, "downers"

On the line below the listing for each brand name (or street name) are given the chemical or generic names of the major active ingredients in that medication.

For each type of medication, up to four subcategories are presented, in the following order:

Prescription Drugs that Call for CAUTION
Prescription Drugs that Are WITHOUT REACTIVATION RISK
Nonprescription Drugs that Call for CAUTION
Nonprescription Drugs that Are WITHOUT REACTIVATION RISK

Text at the beginning of each subcategory gives brief explanation.

A Few Medications that Call for Special Caution

Recovering alcoholics/addicts should take special caution to avoid the few medications identified next. These medications have particularly euphoric effects—to such an extent that the way in which they act in the system may even extend beyond our present understanding.

Many an addictive career has been started by the prescribing of these medications for legitimate medical problems. In addition, many actively addicted individuals drift toward abuse of these medications.

Individuals recovering from substance abuse should either not take any of these at all or observe every possible precaution while using one if recommended as essential by a doctor thoroughly informed about alcoholism/addiction. Alternatives and precautions applicable to the following medications which are used to relieve acute pain are set forth in the Chapter 5 section "Pain." Alternative cough medicines to Tussionex can be found in this chapter's section on "Cough, Cold, or Other Upper Respiratory Medications."

The following are medications calling for special caution by recovering alcohlics/addicts (all are normally prescribed for unusually acute pain except as noted; those listed with the initial letter capitalized are identified by trade name; those with the initial letter given in lowercase are identified by generic name):

Demerol
Dilaudid
Hycodan
Hydrocet
hydrocodone (often in the form hydrocodone bitartrate)
hydromorphone (often in the form hydromorphone hydrochloride)
Hy-phen (formerly Hycodaphen)
Levo-Dromoran
levorphanol (often in the form levorphanol tartrate)
meperidene (often in the form meperidene hydrochloride)
oxycodone (often in the form oxycodone hydrochloride)
Percocet
Percodan
Roxicodone
SK-Oxycodone
Tussionex (cough medicine)
Tylox
Vicodin
Zydone

Analgesics That Are Narcotics or Controlled Substances (Prescription Drugs That Call for CAUTION)

CAUTION: Most significantly, narcotics are addictive drugs that were first nationally regulated in the United States under the Harrison Narcotics Act of 1914. They produce physical and psychological dependence and include opium and its derivatives, heroin, morphine, codeine, and related synthetic drugs that can bring about morphinelike addiction (such as meperidine and methadone). In addition, some state laws also define cocaine and marijuana as narcotics.

Drugs that have been widely abused (nonnarcotics as well as narcotics) are now regulated under a federal law popularly called the Controlled Substances Act (officially, the Drug Abuse Prevention and Control Act of 1970, Public Law 91-513). Provisions of the act are enforced by the Drug Enforcement Administration of the U.S. Department of Justice.

ADDICTION RISKS RANGE FROM HIGHEST FOR SCHEDULE I DRUGS TO LESSER FOR SCHEDULES II THROUGH V

Under the act, drugs are classified as "controlled substances" within its Schedules I, II, III, IV, or V. *Schedule I* drugs pose the highest addiction risks to the public; drugs in *Schedules II through V* pose successively lesser degrees of addiction risks. Schedule I drugs, for instance, are characterized by high potential for abuse, no accepted medical use in the United States, and no accepted medical practices for assuring safe use in the United States. Similarly, Schedule II drugs are marked by high potential for abuse, an accepted medical use in the United States (often with severe restrictions), and severe psychological or physical dependence resulting from abuse.

All the medications in this section are controlled substances in various schedules. (Codeine phosphate, for example, is in Schedule II, and propoxyphene is in Schedule IV; such classifications are indicated by notations in pharmaceutical listings like "C-II" or "CS-II," and "C-IV".) Their major medical use is to relieve unusually severe to extreme pain, so that they are most often medically classified as *analgesics* (pain-relieving medications). They are available only by prescription.

All call for CAUTION on the part of recovering alcoholics/addicts, since they are habit-forming to an extent that varies from extremely habit-forming to very substantially habit-forming. A recovering alcoholic/addict should avoid them whenever possible in order to avoid high risk of reactivating acute substance abuse.

PRECAUTIONS IF YOU MUST TAKE ONE

Only imperative medical need should cause an individual in recovery to use these medications, and, if one must be taken, all the precautions stated elsewhere in this book should be practiced without fail. (For these precautions, see the beginning of this chapter and the section "Pain" in Chapter 5.)

In many cases, these medications are combinations of chemicals that include nonaddictive active ingredients which serve as mild pain relievers or stimulants, such as aspirin, acetaminophen, or caffeine.

Addictive or habit-forming ingredients in these medications include codeine or codeine compounds; opium; barbiturates, such as pentobarbital and butalbital; oxycodone compounds; oxymorphone compounds; hydrocodone compounds; hydromorphone compounds; morphine or morphine compounds; methadone compounds; and compounds of levorphanol, alphaprodine, propoxyphene, meperidine, meprobamate, and pentazocine.

Acetaco Tablets
(codeine phosphate, acetaminophen)
Amacondone Tablets
(hydrocodone bitartrate, acetaminophen)
Anacin-3 with Codeine
(acetaminophen, codeine phosphate)
Anexsia with Codeine
(codeine phosphate, aspirin, caffeine)
Anexsia-D
(hydrocodone bitartrate, aspirin, caffeine)
A.S.A. and Codeine Compound
(codeine phosphate, aspirin, caffeine)
Ascriptin With Codeine
(codeine phosphate, aspirin, magnesium-aluminum hydroxide)
Bancaps HC Capsules
(hydrocodone bitartrate, acetaminophen)
Bayapap with Codeine Elixir
(codeine phosphate, acetaminophen)
Bexophene Capsules
(propoxyphene hydrochloride, aspirin, caffeine)
B&O Supprettes
(opium, belladonna)
Cafergot P-B (antimigraine agent)
(pentobarbital, ergotamine tartrate, caffeine, belladonna alkaloids)
Capital with Codeine Tablets

(codeine phosphate, acetaminophen)
Codap Tablets
(codeine phosphate, acetaminophen)
codeine phosphate
codeine sulfate
Codoxy
(oxycodone hydrochloride, oxycodone terephthalate, aspirin)
Co-Gesic Tablets
(hydrocodone bitartrate, acetaminophen)
Damacet-P
(hydrocodone bitartrate, acteminophen)
Damason-P
(hydrocodone bitartrate, aspirin, caffeine)
Darvocet-N 50
(propoxyphene napsylate, acetaminophen)
Darvocet-N 100
(propoxyphene napsylate, acetaminophen)
Darvon
(propoxyphene hydrochloride)
Darvon-N
(propoxyphene napsylate)
Darvon Compound
(propoxyphene hydrochloride, aspirin, caffeine)
Darvon with A.S.A.
(propoxyphene hydrochloride, aspirin)
Darvon-N with A.S.A.
(propoxyphene napsylate, aspirin)
Demerol
(meperidine hydrochloride)
Demerol APAP
(meperidine hydrochloride, acetaminophen)
Dia-Gesic
(hydrocodone bitartrate, aspirin, acetaminophen, caffeine)
Dicodid
(hydrocodone)
dihydromorphinone hydrochloride
(hydromorphone)
Dilaudid (tablets); Dilaudid-HP (ampuls)
(hydromorphone hydrochloride)
Dolacet Capsules
(hydrocodone bitartrate, acetaminophen)
Dolene Capsules

(propoxyphene hydrochloride)
Dolene AP-65 Capsules
    (propoxyphene hydrochloride, acetaminophen)
Dolene Compound-65 Capsules
    (propoxyphene hydrochloride, aspirin, caffeine)
Dolo-Pap
    (hydrocodone bitartrate, acetaminophen)
Dolophine Hydrochloride Ampoules, Vials, Tablets
    (methadone hydrochloride)
Doxaphene Compound
    (propoxyphene hydrochloride, aspirin, caffeine)
Duradyne DHC
    (hydrocodone bitartrate, acetaminophen)
Duramorph PF
    (morphine)
Emcodeine Tablets
    (codeine phosphate, aspirin)
Empirin with Codeine
    (aspirin, codeine phosphate)
Empracet with Codeine Phosphate
    (acetaminophen, codeine phosphate)
Equagesic
    (meprobamate, aspirin)
Esgic
    (butalbital, caffeine, acetaminophen)
Fiorinal
    (butalbital, aspirin, caffeine)
Fiorinal with Codeine (*Note:* Often prescribed for migraine head-
   aches; occasionally abused by addicts.)
    (butalbital, aspirin, caffeine, codeine)
Hydrocet Capsules
    (hydrocodone bitartrate, acetaminophen)
hydrocodone bitartrate with acetaminophen tablets
Hydrogesic Capsules
    (hydrocodone bitartrate, acetaminophen)
hydromorphone hydrochloride
Hy-Phen Tablets (formerly Hycodaphen)
    (hydrocodone bitartrate, acetaminophen)
Levo-Dromoran
    (levorphanol tartrate)
Lorcet
    (propoxyphene hydrochloride, acetaminophen)

Lorcet-HD
  (hydrocodone bitartrate, acetaminophen)
Lortab ASA
  (hydrocodone bitartrate, aspirin)
Lortab Liquid, Lortab Tablets
  (hydrocodone bitartrate, acetaminophen)
Mepergan
  (meperidine hydrochloride, promethazine)
Mepergran Fortis
  (meperidine hydrochloride, promethazine hydrochloride)
meperidine hydrochloride tablets, injection
methadone hydrochloride tablets, diskets
methadone hydrochloride oral solution
  (methadone hydrochloride, 8 percent alcohol)
Methadose
  (methadone)
Micrainin
  (meprobamate, aspirin)
morphine sulfate (injection; solution; tablets)
MS Contin
  (morphone sulfate)
Nisentil
  (alphaprodine hydrochloride)
Norcet
  (hydrocodone bitartrate, acetaminophen)
Numorphan (suppositories; injection)
  (oxymorphone hydrochloride)
oxycodone hydrochloride, oxycodone terephthalate
Panadol with Codeine
  (acetaminophen, codeine phosphate)
Pantopon
  (opium)
Percocet
  (oxycodone hydrochloride, acetaminophen)
Percodan, Percodan-Demi
  (oxycodone hydrochloride, oxycodone terephthalate, aspirin)
Pethadol
  (meperidine hydrochloride)
Pethidine
  (meperidine hydrochloride)
Phenaphen with Codeine
  (acetaminophen and codeine phosphate)

Phenaphen-650 with Codeine
(acetaminophen and codeine phosphate)
Profene
(propoxyphene)
propoxyphene hydrochloride capsules
propoxyphene napsylate and acetaminophen tablets
Proval #3 Capsules
(codeine phosphate, acetaminophen)
RMS (suppositories)
(morphine sulfate)
Roxanol (oral solution)
(morphine sulfate)
Roxicodone Tablets, Oral Solution
(oxycodone hydrochloride)
SK-APAP with Codeine
(codeine phosphate, acetaminophen)
SK-65 Capsules
(propoxyphene hydrochloride)
SK-65 APAP Tablets
(propoxyphene hydrochloride, acetaminophen)
SK-65 Compound Capsules
(propoxyphene hydrochloride, aspirin, caffeine)
SK-Oxycodone
(oxycodone hydrochloride or oxycodone terephthalate, with
acetaminophen or aspirin)
Sublimaze
(fentanyl)
Synalgos-DC
(dihydrocodeine bitartrate, aspirin, caffeine)
Talacen
(pentazocine hydrochloride, acetaminophen)
Talwin Compound
(pentazocine hydrochloride, aspirin)
Talwin Injection
(pentazocine lactate)
Talwin Nx
(pentazocine hydrochloride, naloxone hydrochloride)
T-Gesic Forte
(hydrocodone bitartrate, acetaminophen)
Tylenol with Codeine; Tylenol with Codeine Elixir
(codeine phosphate, acetaminophen)
Tylox Capsules

(oxycodone hydrochloride, oxycodone terephthalate, acetaminophen)
Ty-Tabs
(codeine phosphate, acetaminophen)
Vicodin Tablets
hydrocodone bitartrate, acetaminophen)
Wygesic
(propoxyphene hydrochloride, acetaminophen)
Zydone Capsules
(hydrocodone bitartrate, acetaminophen)

Analgesics–Antipyretics and Antimigraine Agents That Are Not Narcotics or Addictive Controlled Substances

ANALGESICS–ANTIPYRETICS: PRESCRIPTION DRUGS THAT CALL FOR SOME CAUTION

SOME CAUTION: Recovering alcoholics/addicts should use the medicines in this group only if necessary, and with some caution. Such caution should be exercised because these medications have some mood-altering properties, according to their manufacturers, even though they are nonnarcotic and less euphoric in their effects than narcotics are. The mood-altering qualities of these medications call for SOME CAUTION by recovering alcoholics/addicts, from the standpoint of possibly reactivating their acute substance abuse. These medications are used primarily as analgesics (pain relievers).

butorphanol tartrate
nalbuphine hydrochloride
Nubain
(nalbuphine hydrochloride)
Stadol
(butorphanol tartrate)

ANALGESICS–ANTIPYRETICS AND ANTIMIGRAINE AGENTS: PRESCRIPTION DRUGS WITHOUT REACTIVATION RISK

WITHOUT REACTIVATION RISK: In general, the medications in this group are without reactivation risk for recovering alcoholics when used exactly as prescribed by your doctor. The only (or major) active ingredient in the medications consists of an *analgesic-antipyretic* (to relieve pain and reduce fever). That and any other ingredients are not habit-forming for nonalcoholics, and hence tend to be safe for alcoholics. Main uses of these drugs are indicated by their respective headings (with the *analgesics-antipyretics* used for both analgesic pain relief and antipyretic fever reduction and the *antimigraine agents* being used for migraine headaches).

Analgesics-Antipyretics

> Anaprox
>> (naproxen sodium)
> Dolobid
>> (diflunisal)
> Levoprome
>> (methotrimeprazine)
> Magan
>> (magnesium salicylate)
> Motrin
>> (ibuprofen)
> Nalfon
>> (fenoprofen calcium)
> Ponstel
>> (mefenamic acid)
> Rufen
>> (ibuprofen)
> sodium salicylate
> sodium thiosalicylate

Antimigraine Agents

> Cafergot
>> (ergotamine tartrate, caffeine)
> Inderal; Inderal LA

      (propanolol hydrochloride)
Midrin
      (isometheptene mucate, dichloralphenazone, acetamino-
phen)
Sansert
      (methysergide maleate)
Wigraine
      (ergotamine tartrate, caffeine)

ANALGESICS–ANTIPYRETICS: NONPRESCRIPTION DRUGS THAT CALL FOR CAUTION

CAUTION: These and similar liquid medicines advised to relieve pain and/or reduce fever illustrate a common risk for recovering alcoholics/addicts—and one easily overlooked.

That danger stems from inclusion of alcohol in the liquid medium used for medications of many types. And any alcohol intake whatever can bring high reactivation risk to a recovering person.

In consequence, avoid these medications and any others like them containing alcohol. With any liquid medication, check the label in the case of a nonprescription drug and pass up any that has any alcohol content. (For the pain-relief/fever-relief medications in this group, you can easily substitute a nonliquid form containing no alcohol.) And in the case of any liquid medication prescribed for you, have your doctor specify a no-alcohol-content form and confirm with your pharmacist that it contains no alcohol.

      Peedee Dose Aspirin Alternative
            (10 percent alcohol, acetaminophen)
      St. Joseph Aspirin-Free Elixir (7 percent alcohol), St. Joseph As-
        pirin-Free Infant Drops (10 percent alcohol)
            (alcohol as indicated, acetaminophen)
      Tylenol Elixir (7 percent alcohol), Tylenol Drops (7 percent alco-
        hol), Tylenol Extra Strength Adult Liquid Pain Reliever (8.5
        percent alcohol)
            (alcohol as indicated, acetaminophen)

ANALGESICS-ANTIPYRETICS: NONPRESCRIPTION DRUGS WITHOUT REACTIVATION RISK

WITHOUT REACTIVATION RISK: In general, the medications in this group are without reactivation risk for recovering alcoholics/ addicts when used exactly as prescribed by your doctor. The only (or major) active ingredient in the medications is an analgesic-anti-pyretic (to relieve pain and/or reduce fever). That and any other ingredients are not habit-forming for nonalcoholics, and hence tend to be safe for recovering alcoholics/addicts (from the standpoint of avoiding medications likely to reactivate acute substance abuse).

The prime active ingredient in these medications is typically aspirin or acetaminophen.

Aspirin, acetaminophen, and similar analgesics (such as ibuprofen) are not habit-forming for most persons. However, some strongly addiction-prone individuals have abused aspirin or aceta-minophen by taking it (often in unwisely large quantities) over long periods when its use was not actually justified by their pain. This is an example of addictive behavior with a substance that is not in itself habit-forming.

acetaminophen
Advil
    (ibuprofen)
Anacin
    (aspirin, caffeine)
Anacin-3 (Children's, Regular Strength, Maximum Strength)
    (acetaminophen)
APF Arthritis Pain Formula
    (aspirin)
Arthritis Pain Formula
    (aspirin, magnesium hydroxide, aluminum hydroxide)
aspirin
    (acetylsalicylic acid)
Aspirin-Free Arthritis Pain Formula
    (acetaminophen)
Arthropan
    (choline salicylate)
Ascriptin

(aspirin, magnesium hydroxide, aluminum hydroxide)
Bayer Aspirin, Maximum Bayer Aspirin, Bayer Children's Chewable Aspirin, Arthritis Bayer Timed Release Aspirin
(aspirin)
Bufferin Analgesic Capsules, Extra Strength Bufferin Analgesic Capsules
(aspirin, calcium carbonate, magnesium oxide, magnesium carbonate)
Bufferin Analgesic Tablets, Arthritis Strength Bufferin Analgesic Tablets, Extra Strength Bufferin Analgesic Tablets
(aspirin, aluminum glycinate, magnesium carbonate)
Cama
(aspirin, magnesium oxide, aluminum hydroxide)
Cosprin
(aspirin)
Easprin
(aspirin)
Ecotrin (Maximum Strength, Regular Strength)
(aspirin)
Empirin
(aspirin)
Encaprin
(aspirin)
Excedrin
(acetaminophen, aspirin, caffeine)
Excedrin, Extra Strength
(acetaminophen, caffeine)
Excedrin P.M.
(acetaminophen, diphenhydramine citrate)
Extra Strength Datril
(acetaminophen)
Gemnisyn
(aspirin, acetaminophen)
Liquiprin
(acetaminophen)
Midol, Maximum Strength Midol
(aspirin, cinnamedrine hydrochloride, caffeine)
Momentum
(salsalate, aspirin, phenyltoloxamine citrate)
Nuprin
(ibuprofen)
Panadol, Children's Panadol

(acetaminophen)
Percogesic
    (acetaminophen, phenyltoloxamine citrate)
St. Joseph Aspirin for Children
    (aspirin)
St. Joseph Aspirin-Free for Children, Maximum Strength St.
    Joseph Aspirin-Free
    (acetaminophen)
Synalgos
    (aspirin, caffeine)
Tylenol (Children's, Extra Strength, Maximum Strength)
    (acetaminophen)

Anesthetics

As their main purpose, the anesthetics listed in this section block
the sensation of pain. They range from the medications most often
given to hospital patients for major surgery, to ointments self-applied
by individuals for painful sunburns or rashes. Except where noted,
these anesthetics can be obtained only by prescription.

ANESTHETICS GIVEN ALMOST ENTIRELY
DURING IN-HOSPITAL TREATMENT THAT CALL
FOR CAUTION

CAUTION, BUT FOR USE IN SPECIFIC SITUATIONS: The medications in this group are used to induce anesthesia, or as part of
anesthesia, and are administered most often for surgery. They represent various forms of central nervous system depressants. They call
for CAUTION with respect to the continued abstinence of recovering
alcoholics/addicts. However, recoverees may justifiably agree to the
use of one or more of them—except nitrous oxide—in specific situations in which sufficient caution is taken. Such situations are those
in which an anesthesiologist recommends them as necessary. The
recovering person must exercise caution, first making sure that their
use is necessary and then informing the anesthesiologist of his or her
alcoholism/addiction and consequent potentially idiosyncratic reactions to these medications. (In such idiosyncratic reactions, some

recovering individuals may be insufficiently anesthetized by a normal dose, and others may be overanesthetized by a normal dose.)

Nitrous oxide is singled out as an exception because, in the authors' opinion, it seems to call for special caution in order to safeguard the continued abstinence of recoverees, and it can readily be replaced by many more modern anesthetics that would be safer.

Except for nitrous oxide (which is inhaled as a gas), these anesthetics are administered either by injection or rectally. Before being given one of them a recovering alcoholic/addict should take the following precautions:

1. Tell your doctor and your anesthesiologist about your substance-abuse disease and ask for complete cooperation in your continued recovery. Request specifically that they limit these anesthetics and any narcotic analgesics given postoperatively to minimum amounts and durations.

2. If time permits, plan your protection program with your doctors (including the anesthesiologist) before receiving the anesthetic.

3. If feasible, stay in the hospital after your surgery until any of these anesthetics has been eliminated from your system.

Brevital Sodium
    (methohexital sodium for injection)
methohexital sodium rectal solution
nitrous oxide (inhalant gas)
Pentothal
    (thiopental sodium for injection, or as a rectal suspension)
Surital
    (thiamylal sodium for injection)
thiopental sodium rectal solution
Valium Injectable
    (diazepam, 10 percent ethyl alcohol)
Versed Injection
    (midazolam hydrochloride)

INHALANT GENERAL ANESTHETICS THAT ARE GIVEN ALMOST ENTIRELY DURING IN-HOSPITAL TREATMENT AND THAT ARE WITHOUT REACTIVATION RISK

WITHOUT REACTIVATION RISK: These anesthetics are administered by inhalation—most often for general anesthesia with complete unconsciousness during surgery in a hospital. Some, such as Penthrane, may be given in relatively light dosages for an analgesic (pain-relieving) effect rather than as general anesthesia during surgery or other medical procedure.

They have little or no habit-forming effect and are WITHOUT REACTIVATION RISK for individuals recovering from substance abuse.

Ethrane
  (enflurane)
Fluothane
  (halothane)
Forane
  (isoflurane)
halothane
Penthrane
  (methoxyflurane)

OTHER ANESTHETICS OFTEN GIVEN DURING IN-HOSPITAL TREATMENT THAT ARE WITHOUT REACTIVATION RISK

WITHOUT REACTIVATION RISK: These anesthetics are often administered in the course of major surgery in a hospital. Most of them are typically administered by means of a *spinal tap*, with injection of anesthetic to make the lower body painfree.

These painkillers are termed *spinal, epidural, caudal,* or *saddle block anesthetics* when given by a tap or injection into the lower spine. When administered in this way, these drugs act as regional or local anesthetics. A number of the anesthetics listed in this section are also given by injection in other parts of the body to produce local anesthesia in those areas. Some of them are at times used by dentists for local anesthesia in the mouth and jaws.

Such regional or local anesthetics do not affect the entire system and influence consciousness. For this and other reasons, they are WITHOUT REACTIVATION RISK for individuals recovering from substance abuse.

Carbocaine Hydrochloride
    (mepivacaine hydrochloride)
Carbocaine Hydrochloride 2 percent with Neo-Cobefrin 1:20,000 Injection
    (mepivacaine hydrochloride; levonordefrin)
Duranest Hydrochloride; Duranest Hydrochloride with Epinephrine
    (etidocaine hydrochloride; epinephrine bitartrate)
lidocaine hydrochloride injection
Marcaine Hydrochloride; Marcaine Hydrochloride with Epinephrine
    (bupivacaine hydrochloride; epinephrine bitartrate)
Marcaine Spinal
    (bupivacaine hydrochloride; dextrose)
Nesacaine Solutions, Nesacaine-CE Solutions
    (chloroprocaine hydrochloride)
Novocain Hydrochloride for Spinal Anesthesia, Novocain Hydrochloride
    (procaine hydrochloride)
Pontocaine Hydrochloride for Spinal Anesthesia
    (tetracaine hydrochloride)
Sarapin
    (*sarracenia purpurea* plant distillate for injection [to relieve neuromuscular or neuralgic pain])
Sensorcaine Hydrochloride; Sensorcaine Hydrochloride with Epinephrine 1:200,000
    (bupivacaine hydrochloride; epinephrine bitartrate)
Xylocaine Sterile Solution
    (lidocaine hydrochloride)
Xylocaine Hydrochloride with Epinephrine
    (lidocaine hydrochloride; epinephrine bitartrate)
Xylocaine Solution with Dextrose
    (lidocaine hydrochloride; dextrose)
Xylocaine Solution with Glucose
    (lidocaine hydrochloride; glucose)

ANESTHETICS THAT ARE MOST OFTEN USED IN OUTPATIENT TREATMENT AND THAT ARE WITHOUT REACTIVATION RISK

WITHOUT REACTIVATION RISK: The following anesthetics are applied *topically*, to the skin or the mucous membranes, most often by doctors providing treatment or examination. They do not enter the system and influence consciousness or mood to any appreciable extent. They are consequently WITHOUT REACTIVATION RISK for recovering alcoholics or addicts.

Ophthalmologists also use topical anesthetics like these in examination or treatment of certain eye conditions. Such infrequently encountered anesthetics are not listed here, but can also be considered WITHOUT REACTIVATION RISK by persons in recovery when seeking ophthalmic care.

Anestacon
   (lidocaine hydrochloride)
Cetacaine Topical Anesthetic
   (benzocaine, tetracaine hydrochloride, butyl aminobanzoate)
Dyclone
   (dyclonine hydrochloride)
Hurricaine Topical Anesthetic (Spray, Gel, Liquid; nonprescription, but usually doctor-applied)
   (benzocaine)
Sucrets Maximum Strength Spray (nonprescription sore throat remedy; CAUTION called for because of alcohol content)
   (alcohol, dyclonine hydrochloride)

NONPRESCRIPTION ANESTHETICS THAT ARE SELF-APPLIED TO LOCAL AREAS BY PATIENTS FOR MINOR CONDITIONS AND THAT ARE WITHOUT REACTIVATION RISK

WITHOUT REACTIVATION RISK: These nonprescription anesthetics are advised for local application by the patient to relieve minor conditions such as sunburn or other burns on the skin, rashes, hemorrhoids, mouth sores, or sore throats. Only if large amounts of some of the active anesthetic ingredients are absorbed into the system is there any excitant or depressant effect of the drug on the central nervous system. These medications are therefore WITHOUT REACTIVATION RISK to recovering individuals.

Anbesol Gel, Liquid (for external use only)
    (70 percent alcohol, benzocaine, phenol)
Bactine Antiseptic/Anesthetic First Aid Spray
    (lidocaine hydrochloride, benzalkonium chloride)
BiCozene Creme
    (benzocaine, resorcinol)
Campho-Phenique Cold Sore Gel, Liquid
    (phenol, camphor)
Cēpacol Anesthetic Lozenges
    (benzocaine, cetylpyridinium chloride)
Cēpastat Sore Throat Lozenges
    (phenol, menthol)
Chloraseptic Children's Lozenges
    (benzocaine)
Chloraseptic Lozenges, Liquid, Spray
    (phenol, sodium phenolate)
Dermoplast Lotion, Spray
    (benzocaine)
Foille First Aid Liquid, Ointment, Spray
    (benzocaine, chloroxylenol)
Herbal Ice
    (benzocaine, camphor, menthol)
Ivarest Medicated Cream, Lotion
    (benzocaine, calamine)
Kank-A Medicated Cream, Lotion
    (benzocaine, compound benzoin tincture, cetylpyridinium chloride)
Lubraseptic Jelly
    (phenyl phenol, amyl phenol)
Medicone Dressing Cream, Rectal Ointment, Rectal Suppositories
    (benzoczine, hydroxyquinoline sulfate)
Medi-Quik Aerosol Spray
    (lidocaine, benzalkonium chloride)
Nupercainal Cream, Ointment
    (dibucaine)
Orajel, Baby, Maximum Strength
    (benzocaine)
Orajel Mouth-Aid

(benzocaine, benzalkonium chloride)
ProctoFoam/nonsteroid
   (pramoxine hydrochloride)
Solarcaine
   (benzocaine, triclosan)
Swab and Gargle Solution
   (benzocaine, iodine, phenol, thymol)
Tronolane Anesthetic Cream/Suppositories for Hemorrhoids
   (pramoxine hydrochloride)
Tronothane Hydrochloride Cream
   (pramoxine hydrochloride)
Unga-Eze
   (benzocaine, carbolic acid, zinc oxide)
Xylocaine 2.5 Ointment
   (lidocaine)

Antiallergy Medications (Antihistamines/Antipruritics/Mast-Cell Stabilizers)

Relief of allergy symptoms represents a major use of the medications described in this section. They are used to relieve the allergic symptoms affecting the nasal membranes, bronchial breathing passageways, and eyelid tissues (with runniness, irritation, swelling, or congestion). They are also used to relieve symptoms affecting the skin (with itching and rashes; such effect on itching is termed *antipruritic action*. These medicines are all either taken by mouth or inhaled as nasal sprays.

Almost all the medications listed in this group are antihistamines or contain an antihistamine as an active ingredient. Most antihistamines may cause sleepiness as a side effect. People react in differing ways with regard to this side effect. Some don't get sleepy at all, and some are "zonked out."

It is our feeling that this effect is not a risk to the recovering alcoholic/addict, and that, when medically appropriate, the recoveree can safely take antihistamines. However, there are recently developed antihistamines that do not have this side effect (Seldane, for example). The recovering alcoholic/addict would do well to request one of these when an antihistamine (or combination drug containing antihistamine) is to be prescribed.

ANTIALLERGY MEDICATIONS: PRESCRIPTION DRUGS THAT ARE WITHOUT REACTIVATION RISK IN THIS USE

WITHOUT REACTIVATION RISK IN THIS USE: Most of the medications listed in this group are antihistamines. As explained, antihistamines are without reactivation risk when used for the relief of allergy symptoms by individuals in recovery.

One medication listed contains cromolyn sodium, which is not an antihistamine but a type of drug known as a *mast-cell stabilizer.* (It is also identified as a *mast-cell stabilizer* in the listing.) Like antihistamines, mast-cell stabilizers reduce the effect of the substance histamine that causes the symptoms of allergic reactions. Mast-cell stabilizers have little or no sedative properties and also tend to be without reactivation risk in this use by recovering alcoholics/addicts.

Alermine
    (chlorpheniramine maleate)
Aller-Chlor
    (chlorpheniramine maleate)
Allerid-O.D.
    (chlorpheniramine maleate)
Atrohist Sprinkle Capsules
    (brompheniramine maleate, phenyltoloxamine citrate, phenylephrine hydrochloride)
Bayidyl
    (triprolidine hydrdochloride)
Bena-D
    (diphenhydramine hydrochloride)
Benahist
    (diphenhydramine hydrochloride)
Bendylate
    (diphenhydramine hydrochloride)
Bromamine
    (brompheniramine maleate)
Brombay
    (brompheniramine maleate)
Bromfed Capsules, Tablets

(brompheniramine maleate, pseudoephedrine hydrochloride)
Bromphen
    (brompheniramine maleate)
brompheniramine maleate tablets, elixir
Chlo-Amine
    (chlorpheniramine maleate)
Chlor-100
    (chlorpheniramine maleate)
Chlor-Mal
    (chlorpheniramine maleate)
Chlor-Niramine
    (chlorpheniramine maleate)
chlorpheniramine maleate tablets, capsules, syrup
Chlor-Pro
    (chlorpheniramine maleate)
Chlorspan
    (chlorpheniramine maleate)
Chlortab
    (chlorpheniramine maleate)
cyproheptadine hydrochloride tablets, syrup
Diahist
    (diphenhydramine hydrochloride)
Dihydrex
    (diphenhydramine hydrochloride)
Dimentabs
    (diphenhydramine hydrochloride)
Diphen
    (diphenhydramine hydrochloride)
Diphenacen
    (diphenhydramine hydrochloride)
Diphenadril
    (diphenhydramine hydrochloride)
diphenhydramine hydrochloride capsules, elixir, syrup
Dormarex
    (pyrilamine maleate)
Extendryl Tablets, Capsules, Syrup
    (phenylephrine hydrochloride, chlorpheniramine maleate,
    methscopolamine nitrate)
Fenylhist
    (diphenhydramine hydrochloride)
Fynex
    (diphenhydramine hydrochloride)

Hal-Chlor
    (chlorpheniramine maleate)
Hispril Spansule Capsules
    (diphenylpyraline hydrochloride)
Histrey
    (chlorpheniramine maleate)
Hydril
    (diphenhydramine hydrochloride)
Hyrexin-50
    (diphenhydramine hydrochloride)
Kronofed-A Kronocaps, Junior Kronofed-A Kronocaps
    (pseudoephedrine hydrochloride, chlorpheniramine maleate)
Nasahist B
    (brompheniramine maleate)
Nasalcrom (this is a "mast-cell stabilizer")
    (cromolyn sodium)
Nolahist
    (phenindamine tartrate)
Noradryl, Nordryl
    (diphenhydramine hydrochloride)
Oraminic II
    (brompheniramine maleate)
Optimine Tablets
    (azatadine maleate)
PBZ Tablets, Elixir, PBZ-SR Tablets
    (tripelennamine hydrochloride, tripelenneamine citrate);
    Elixir, tripelennamine citrate only)
Periactin Syrup, Tablets
    (cyproheptadine hydrochloride)
Phenetron
    (chlorpheniramine maleate)
Polarmine Repetabs
    (dexchlorpheniramine maleate)
Robalyn
    (diphenhydramine hydrochloride)
Seldane
    (terfenadine)
Tacaryl Tablets, Chewable Tablets, Syrup
    (methdilazine hydrochloride)
Tavist, Tavist-1 Tablets
    (clemastine fumarate)
Tavist-D

(clemastine fumarate, phenylpropanolamine hydrochloride)
TD Alermine
(chlorpheniramine maleate)
Teldrin Timed-Release Allergy Capsules
(chlorpheniramine maleate, benzyl alcohol)
Temaril Tablets, Syrup, Spansule Capsules
(trimeprazine tartrate) (anti-itch)
tripelennamine hydrochloride tablets
triprolidine hydrochloride syrup
Trymegen
(chlorpheniramine maleate)
Tusstat
(diphenhydramine hydrochloride)
Valdrene
(diphenhydramine hydrochloride)
Veltane
(brompheniramine maleate)
Wehdryl
(diphenhydramine hydrochloride)

ANTIALLERGY MEDICATIONS: NONPRESCRIPTION DRUGS THAT ARE WITHOUT REACTIVATION RISK IN THIS USE

WITHOUT REACTIVATION RISK IN THIS USE: Most of the non-prescription medications listed in this group contain an antihistamine as an ingredient. For the indicated use of relieving allergic reactions, antihistamines are without reactivation risk for recovering alcoholics/addicts (from the standpoint of not tending to reactivate acute substance abuse), as explained at the start of this "Antiallergy Medications" section. Among other ingredients in these drugs are decongestants, astringents, or mild anti-irritants—all of which are safe for recovering individuals.

Take Care Not to Overuse Decongestant Nasal Sprays: For any persons, an addictivelike overuse of decongestant nasal sprays such as those listed here can develop through carelessness. After initial use, nasal passages first shrink and give relief from congestion. But the tissues then may swell seemingly more than before, leading to a second use, followed by relief and then more swelling, followed by a third use in less time than before, followed by still more swelling, which in turn is followed by a fourth use in still less time and then still more swelling, and so on. This is termed *rebound effect*.

Such overuse can be avoided by using a decongestant nasal spray no oftener and for no longer a time span than specified in the directions.

Actidil Tablets, Syrup
    (triprolidine hydrochloride)
Ayr Saline Nasal Drops, Mist
    (sodium chloride [table salt], water)
Benadryl Capsules, Kapseals, Elixir, Tablets
    (diphenhydramine hydrochloride)
Bromfed Syrup
    (brompheniramine maleate, pseudoephedrine hydrochloride)
Dimetapp Tablets, Elixir, Extentabs
    (brompheniramine maleate, phenylpropanolamine hydrochloride)
Fedrazil Tablets
    (pseudoephedrine hydrochloride, chlorcyclizine hydrochloride)
Vicks Sinex Decongestant Nasal Spray
    (phenylephrine hydrochloride, cetylpyridinium chloride)
Vicks Sinex Long-Acting Decongestant Nasal Spray
    (oxymetazoline hydrochloride)
Visine A.C. Eye Drops
    (tetrahydrozoline hydrochloride, zinc sulfate)

Antiarthritic Agents

WITHOUT REACTIVATION RISK: Relief of arthritic pain and/or inflammation in the joints is the main purpose for which physicians advise the medications in this group. Some are also used to relieve *muscular pain*, the pain from conditions like bursitis and tendonitis, or the pain resulting from gout. They are also used in some cases to treat migraine headaches or menstruation.

Active ingredients in these medications are often safe analgesics (pain relievers) or nonsteroidal anti-inflammatory agents.

None of these medications has habit-forming or addictive effect. They are hence all without reactivation risk for recovering alcoholics/

addicts (but only in the dosages specified, and as and when directed by a doctor).

Some of the drugs listed in the "Analgesics" section of this chapter are also prescribed by doctors for arthritic relief, others for non-arthritic pain.

Among widely used antiarthritic medications of this type (and the generic name of a major active ingredient in each) are Indocin (indomethacin), Motrin (ibuprofen), and Naprosyn (naproxen).

Antiasthmatics (Bronchodilators)

Antiasthmatics (bronchodilators) act by dilating the air passageways in the lung called *bronchioles*. They are usually prescription drugs. Asthma attacks and some kinds of lung infections can cause the openings in the bronchiole tubes to constrict and to be further narrowed by increased mucus. Antiasthmatic drugs are formulated to relieve the constriction and obstruction within the bronchioles.

ANTIASTHMATICS: PRESCRIPTION AND NONPRESCRIPTION DRUGS THAT CALL FOR CAUTION

CAUTION: The following antiasthmatic medications call for caution to safeguard the continued abstinence of recovering alcoholics/addicts because they contain phenobarbital (an addictive barbiturate) and/or alcohol. They are prescription drugs unless otherwise noted.

Quadrinal (a systemic drug, taken orally)
  (ephedrine hydrochloride, phenobarbital, theophylline calcium salicylate, potassium iodide)
Tedral Elixir (a systemic drug, taken orally)
  (15 percent alcohol, ephedrine hydrochloride, phenobarbital, theophylline)
Tedral Suspension, Tedral SA (systemic drugs, taken orally)
  (ephedrine hydrochloride, phenobarbital, theophylline)
Primatene Mist (a nonprescription inhalant drug)
  (34 percent alcohol, epinephrine)

ANTIASTHMATICS: PRESCRIPTION AND NONPRESCRIPTION DRUGS THAT ARE WITHOUT REACTIVATION RISK

WITHOUT REACTIVATION RISK: All other antiasthmatics that do not contain barbiturates or alcohol are without reactivation risk for recovering alcoholics/addicts. It would be wise to check ingredients of any antiasthmatic (bronchodilator) drug before taking it to make sure it contains no possibly addictive chemicals.

There are many such antiasthmatics that are without reactivation risk. A few examples in wide use are the following:

> *Inhalant antiasthmatics* include Brethaire Inahler (terbutaline sulfate), Proventil Inhaler (albuterol), and Ventolin Inhaler (albuterol).
>
> *Systemic Antiasthmatics* include Choledyl SA Tablets (oxtriphylline), Slo-Bid Gyrocaps (anhydrous theophylline), and Theo-Dur (anhydrous theophylline).

Antibiotics

WITHOUT REACTIVATION RISK: Antibiotics are not mood-altering and are thus without reactivation risk for the recovering alcoholic/addict, in the sense of raising no risk of reactivating acute substance abuse. Antibiotics interfere with the growth of bacteria and are used to treat bacterial infections. They are available only by prescription, in almost all cases. Major types and their general uses follow.

Erythromycins are broad-spectrum antibiotics generally prescribed for respiratory tract infections, skin and soft tissue infections, venereal disease, and conjunctivitis, as well as urethral, endocervical, and rectal infections. Among erythromycins in wide use are E-Mycin, Eryc, Erythrocin Stearate, and PCE.

Penicillin antibiotics are also effective against certain respiratory tract infections, gastrointestinal and genitourinary tract infections, skin infections, and venereal disease. They are used as well against some forms of staphylococcal and streptococcal infections. Penicillins widely used include Amcill (ampicillin), Amoxil (amoxicillin), Pentids (Penicillin G potassium), and Prostaphlin (oxacillin sodium).

Tetracyclines are other broad-spectrum antibiotics used with certain respiratory infections, urinary and gynecological infections, and some venereal diseases. Widely used teteracyclines include Achromysin (tetracycline hydrochloride) and Vibramycin (doxycycline).

Cephalosporins are broad-based antibiotics prescribed mainly to fight a variety of infectious organisms within the urinary tract, respiratory tract, skin, intestinal tract, and bones and joints. They are also used for genital infections. Cephalosporins in wide use include Keftabs (cephalexin), Ceclor (ceflacor), and Duricef (cefadroxil).

Sulfanamides (sulfa drugs) are antibiotics commonly used for the treatment of urinary tract infections caused by susceptible microorganisms, certain types of meningitis, and various eye and ear infections. Commonly used sulfa drugs include Bactrim (sulfamethoxazole, trimethoprim), Gantrisin (sulfisoxazole), and Septra (sulfamethoxazole, trimethoprim).

Anticancer Agents (Antineoplastics)

WITHOUT REACTIVATION RISK: Treatment of one or more of the many forms of cancer is the major purpose for which medications of this type are used. In general, they can be obtained only by prescription.

All these anticancer medications are without reactivation risk for recovering alcoholics/addicts, from the standpoint of not endangering their freedom from substance abuse, if the medications are included in the following subtypes: alkylating agents, antimetabolites, antineoplastic antibiotics, hormones, and an additional broad subtype generally consisting of medications that reduce or end the growth of cancerous cells.

For other extremely important advice on actions that safeguard recovery in the case of a formerly active alcoholic/addict who has cancer, readers should see also the section on cancer in Chapter 10, "Dealing with Chronic Illness."

This group of medications does not include other drugs of highly significant types that are also very often given to recovering alcoholics/addicts who have cancer. These are pain-relieving or pain-killing drugs. Vital information on such drugs is given in the sections in this chapter on analgesics and can be readily located by using the index. Other vital information about use of these pain medications by recovering individuals who have cancer is given in Chapter 10.

Examples of anticancer medications in wide use include: Adriamycin (an antineoplastic antibiotic containing doxorubicin hydrochloride), Leukeran (an alkylating agent containing chlorambucil), methotrexate (an antimetabolite), Platinol (an antineoplastic agent containing cisplatin), Cytoxan (an alkylating agent containing cyclophosphamide), Efudex (an antimetabolite containing fluorouracil), Mutamysin (an antineoplastic antibiotic containing mitomycin), and Teslac (a hormone containing testolactone).

Anticoagulants

WITHOUT REACTIVATION RISK: Anticoagulants are without reactivation risk for recovering alcoholics/addicts from the standpoint of their continued abstinence. Anticoagulants reduce the ability of blood to clot. Heparin is such a drug; it acts by inhibiting the reactions that lead to blood clotting. Such medications are used to prevent clotting or coagulation of the blood within the circulatory system—as in the treatment of phlebitis, for example.

Anticonvulsants

For the most part, the anticonvulsants in this group of medications are used in attempts to prevent convulsions for patients who have any seizure disorder (including epilepsy).

In a less frequent use of special importance, some of these medications—such as phenytoin (Dilantin)—are given to alcoholics during detoxification to prevent the convulsions that sometimes result from alcohol withdrawal. (These alcoholic seizures are described in Chapter 1.) A few recovering alcoholics or addicts evidence continued tendencies to suffer seizures from time to time after withdrawal and may need to take an anticonvulsant regularly on a continuing basis to prevent or relieve such seizures.

All of these anticonvulsants may be obtained only by prescription.

ANTICONVULSANTS: PRESCRIPTION MEDICATIONS THAT ARE WITHOUT REACTIVATION RISK

WITHOUT REACTIVATION RISK: Inasmuch as the anticonvulsants listed next do not contain habit-forming or addictive ingredients, they are without reactivation risk for recovering alcoholics/addicts, from the standpoint of a renewed outbreak of their acute substance abuse.

Celontin Kapseals, Half-Strength Kapseals
(methsuximide)
Depakene Capsules, Syrup
(valproic acid)
Depakote Tablets
(divalproex sodium)
Diamox Tablets, Diamox Sequels Capsules
(acetazolimide)
Dilantin Kapseals
(phenytoin sodium)
Dilantin Infatabs
(phenytoin)
Dilantin with Phenobarbital
(phenytoin, phenobarbital) (*Note:* Though it is a barbiturate, phenobarbital is weak in its habit-forming potential and is without reactivation risk for recovering alcoholics or addicts when used as indicated here for seizure control.)
Diphenylan
(phenytoin)
Gemonil Tablets
(metharbital) (*Note:* Though it is a barbiturate, metharbital is weak in its habit-forming potential and is without reactivation risk for recovering alcoholics or addicts when used as indicated here for seizure control.)
Mesantoin
(mephenytoin)
Milontin Kapseals
(phensuximide)
Mysoline
(primidone)
Paradione

(paramethadione)
Peganone
    (ethotoin)
Phenurone Tablets
    (phenacemide)
phenytoin
Tegretol Tablets, Chewable Tablets
    (carbamazepine)
Tridione
    (trimethadione)
Zarontin Capsules, Syrup
    (ethosuximide)

Antidiabetics (Hypoglycemic Agents)

WITHOUT REACTIVATION RISK: Control of the disease diabetes mellitus is the main purpose for which the medicines of this type are recommended.

None of these medications tends to be habit-forming or addictive. They are therefore without reactivation risk for recovering alcoholics/ addicts, from the standpoint of recovery from addiction.

However, taking incorrect dosages of these medications, or neglecting to take them, can result in unconsciousness or even death. It is hence unusually important to follow competent medical direction with scrupulous care in use of these medications.

Among widely used antidiabetics are many brands of insulin available as prescription or nonprescription drugs taken by injection and noninsulin prescription medications containing active ingredients such as chlorpropamide, glyburide, and glipizide and taken orally.

Antidyskinetics (Antiparkinsonism Agents)

WITHOUT REACTIVATION RISK: One major reason for prescribing a medication in this group is to relieve the constant shaking of the extremities, or *palsy*, resulting from the condition commonly called *Parkinson's disease* (or parkinsonism). The term *antidyskinetics* refers to this effect of reducing the shaking, or *dyskinetics*, of palsy.

Other reasons for prescribing one of the medications include relieving severe side effects caused by other medicines. These include psychiatric medications for treating mental illness (such as phenothiazines) or medications such as reserpine that are given to lower high blood pressure.

For a recovering alcoholic/addict, any of these medications is without reactivation risk with respect to the individual's continued recovery when taken for its prescribed purpose. This is true because none tends to be habit-forming or addictive. All are available only by prescription, however, and should be used only as prescribed.

Among widely used antidyskinetics are Cogentin (containing benztropine mesylate), Artane (containing trihexyphenidyl hydrochloride), and Benadryl (given intravenously and containing diphenhydramine hydrochloride).

Antifungal Agents; Antiviral Agents

WITHOUT REACTIVATION RISK: Clearing up fungus infections of various types—or certain viral infections—is the main purpose of recommending use of the medications of this type. For recovering alcoholics/addicts, they are all without reactivation risk, from the standpoint of not tending to have habit-forming or addictive effects. Subgroups of medications of this type are as follows.

SYSTEMIC ANTIFUNGAL MEDICATIONS

Systemic antifungal medications tend to be prescribed only for deep-seated or very serious cases of fungal infections. A number of them can have serious side effects on the system. They are taken by mouth or by injection and include Fulvicin (containing griseofulvin) and Fungizone (containing amphotericin).

TOPICAL ANTIFUNGAL MEDICATIONS

For relatively less serious fungal infections, these topical medications are applied locally to the area affected—to the feet or the groin for complaints like athlete's foot, jock itch, or ringworm; to the vagina for various types of vaginal infections. Drugs among them that have possibly injurious effects or side effects can be obtained only by prescription (and include, for example, those containing clioquinol or clortrimazole). Others with milder effects are nonprescription drugs (such as Desenex, containing undecylenic acid; and Tinactin, containing tolnaftate).

ANTIVIRAL MEDICATIONS

The fewer medications of the antiviral subgroup are prescribed to relieve viral infections. Those with acyclovir as the major active ingredient relieve the symptoms of genital herpes (infection due to type 2 herpes simplex virus.) Others such as Herplex (containing idoxuridine) or Vira-A (containing vidarabine) are used for treatment of various types of infections caused by the Herpes Simplex Virus.

Antigout Agents

WITHOUT REACTIVATION RISK: These medications are prescribed mainly to relieve the painful arthritic condition of the joints known as gout (which occurs chiefly in the hands, feet, and big toe). Gout results largely from a metabolic problem leading to excessive uric acid in the blood. These drugs help relieve acute attacks of gout or help prevent future acute attacks.

Antigout agents are available only by prescription, since they can have hazardous or disabling side effects. However, none of them tends to be habit-forming or addictive. They are hence without reactivation risk for recovering alcoholics/addicts, in the sense that they have little or no effect in reactivating acute substance abuse.

Widely used antigout agents include drugs containing as their major active ingredient allopurinol, colchicine, probenecid, or sulfinpyrazone. Antiarthritic medications are also widely used to treat the symptoms of gout.

Antihypertensive Agents (High Blood Pressure Medications)

WITHOUT REACTIVATION RISK: Medications of all the major varieties that are used to treat hypertension (abnormally high blood pressure) are without reactivation risk for recovering alcoholics/addicts, in that they do not endanger continued abstinence. Main types of antihypertensives and examples of each in wide use are as follows.

ACE Inhibitors cause blood vessels to dilate through action on enzymes in the blood. Examples include Capoten (capotril) and Vasotec (enalapril maleate).

Beta-Blocking Agents decreases the force of heart contractions. Among examples are Corgard (nadolol), Inderal (propanolol hydrochloride), Lopressor (metoprolol tartrate), and Tenormin (stenolol).

Calcium Channel Blockers block constriction of blood vessels through action on heart muscle and smooth muscle. Examples include Calan (verapamil hydrochloride), Isoptin (verapamil hydrochloride), and Procardia (nifedapine).

Diuretics result in decreased blood volume through their effect on the kidneys. Among widely used examples are hydrochlorothiazide (often called HCTZ), Lasix (furosimide), and Maxzide (triamterene, hydrochlorothiazide).

Combination Antihypertensive Medications include Capozide (capotril, hydrochlorothiazide), Corzide (nadolol, bendroflumethiazide), and Diazide (hydrochlorothiazide, triamterine).

Antiplatelet Agents

WITHOUT REACTIVATION RISK: Antiplatelet agents are without reactivation risk for recovering alcoholics/addicts from the standpoint of their continued abstinence. These medications interfere with the platelet function in clotting. Studies recently made public have indicated the possible benefit of aspirin as a drug that interferes with clotting and the progression of *atherosclerosis* (obstruction of the arteries by cholesterol deposits, resulting in atherosclerosis). Commonly used brand names for aspirin are Bayer, Bufferin, and Empirin.

Corticosteroids

WITHOUT REACTIVATION RISK, BUT EXERCISE CAUTION WHEN TAKING: Corticosteroids are a class of medications that are all related to hormones made by the adrenal gland. These hormones play a complex role in the balance of many physiologic functions.

Medically, corticosteroids are used in multiple ways and for many different conditions. Asthma, poison ivy, lupus erythematosus, certain types of arthritis, allergies, and multiple sclerosis are among the conditions treated by corticosteroids. Corticosteroids are available as pills, as injections, and as creams and ointments.

Many people confuse these drugs with the other class of "steroids"—the hormones used by bodybuilders and athletes to build muscle. They are not the same, and, for our purposes, only corticosteroids need be discussed.

Cortisone is the best-known corticosteroid. Prednisone is an often-prescribed oral form.

Cortisone and related steroids can have an effect on mood when taken internally. They can make one feel "hyper," "spacy," extremely energetic, and sometimes uncomfortably "high." Some people report difficulty sleeping after taking these steroids, although they seem to require less sleep.

In general, corticosteroids do often interact with mood but in a way that is without reactivation risk concerning one's sobriety as a recovering alcoholic/addict. Each individual's reaction to cortisone is different, though, and *caution should be exercised when using these drugs.*

Corticosteroids Taken Orally or by Injection

A-hydroCort Vials
    (hydrocortisone sodium succinate)
A-methaPred Vials
    (methylprednisolone sodium succinate)
Aristocort Tablets
    (triamcinolone)
Aristocort Vials
    (triamcinolone diacetate)
Aristospan Vials
    (triamcinolone hexacetonide)
Celestone Tablets, Syrup
    (betamethasone)
Celestone Vials
    (betamethasone sodium phosphate)
Celestone Soluspan
    (betamethasone sodium phosphate, betamethasone acetate)

Cortef Tablets
    (hydrocortisone)
Cortef Acetate Vials
    (hydrocortisone acetate suspension)
Cortef Oral Suspension
    (hydrocortisone cypionate)
cortisone acetate tablets, vials
Decadron Tablets, Elixir
    (dexamethasone)
Decadron Phosphate Syringes
    (dexamethasone sodium phosphate)
Delta-Cortef Tablets
    (prednisolone)
dexamethasone sodium phosphate
Decadron-LA Suspension Vials
    (dexamethasone acetate)
Deltasone Tablets
    (prednisone)
Depo-Medrol Syringes, Vials
    (methylprednisolone acetate suspension)
Florinef Tablets
    (fludrocortisone acetate)
Haldrone Tablets
    (paramethasone acetate)
Hexadrol Tablets
    (dexamethasone)
Hexadrol Phosphate Injection Vials, Syringes
    (dexamethasone sodium phosphate)
Hydeltrosoc
    (prednisolone)
Kenalog-10, Kenalog-40
    (triamcinoline)
Medrol Tablets
    (methylprednisolone)
Pediapred
    (prednisolone sodium phosphate)
prednisolone acetate vials,
prednisolone sodium phosphate vials
Solu-Cortef Vials
    (hydrocortisone sodium succinate)
Solu-Medrol Vials
    (methylprednisolone sodium succinate)

Corticosteroids Taken by Inhalation

Aerobid
   (flunisolide)
Azmacort
   (triamcinolone acetonide)
Beclovent
   (beclomethasone dipropionate)
Beconase
   (beclomethasone dipropionate)
Nasalide
   (flunisolide)
Resphihaler Decadron Phosphate
   (dexamethasone sodium phosphate)
Vancenase
   (beclomethasone dipropionate)
Vanceril Inhaler
   (beclomethasone dipropionate)

Corticosteroids Given Rectally

Cortenema
   (hydrocortisone retention enema)
Corticaine Cream
   (hydrocortisone acetate, dibucaine)
Corticaine Suppositories
   (hydrocortisone acetate)

Cough, Cold, or Other Upper Respiratory Medications

Relieving the symptoms of coughs, colds, flu, sore throats, and other ailments of the upper respiratory tract is the main purpose for which you might be advised to take these medications.

Most drugs in this very large group consist of combinations of active ingredients. Each ingredient acts to relieve one type of symptom. A combination medicine in this group is accordingly designed to relieve certain sets of symptoms characteristic of certain types of flus, colds, or sore throats. Types of ingredients common in medications of this broad type, and the symptoms they relieve, are as follows:

Type of Ingredient	Symptoms Relieved
Antihistamines	Runniness of nose, inflamation of mucous membranes
Cough suppressant	Tickle or scratchiness in throat that provokes coughing
Decongestant	Swollen tissues in nose, thorat, sinuses, and lungs that close down air passages for breathing
Expectorant	Thick mucus sticking in throat (expectorant helps loosen such mucus so that it may be coughed up and spit out)
Analgesic/antipyretic	Headache, other aches or soreness, and possible fever of these upper-respiratory ailments

Types of ingredients which call for caution by recovering alcoholics or addicts consist mainly of:

—Cough Suppressants (also termed antitussives) that are habit-forming narcotic chemicals.

—Analgesics (pain relievers) that are narcotics and strongly habit-forming, such as hydrocodone or codeine (you should also realize that, though other analgesics such as aspirin and acetaminophen are not habit-forming for most persons, some persons who are strongly addiction-prone have abused them by taking them to excess when not needed to relieve pain).

—Alcohol (included in liquid forms of some of these medications as a mild analgesic, in proportions ranging from less than 1 percent to more than 25 percent; recovering alcoholics or addicts should avoid ingesting medicines with any alcohol content whatever. They should of course avoid them in order to avoid risk of reactivating their acute addiction, as explained earlier.)

Identifications and warnings for these and all dangerous ingredients are clearly given in the listings given in this section.

Many of the medications described here contain an antihistamine as an active ingredient. Most antihistamines may cause sleepiness as a side effect. People are affected to different degrees with regard to this side effect. Some don't get sleepy at all, and some get "zonked out."

It is our feeling that this effect is not a risk to the recovering alcoholic/addict, and that, when medically appropriate, the recoveree can safely take antihistamines. However, there are recently developed antihistamines that do not have this side effect (Seldane, for example). The recovering alcoholic/addict would do well to request one of these when an antihistamine (or combination drug containing antihistamine) is to be prescribed.

Moreover, with the many drugs for colds and general upper respiratory conditions, there is potential for differing side effects. Some decongestants can cause a jittery, "hyper," or nervous feeling that is quite uncomfortable. Other combination drugs can cause a "spacy" or weird feeling, and, of course, some can cause sleepiness. For recovering alcoholics/addicts, the safest approach to these medications is to use them only when clearly necessary, and to start with lower-than-normal doses. These suggestions should be discussed with your physician.

TYPES OF INGREDIENTS GIVEN IMMEDIATELY AFTER BRAND NAME

Each type of active ingredient in a medication is listed within brackets immediately following the brand name for that medication, for example, ". . . [antihistamine, cough suppressant, decongestant, expectorant, analgesic]." These types of ingredients are abbreviated as follows:

antihist. (antihistamine)
cough supp. (cough suppressant)
decong. (decongestant)
expect. (expectorant)

Given in parentheses below the line (or lines) reporting the brand name and types of ingredients are the chemical or generic names of each active ingredient in the medication.

COUGH, COLD, OR OTHER UPPER RESPIRATORY MEDICATIONS: PRESCRIPTION DRUGS THAT CALL FOR CAUTION

CAUTION: Each of the following medications calls for caution on the part of recovering alcoholics/addicts because one or more ingredients are potentially addictive.

Addictive or habit-forming ingredients in them include alcohol; codeine and its compounds, including codeine phosphate and sulfate; hydrocodone compounds, including hydrocodone bitartrate; and hydromorphone compounds, including hydromorphone hydrochloride.

Actifed with Codeine Syrup [antihist., cough supp., decong.]
    (4.3 percent alcohol, triprolidine hydrochloride, pseudoephedrine hydrochloride, codeine phosphate)
Ambenyl Syrup [antihist., cough supp.]
    (5 percent alcohol, bromodiphenhydramine hydrochloride, codeine phosphate)
Calcidrine Syrup [cough supp., expect.]
    (6 percent alcohol, codeine, calcium iodide)
Cetro-Cirose Liquid [cough supp., expect.]
    (1.5 percent alcohol, codeine phosphate, potassium guaiacolsulfonate, fluid extract ipecac)
Citra Forte Syrup [cough supp., antihistamine]
    (2 percent alcohol, hydrocodone bitartrate, pheniramine maleate, pyrilamine maleate, ascorbic acid, potassium citrate)
codeine sulfate tablets [cough supp.]
Codiclear DH Syrup [cough supp., expect.]
    (hydrocodone bitartrate, potassium guaiacolsulfonate)
Dilaudid Syrup [cough supp., expect.]
    (5 percent alcohol, hydromorphone hydrochloride, guaifenesin)
Dimetane-DC Syrup [antihist., cough supp., decong.]
    (0.95 percent alcohol, brompheniramine maleate, phenylpropanolamine hydrochloride, codeine phosphate)
Donatussin DC Syrup [cough supp., decong., expect.]
    (hydrocodone bitartrate, phenylephrine hydrochloride, guaifenesin)
Entex Liquid [decong., expect.]

(5 percent alcohol, phenylephrine hydrochloride, phenylpropanolamine hydrochloride, guaifenesin)

Entuss Liquid [cough supp., expect.]
 (alcohol, hydrocodone bitartrate, potassium guaiacolsulfonate)

Entuss Tablets [cough supp., expect.]
 (hydrocodone bitartrate, guaifenesin)

Entuss-D Liquid, Tablets [cough supp., decong., expect.]
 (hydrocodone bitartrate, pseudoephedrine hydrochloride, guaifenesin)

Histalet X Syrup [antihist., decong., expect.]
 (15 percent alcohol, pseudoephedrine hydrochloride, chlorpheniramine maleate, guaifenesin)

Histaspan-D Capsules [antihist., decong., anticholinergic]
 (alcohol, chlorpheniramine maleate, phenylephrine hydrochloride, pyrilamine maleate)

Histaspan-Plus Capsules [antihist., decong.]
 (alcohol, chlorpheniramine maleate, phenylephrine hydrochloride)

Hycodan Tablets and Syrup [cough supp., anticholinergic]
 (hydrocodone bitartrate, homatropine methylbromide)

Hycomine Compound Tablets [antihist., cough supp., decong., analgesic]
 (hydrocodone bitartrate, chlorpheniramine maleate, phenylephrine hydrochloride, acetaminophen, caffeine)

Hycomine Syrup; Hycomine Pediatric Syrup [cough supp., decong.]
 (hydrocodone bitartrate, phenylpropanolamine hydrochloride)

Hycotuss Expectorant [cough supp., expect.]
 (10 percent alcohol, hydrocodone bitartrate, guaifenesin)

Kwelkof Liquid [cough supp., expect.]
 (hydrocodone bitartrate, guaifenesin)

Naldecon-CX Suspension [cough supp., decong., expect.]
 (codeine phosphate, phenlypropanolamine hydrochloride, guaifenesin)

Norisodrine with Calcium Iodide Syrup [expect., bronchodilator]
 (6 percent alcohol, isoproterenol sulfate, anhydrous calcium iodide)

Novahistine DH Liquid [antihist., cough supp., decong.]
 (5 percent alcohol, codeine phosphate, pseudoephedrine hydrochloride)

Novahistine Expectorant [cough supp., decong., expect.]
(7.5 percent alcohol, codeine phosphate, pseudoephedrine hydrochloride, guaifenesin)
Nucofed Capsules, Syrup [cough supp., decong.]
(codeine phosphate, psuedoephedrine hydrochloride)
Nucofed Expectorant (cough supp., decong., expect.)
(12.5 percent alcohol, codeine phosphate, pseudoephedrine hydrochloride, guaifenesin)
Nucofed Pediatric Expectorant [cough supp., decong., expect.]
(6 alcohol, codeine phosphate, psuedoephedrine hydrochloride, guaifenesin)
Organidin Elixir [expect.]
(21.75 percent alcohol, iodinated glycerol)
Pediacof Syrup [antihist., cough supp., decong., expect.]
(5 percent alcohol, codeine phosphate, phenylephrine hydrochloride, chlorpheniramine maleate, potassium iodide)
Phenergan VC with Codeine Syrup [antihist., cough supp., decong., expect.]
(7 percent alcohol, promethazine hydrochloride, phenylephrine hydrochloride, codeine phosphate)
Phenergan with Codeine Syrup [antihist., cough supp., expect.]
(7 percent alcohol, promethazine hydrochloride, codeine phosphate)
Phenergan with Dextromethorphan Syrup [antihist., cough supp., expect.]
(7 percent alcohol, promethazine hydrochloride, detromethorphan hydrobromide)
Polaramine Syrup [antihist.]
(6 percent alcohol, dexchlorpheniramine maleate)
Promist HD Liquid [cough supp., decong., antihist.]
(5 percent alcohol, hydrocodone bitartrate, pseudoephedrine hydrochloride, chlorpheniramine maleate)
P-V-Tussin Syrup [antihist., cough supp., decong., expect.]
(5 percent alcohol, phenylephrine hydrochloride, pyrilamine maleate, chlorpheniramine maleate, ammonium chloride)
P-V-Tussin Tablets [antihist., cough supp., expect.]
(hydrocodone bitartrate, phenindamine tartrate, guaifenesin)
Robitussin A-C Syrup [cough supp., expect.]
(3.5 percent alcohol, codeine phosphate, guaifenesin)
Robitussin-DAC Syrup [cough supp., decong., expect.]
(1.45 percent alcohol, codeine phosphate, pseudoephedrine hydrochloride, guaifenesin)

Rondec-DM Syrup, Drops [antihist., cough supp., decong.]
(less than 0.6 percent alcohol, carbinoxamine maleate, pseudoephedrine hydrochloride, dextromethorphan hydrobromide)

Ru-Tuss Expectorant [antihist., cough supp., decong., expect.]
(5 percent alcohol, codeine phosphate, phenylephrine hydrochloride, chlorpheniramine maleate, ammonium chloride)

Ru-Tuss with Hydrocodone Liquid [antihist., cough supp., decong.]
(5 percent alcohol, hydrocodone bitartrate, phenylephrine hydrochloride, phenylpropanolamine hydrochloride, pheniramine maleate, pyrilamine maleate)

Ryna-C Liquid [antihist., cough supp., decong.]
(codeine phosphate, pseudoephedrine hydrochloride, chlorpheniramine maleate)

Ryna-CX Liquid [cough supp., decong., expect.]
(codeine phosphate, pseudoephedrine hydrochloride, guaifenesin)

S-T Forte Sugar-Free, Syrup [cough supp., decong., antihist., expect.]
(5 percent alcohol, hydrocodone bitartrate, phenylephrine hydrochloride, phenylpropanolamine hydrochloride, pheniramine maleate, guaifenesin)

terpin hydrate with codeine elixir [cough supp., expect.]
(40 percent alcohol)

Triaminic Expectorant with Codeine [cough supp., decong., expect.]
(5 percent alcohol, codeine phosphate, phenylpropanolamine hydrochloride, guaifenesin)

Tussar SF (Sugar-Free) Cough Syrup [antihist., cough supp., expect.]
(12 percent alcohol, codeine phosphate, chlorpheniramine maleate, guaifenesin, carbetapentane citrate, sodium citrate, citric acid, methylparaben)

Tussar-2 Cough Syrup [antihist., cough supp., expect.]
(5 percent alcohol, codeine phosphate, chlorpheniramine maleate, guaifenesin, carbetapentane citrate, sodium citrate, citric acid, methylparaben)

Tussend Expectorant [cough supp., decong., expect.]
(12.5 percent alcohol, hydrocodone bitartrate, pseudoephedrine hydrochloride, guaifenesin)

Tussend Tablets, Liquid [cough supp., decong.]

(5 percent alcohol, hydrocodone bitartrate, pseudoephedrine hydrochloride)
Tussionex Capsules, Tablets, Suspension [cough supp.]
(hydrocodone, phenyltoloxamine; Suspension, 0.59 percent alcohol)
Tussi-Organidin Liquid [cough supp., expect.]
(codeine phosphate, iodinated glycerol)
Tuss-Ornade Liquid [cough supp., decong.]
(5 percent alcohol, caramiphen edisylate, phenylpropanolamine hydrochloride)

COUGH, COLD, OR OTHER UPPER RESPIRATORY MEDICATIONS: PRESCRIPTION DRUGS THAT ARE WITHOUT REACTIVATION RISK

WITHOUT REACTIVATION RISK: Generally speaking, the prescription medications in this group are WITHOUT REACTIVATION RISK for recovering alcoholics or addicts when taken exactly as prescribed by a doctor.

Many of the medications in this group contain an antihistamine as an active ingredient. Most antihistamines may cause sleepiness as a side effect, but people react in differing ways with regard to this side effect.

It is our feeling that this effect is not a risk to the recovering alcoholic/addict, and that, when medically appropriate, the recoveree can safely take antihistamines. However, there are recently developed antihistamines that do not have this side effect (Seldane, for example). The recovering alcoholic/addict would do well to request one of these when an antihistamine (or combination drug containing antihistamine) is to be prescribed.

Moreover, with the many drugs for colds and general upper respiratory conditions, there is potential for differing side effects. Some decongestants can cause a jittery, "hyper," or nervous feeling that is quite uncomfortable. Other combination drugs can cause a "spacy" or weird feeling, and, of course, some can cause sleepiness. For recovering alcoholics/addicts, the safest approach to these medications is to use them only when clearly necessary, and to start with lower-than-normal doses. These suggestions should be discussed with your physician.

A common pain-reliever/fever-reducer drug in some of these medications—which is either aspirin or acetaminophen in almost all cases—may be subject to abuse by some addiction-prone persons, who take such a drug unnecessarily or to excess.

Clistin-D Tablets [antihist., decong., analgesic]
    (phenylephrine hydrochloride, carbinoxamine maleate, acetaminophen)
Comhist Tablets, Comhist LA Capsules [antihist., decong.]
    (chlorpheniramine maleate, phenyltoloxamine citrate, phenylephrine hydrochloride)
Deconamine Tablets, SR Capsules, Syrup [antihist., decong.]
    (chlorpheniramine maleate, d-pseudoephedrine hydrochloride)
Delsym Syrup [cough supp.]
    (dextromethorphan hydrobromide)
Entex Capsules [decong., expect.]
    (phenylephrine hydrochloride, phenylpropanolamine hydrochloride, guaifenesin)
Entex LA Tablets [decong., expect.]
    (phenylpropanolamine hydrochloride, guaifenesin)
Fedahist Gyrocaps, Tablets, and Syrup [antihist., decong.]
    (pseudoephedrine hydrochloride, chlorpheniramine maleate)
Isoclor Capsules [antihist., decong.]
    (chlorpheniramine maleate, pseudoephedrine hydrochloride)
Naldecon Tablets, Syrup, Pediatric Syrup, Drops [antihist., decong.]
    (phenyltoloxamine citrate, chlorpheniramine maleate, phenylephrine hydrochloride, phenylpropanolamine hydrochloride)
Nolamine Tablets [antihist., decong.]
    (phenindamine tartrate, chlorpheniramine maleate, phenylpropanolamine hydrochloride)
Novafed A Capsules [antihist., decong.]
    (chlorpheniramine maleate, pseudoephedrine hydrochloride)
Organidin Tablets, Solution [expect.]
    (iodinated glycerol)
Ornade Capsules [antihist., decong.]
    (chlorpheniramine maleate, phenylpropanolamine hydrochloride)
Phenergan-D Tablets [antihist., decong.]

(promethazine hydrochloride, pseudoephedrine hydrochloride)

potassium iodide [expect.]

Rondec Tablets, Rondec TR Tablets, Syrup, Drops [antihist., decong.]

(carbinoxamine maleate, pseudoephedrine hydrochloride)

Ru-Tuss II Capsules [antihist., decong.]

(chlorpheniramine maleate, phenylpropanolamine hydrochloride)

Ru-Tuss Tablets [antihist., decong., anticholinergic]

(chlorpheniramine maleate, phenylpropanolamine hydrochloride, phenylephrine hydrochloride, hyoscyamine sulfate, atropine sulfate, scopolamine hydrobromide)

Rynatan Tablets, Pediatric Suspension [antihist., decong.]

(chlorpheniramine tannate, pyrilamine tannate, phenylephrine tannate)

Rynatuss Tablets, Pediatric Suspension [antihist., cough supp., decong.]

(chlorpheniramine tannate, phenylephrine tannate, carbetapentane tannate, ephedrine tannate)

Sinubid Tablets [antihist., decong., analgesic]

(phenyltoloxamine citrate, phenylpropanolamine hydrochloride, acetaminophen)

Tavist-D Tablets [antihist., decong.]

(clemastine fumarate, phenylpropanolamine hydrochloride)

Tessalon Capsules [cough supp.]

(benzonatate)

Triaminic TR Tablets, Oral Infant Drops [antihist., decong.]

(pheniramine maleate, pyrilamine maleate, phenylpropanolamine hydrochloride)

Trinalin Tablets [antihist., decong.]

(azatadine maleate, pseudoephedrine sulfate)

Tussi-Organidin DM Liquid [cough supp., expect.]

(dextromethorphan hydrobromide, iodinated glycerol)

Tyzine Nasal Solution, Drops [decong.]

(tetrahydrozoline hydrochloride)

COUGH, COLD, OR OTHER UPPER RESPIRATORY MEDICATIONS: NONPRESCRIPTION DRUGS THAT CALL FOR CAUTION

CAUTION: These and similar liquid medicines commonly advised for upper respiratory infections (and particularly for coughs and sore throats) illustrate a frequent major need for CAUTION by recovering alcoholics/addicts—and a need that can easily be overlooked until too late.

That need stems from the inclusion of alcohol in the liquid medium used in medicines of many types. And any alcohol intake whatever can of course bring high reactivation risk to a recovering alcoholic/addict (as explained earlier).

In consequence, avoid these medications and any others like them containing alcohol. With any liquid medication, check the label and pass it up if it has any alcohol content whatever. Substitute another that is completely free of alcohol, perhaps double-checking with your pharmacist or physician to make absolutely sure that it is free of alcohol (and of any habit-forming chemical).

Read labels with extreme care, especially for medicines of this type. For instance, as shown in the listing for this group, "Congespirin Liquid" contains 10 percent alcohol (and is hence deemed potentially dangerous for recovering alcoholics/addicts). However, a related medicine similarly deemed safe (inasmuch as it contains no alcohol) has the closely similar name *Congespirin Syrup.*

Ambenyl-D Decongestant Cough Formula [cough supp., decong., expect.]
   (9.5 percent alcohol, dextromethorphan hydrobromide, pseudoephedrine hydrochloride, guaifenesin)
Bayer Cough Syrup for Children [cough supp., decong.]
   (5 percent alcohol, dextromethorphan hydrobromide, phenylpropanolamine hydrochloride)
Benylin Cough Syrup [antihist.]
   (5 percent alcohol, diphenhydramine hydrochloride)
Benylin DM Syrup [cough supp.]
   (5 percent alcohol, dextromethorphan hydrobromide)
Cheracol D Cough Formula [cough supp., expect.]
   (4.75 percent alcohol, dextromethorphan hydrobromide, guaifenesin)

Cheracol Plus Head Cold/Cough Formula [antihist., cough supp., decong.]
(8 percent alcohol, chlorpheniramine maleate, dextromethorphan hydrobromide, phenylpropanolamine hydrochloride)
Chlor-Trimeton Allergy Syrup [antihist.]
(7 percent alcohol, chlorpheniramine maleate)
Comtrex Liquid [antihist., cough supp., decong., analgesic]
(20 percent alcohol, chlorpheniramine maleate, dextromethorphan hydrobromide, phenylpropanolamine hydrochloride, acetaminophen)
Congespirin for Children Aspirin-Free Liquid [decong., analgesic]
(10 percent alcohol, phenylpropanolamine hydrochloride, acetaminophen)
Contac Jr. Children's Cold Medicine [cough supp., decong., analgesic]
(10 percent alcohol, dextromethorphan hydrobromide, phenylpropanolamine hydrochloride, acetaminophen)
Contac Severe Cold Formula Night Strength [antihist., cough supp., decong., analgesic]
(25 percent alcohol, doxylamine succinate, dextromethorphan hydrobromide, pseudoephedrine hydrochloride, acetaminophen)
Coricidin Cough Syrup [cough supp., decong., expect.]
(less than 0.5 percent alcohol, dextromethorphan hydrobromide, phenylpropanolamine hydrochloride, guaifenesin)
Coryban-D Cough Syrup [cough supp., decong., expect., analgesic]
(7.5 percent alcohol, dextromethorphan hydrobromide, phenylephrine hydrochloride, guaifenesin, acetaminophen)
CoTylenol Liquid Cold Medication [antihist., cough supp., decong., analgesic]
(7.5 percent alcohol, chlorpheniramine maleate, dextromethorphan hydrobromide, pseudoephedrine hydrochloride, acetaminophen)
Cremacoat 1 Throat-Coating Cough Medicine [cough supp.]
(10 percent alcohol, dextromethorphan hydrobromide)
Cremacoat 2 Throat-Coating Cough Medicine [expect.]
(10 percent alcohol, guaifenesin)
Cremacoat 3 Throat-Coating Cough Medicine [cough supp., decong., expect.]
(10 percent alcohol, dextromethorphan hydrobromide, phenylpropanolamine hydrochloride, guaifenesin)

Cremacoat 4 Throat-Coating Cough Medicine [antihist., cough supp., decong.]
(10 percent alcohol, doxylamine succinate, dextromethorphan hydrobromide, phenylpropanolamine hydrochloride)

Daycare Liquid [cough supp., decong., analgesic]
(10 percent alcohol, dextromethorphan hydrobromide, phenylpropanolamine hydrochloride, acetaminophen)

Demazin Syrup [antihist., decong.]
(7.5 percent alcohol, chlorpheniramine maleate, phenylephrine hydrochloride)

Dimetane Decongestant Tablets and Elixir [antihist., decong.]
(2.3 percent alcohol, brompheniramine maleate, phenylephrine hydrochloride)

Dimetane Elixir [antihist.]
(3 percent alcohol, brompheniramine maleate)

Dorcol Pediatric Cough Syrup [cough supp., decong., expect.]
(5 percent alcohol, dextromethorphan hydrobromide, phenylpropanolamine hydrochloride, guaifenesin)

Dristan Nasal Spray [antihist., decong.]
(0.4 percent alcohol, pheniramine maleate, phenylephrine hydrochloride)

Dristan Ultra Colds Formula Nighttime Liquid [antihist., cough supp., decong., analgesic]
(25 percent alcohol, chlorpheniramine maleate, dextromethorphan hydrobromide, pseudoephedrine hydrochloride, acetaminophen)

Formula 44 Cough Mixture [antihist., cough supp.]
(10 percent alcohol, doxylamine succinate, dextromethorphan hydrobromide)

Formula 44D Decongestant Cough Mixture [cough supp., decong., expect.]
(10 percent alcohol, dextromethorphan hydrobromide, phenylpropanolamine hydrochloride, guaifenesin)

Halls Menthol-Lyptus Decongestant Cough Formula [cough supp., decong.]
(22 percent alcohol, dextromethorphan hydrobromide, phenylpropanolamine hydrochloride)

Head & Chest Decongestant/Expectorant Cold Medicine Liquid [decong., expect.]
(5 percent alcohol, phenylpropanolamine hydrochloride, guaifenesin)

Naldecon-DX Pediatric Syrup [cough supp., decong., expect.]
    (5 percent alcohol, dextromethorphan hydrobromide, phenylpropanolamine hydrochloride, guaifenesin)
Naldecon-EX Pediatric Drops [decong., expect.]
    (0.6 percent alcohol, phenylpropanolamine hydrochloride, guaifenesin)
Novahistine Cough and Cold Formula [antihist., cough supp., decong.]
    (5 percent alcohol, chlorpheniramine maleate, dextromethorphan hydrobromide, pseudophedrine hydrochloride)
Novahistine Cough Formula [cough supp., expect.]
    (7.5 percent alcohol, dextromethorphan hydrobromide, guaifenesin)
Novahistine DMX Liquid [cough supp., decong.]
    (10 percent alcohol, dextromethorphan hydrobromide, pseudoephedrine hydrochloride)
Novahistine Elixir [antihist., decong.]
    (5 percent alcohol, chlorpheniramine maleate, phenylephrine hydrochloride)
Nyquil Nighttime Colds Medicine [antihist., cough supp., decong., analgesic]
    (25 percent alcohol, doxylamine succinate, dextromethorphan hydrobromide, pseudoephedrine hydrochloride, acetaminophen)
Pertussin Complex D Cough and Cold Formula [antihist., cough supp., decong.]
    (9.5 percent alcohol, chlorpheniramine maleate, dextromethorphan hydrobromide, phenylpropanolamine hydrochloride)
Pertussin 8-Hour Cold Formula [cough supp.]
    (9.5 percent alcohol, dextromethorphan hydrobromide)
Pertussin Original Wild Berry Cold Formula [cough supp., expect.]
    (8.5 percent alcohol, dextromethorphan hydrobromide, guaifenesin)
Quelidrine Syrup [antihist., cough supp., decong., expect.]
    (2 percent alcohol, chlorpheniramine maleate, dextromethorphan hydrobromide, phenylephrine hydrochloride, ephedrine hydrochloride)
Robitussin [expect.]
    (3.5 percent alcohol, guaifenesin)
Robitusson-CF [cough supp., decong., expect.]

(4.75 percent alcohol, dextromethorphan hydrobromide, phenylpropanolamine hydrochloride, guaifenesin)

Robitusson-DM [cough supp., expect.]

(1.4 percent alcohol, dextromethorphan hydrobromide, guaifenesin)

Robitusson Night Relief Colds Formula [antihist., cough supp., decong., analgesic]

(25 percent alcohol, pyrilamine maleate, dextromethorphan hydrobromide, phenylephrine hydrochloride, acetaminophen)

Robitusson-PE [decong., expect.]

(1.4 percent alcohol, pseudoephedrine hydrochloride, guaifenesin)

Ru-Tuss Liquid [antihist., decong.]

(5 percent alcohol, chlorpheniramine maleate, phenylephrine hydrochloride)

Sudafed Cough Syrup [cough supp., decong., expect.]

(2.4 percent alcohol, dextromethorphan hydrobromide, pseudoephedrine hydrochloride, guaifenesin)

terpin hydrate elixir [expect.]

(42.5 percent alcohol, terpin hydrate)

Triaminic Expectorant [decong., expect.]

(5 percent alcohol, phenylpropanolamine hydrochloride, guaifenesin)

Trind [antihist., decong.]

(5 percent alcohol, chlorpheniramine maleate, phenylpropanolamine hydrochloride)

Trind-DM [antihist., cough supp., decong.]

(5 percent alcohol, chlorpheniramine maleate, dextromethorphan hydrobromide, phenylpropanolamine hydrochloride)

Vicks Cough Syrup (cough supp., expect.)

(5 percent alcohol, dextromethorphan hydrobromide, guaifenesin)

COUGH, COLD, OR OTHER UPPER RESPIRATORY MEDICATIONS: NONPRESCRIPTION DRUGS THAT ARE WITHOUT REACTIVATION RISK

WITHOUT REACTIVATION RISK: In general, the nonprescription medications in this group are WITHOUT REACTIVATION RISK for recovering alcoholics/addicts when taken exactly as advised— ideally, by a doctor.

Many of the medications in this group contain an antihistamine as an active ingredient. Most antihistamines may cause sleepiness as a side effect. People react in differing ways with regard to this side effect. Some don't get sleepy at all, and some get "zonked out."

It is our feeling that this effect is not a risk to the recovering alcoholic/addict, and that, when medically appropriate, the re-coveree can safely take antihistamines. However, there are recently developed antihistamines that do not have this side effect (Seldane, for example). The recovering alcoholic/addict would do well to re-quest one of these when an antihistamine (or combination drug containing antihistamine) is to be prescribed.

Moreover, with the many drugs for colds and general upper respi-ratory conditions, there is potential for differing side effects. Some decongestants can cause a jittery, "hyper," or nervous feeling that is quite uncomfortable. Other combination drugs can cause a "spacy" or weird feeling, and, of course, some can cause sleepiness. For recovering alcoholics/addicts, the safest approach to these medica-tions is to use them only when clearly necessary, and to start with lower-than-normal doses. These suggestions should be discussed with your physician.

A common pain-reliever/fever-reducer drug in some of these medi-cations—which is either aspirin or acetaminophen in almost all cases—may be subject to abuse by some addiction-prone persons, who take such a drug unnecessarily or to excess.

Special Effects of Nasal Sprays Call for Caution: Many nasal sprays act by constricting the nasal membranes. As a result of what might be called a *rebound effect* when the nasal spray wears off, there is often more swelling and obstruction. This leads to more and more frequent use of the nasal spray, and can in time produce addictivelike behavior. People have been known to develop into "nasal-spray addicts" as a result. Individuals recovering from alcoholism or addiction should hence be especially careful to stop use of a nasal spray if such addictivelike behavior starts to develop. However, compulsive overdependence on such nasal sprays can appear in anyone who is not careful about using the sprays according to directions.

Actifed Syrup, Tablets [antihist., decong.]
    (pseudoephedrine hydrochloride, tripolidine hydrochloride)
Afrin Nasal Spray, Drops [decong.]
    (oxymetazoline hydrochloride)
Afrinol Repetabs Tablets [decong.]
    (pseudoephedrine sulfate)
Alka-Seltzer Plus Cold Medicine [antihist., decong., aspirin]
    (chlorpheniramine maleate, phenylpropanolamine hydrochloride)
Allerest Children's Chewable Tablets, Timed Release Capsules [antihist., decong.]
    (chlorpheniramine maleate, phenylpropanolamine hydrochloride)
Allerest Headache Strength Tablets, Sinus Pain Formula Tablets, [antihist., decong., analgesic]
    (chlorpheniramine maleate, phenylpropanolamine hydrochloride, acetaminophen)
A.R.M. Allergy Relief Medicine Tablets [antihist., decong.]
    (chlorpheniramine maleate, phenylpropanolamine hydrochloride)
Bayer Children's Cold Tablets [decong., aspirin]
    (phenylpropanolamine hydrochloride, aspirin)
Benzedrex Inhaler [decong.]
    (propylhexadrine)
Breonesin Capsules [expect.]
    (guaifenesin)
Chlor-Trimeton Allergy Tablets (antihist.)
    (chlorpheniramine maleate)
Chlor-Trimeton Decongestant Tablets [antihist., decong.]
    (chlorpheniramine maleate, pseudoephedrine sulfate)
Comtrex Caplets, Tablets [antihist., cough supp., decong., analgesic]
    (chlorpheniramine maleate, dextromethorphan hydrobromide, phenylpropanolamine hydrochloride, acetaminophen)
Congespirin Chewable Cold Tablets [decong., aspirin]

(phenylephrine hydrochloride, aspirin)

Congespirin for Children Aspirin-Free Chewable Cold Tablets [decong., analgesic]

(phenylephrine hydrochloride, acetaminophen)

Congespirin for Children Cough Syrup [cough supp.]

(dextromethorphan hydrobromide)

Contac Cough Capsules [cough supp., decong.]

(dextromethorphan hydrobromide, pseudoephedrine hydrochloride)

Contac Decongestant Capsules [antihist., decong.]

(chlorpheniramine maleate, phenylpropanolamine hydrochloride)

Contac Severe Cold Formula Capsules [antihist., cough supp., decong., analgesic]

(chlorpheniramine maleate, dextromethorphan hydrobromide, pseudoephedrine hydrochloride, acetaminophen)

Coricidin Decongestant Nasal Mist [decong.]

(phenylephrine hydrochloride)

Coricidin Demilets Tablets for Children, Sinus Tablets [antihist., decong., analgesic]

(chlorpheniramine maleate, phenylpropanolamine hydrochloride, acetaminophen)

Coricidin Medilets Tablets for Children [antihist., decong.]

(chlorpheniramine maleate, phenylpropanolamine hydrochloride)

Coricidin Tablets [antihist., aspirin]

(chlorpheniramine maleate, aspirin)

Coricidin "D" Tablets [antihist., decong., aspirin]

(chlorpheniramine maleate, phenylpropanolamine hydrochloride, aspirin)

Coryban-D Capsules [antihist., decong., caffeine]

(chlorpheniramine maleate, phenylpropanolamine hydrochloride, caffeine)

CoTylenol Children's Chewable Tablets [antihist., decong., analgesic]

(chlorpheniramine maleate, phenylpropanolamine hydrochloride, acetaminophen)

Daycare Capsules [cough supp., decong., analgesic]

(dextromethorphan hydrobromide, phenylpropanolamine hydrochloride, acetaminophen)

Demazin Repetabs Tablets, Syrup [antihist., decong.]

(chlorpheniramine maleate, phenylephrine hydrochloride)

Dimacol Capsules [cough supp., decong., expect.]
(dextromethorphan hydrobromide, pseudoephedrine hydrochloride, guaifenesin)
Disophrol Tablets [antihist., decong.]
(dexbrompheniramine maleate, pseudoephedrine sulfate)
Dristan Advanced Formula Tablets [antihist., decong., analgesic]
(chlorpheniramine maleate, phenylephrine hydrochloride, acetaminophen)
Dristan Long-Lasting Nasal Spray, Long-Lasting Menthol Nasal Spray [decong.]
(oxymetazoline hydrochloride)
Dristan Menthol Nasal Spray [antihist., decong.]
(pheniramine maleate, phenylephrine hydrochloride)
Dristan Ultra Colds Formula Capsules, Tablets [antihist., cough supp., decong., analgesic]
(chlorpheniramine maleate, dextromethorphan hydrobromide, pseudoephedrine hydrochloride, acetaminophen)
Drixoral Sustained-Action Tablets [antihist., decong.]
(dexbrompheneramine maleate, pseudoephedrine sulfate)
Duration 12-Hour Nasal Spray [decong.]
(oxymetazoline)
Duration Mild 4-Hour Nasal Spray [decong.]
(phenylephrine hydrochloride)
Extend 12 Liquid [cough supp.]
(dextromethorphan hydrobromide)
Formula 44 Discs [cough supp., local anesthetic]
(dextromethorphan hydrobromide, benzocaine)
(Four) 4-Way Cold Tablets [antihist., decong., aspirin]
(chlorpheniramine maleate, phenylpropanolamine hydrochloride, aspirin)
(Four) 4-Way Nasal Spray [antihist., decong.]
(pyrilamine maleate, phenylephrine hydrochloride, naphazoline hydrochloride)
(Four) 4-Way Long Acting Nasal Spray [decong.]
(oxymetazoline hydrochloride)
Head & Chest Cold Medicine Tablets, Capsules [decong., expect.]
(phenylpropanolamine hydrochloride, guaifenesin)
Headway Capsules, Tablets [antihist., decong., analgesic]
(chlorpheniramine maleate, phenylpropanolamine hydrochloride, acetaminophen)
Hold Children's Lozenges [cough supp., decong.]

(dextromethorphan hydrobromide, phenylpropanolamine hydrochloride)

Hold Lozenges [cough supp.]
(dextromethorphan hydrobromide)

Neo-Synephrine (solution) [decong.]
(phenylephrine hydrochloride)

Neo-Synephrine 12 Hour Nasal Spray, Vapor Nasal Spray, Nose Drops, Children's Nose Drops [decong.]
(oxymetazoline hydrochloride)

Neo-Synephrine II Long Acting Nasal Spray, Vapor Nasal Spray, Nose Drops, Children's Nose Drops [decong.]
(xylometazoline hydrochloride)

Neo-Synephrinol Day Relief Capsules [decong.]
(pseudoephedrine hydrochloride)

Nostril Nasal Decongestant [decong.]
(phenylephrine hydrochloride)

Nostrilla Long-Acting Nasal Decongestant [decong.]
(oxymetazoline hydrochloride)

NTZ Nasal Spray, Nose Drops [decong.]
(oxymetazoline hydrochloride)

Ornacol Capsules [cough supp., decong.]
(dextrometorphan hydrobromide, phenylpropanolamine hydrochloride)

Ornex Capsules [decong., analgesic]
(phenylpropanolamine hydrochloride, acetaminophen)

Otrivin Nasal Spray, Nose Drops [decong.]
(xylometazoline hydrochloride)

Privine Nasal Solution, Spray [decong.]
(naphazoline hydrochloride)

Pyrroxate Capsules [antihist., decong., analgesic]
(chlorpheniramine maleate, phenylpropanolamine hydrochloride, acetaminophen)

Ryna Liquid [antihist., decong.]
(chlorpheniramine maleate, pseudoephedrine hydrochloride)

Sinarest Tablets [antihist., decong., analgesic]
(chlorpheniramine maleate, phenylpropanolamine hydrochloride, acetaminophen)

Sine-Aid Sinus Headache Tablets, Extra-Strength Sine-Aid Caplets [decong., analgesic]
(pseudoephedrine hydrochloride, acetaminophen)

Sine-Off Extra-Strength Non-Aspirin Capsules [antihist., decong., analgesic]
(chlorpheniramine maleate, phenylpropanolamine hydrochloride, acetaminophen)

Sine-Off Extra-Strength No-Drowsiness Formula Capsules [decong., analgesic]
(phenylpropanolamine hydrochloride, acetaminophen)

Sine-Off Tablets—Aspirin Formula [antihist., decong., aspirin]
(chlorpheniramine maleate, phenylpropanolamine hydrochloride, aspirin)

Sinex Long-Acting Decongestant Nasal Spray [decong.]
(oxymetazoline hydrochloride)

Sinutab Capsules, Tablets [antihist., decong., analgesic]
(chlorpheniramine maleate, pseudoephedrine hydrochloride, acetaminophen)

Sinutab II Maximum Strength, No-Drowsiness Formula Capsules, Tablets [decong., analgesic]
(pseudoephedrine hydrochloride, acetaminophen)

Spec-T Sore Throat/Cough Suppressant Lozenges [cough supp., local anesthetic]
(dextromethorphan hydrobromide, benzocaine)

Spec-T Sore Throat/Decongestant Lozenges [decong., local anesthetic]
(phenylephrine hydrochloride, phenylpropanolamine hydrochloride, benzocaine)

St. Joseph Cold Tablets for Children [decong., aspirin]
(phenylpropanolamine hydrochloride, aspirin)

Sucrets Cold Decongestant Formula [decong.]
(phenylpropanolamine hydrochloride)

Sucrets Cough Control Formula [cough supp.]
(dextromethorphan hydrobromide)

Sudafed Cough Syrup, Sustained Action Capsules, Tablets [decong.]
(pseudoephedrine hydrochloride)

Sudafed Plus Syrup, Tablets [antihist., decong.]
(chlorpheniramine maleate, pseudoephedrine hydrochloride)

Teldrin Multi-Symptom Capsules [antihist., decong., analgesic]
(chlorpheniramine maleate, pseudoephedrine hydrochloride, acetaminophen)

Triaminic Chewable Tablets, Cold Tablets, Cold Syrup, Triaminic-12 Tablets [antihist., decong.]

(chlorpheniramine maleate, phenylpropanolamine hydrochloride)

Triaminic-DM Cough Formula [cough supp., decong.]
(dextromethorphan hydrobromide, phenylpropanolamine hydrochloride)

Triaminicin Tablets [antihist., decong., aspirin, caffeine]
(chlorpheniramine maleate, phenylpropanolamine hydrochloride, aspirin, caffeine)

Triaminicol Multi-Symptom Cold Tablets, Syrup [antihist., cough supp., decong.]
(chlorpheniramine maleate, dextromethorphan hydrobromide, phenylpropanolamine hydrochloride)

Tussagesic Suspension, Tablets [antihist., cough supp., decong., expect., analgesic]
(pheniramine maleate, pyrilamine maleate, dextromethorphan hydrobromide, phenylpropanolamine hydrochloride, terpin hydrate, acetaminophen)

Tylenol Maximum Strength Sinus Medication, Capsules, Tablets [decong., analgesic]
(pseudoephedrine hydrochloride, acetaminophen)

Ursinus Inlay-Tabs [antihist., decong., aspirin]
(pheniramine maleate, pyrilamine maleate, phenylpropanolamine hydrochloride, aspirin)

Vatronol Nose Drops [decong.]
(ephedrine sulfate)

Vicks Cough Silencers Cough Drops [cough supp., local anesthetic]
(dextromethorphan hydrobromide, benzocaine)

Vicks Inhaler [decong.]
(1-desoxyephedrine)

Dental Preparations

Except where alcohol is an ingredient, the drugs listed in this section are safe for alcoholics/addicts to use without risk of reactivating their addiction.

DENTAL PREPARATIONS: PRESCRIPTION DRUGS THAT ARE WITHOUT REACTIVATION RISK

WITHOUT REACTIVATION RISK: The prescription medications listed here are of two types: corticosteroidal pastes and fluoride supplements. Ingestion of fluoride during tooth development leads to significantly harder teeth that are more resistant to decay. Excessive amounts of fluoride can cause *dental fluorosis,* or mottling of the teeth.

These drugs have no mood-altering effects and can be used by recovering alcoholics/addicts without danger of reactivating their addiction.

Fluoritab Tablets
(sodium fluoride)
Fluoritab Liquid
(sodium fluoride)
Kenalog in Orabase
(triamcinolone acetonide)
Luride Drops
(sodium fluoride)
Mulvidren-F Softab
(sodium fluoride and vitamins)
Orabase HCA
(hydrocortisone)
Phos-Flur Oral Rinse/Supplement
(aciduated phosphate fluoride)
Prevident Brush-On Gel
(sodium fluoride)
Thera-Flur Gel Drops
(sodium fluoride)

DENTAL PREPARATIONS: NONPRESCRIPTION DRUGS THAT CALL FOR CAUTION

CAUTION: The two nonprescription preparations listed here call for CAUTION on the part of recovering alcoholics/addicts because of their alcohol content.

Anbesol Gel Antiseptic Anesthetic
(benzocaine, phenol, 70 percent alcohol)
Point-Two Dental Rinse
(sodium fluoride, 6 percent alcohol)

DENTAL PREPARATIONS: NONPRESCRIPTION DRUGS THAT ARE WITHOUT REACTIVATION RISK

WITHOUT REACTIVATION RISK: The nonprescription preparations in this group are without reactivation risk for recovering alcoholics/addicts. Included here are oral anesthetics and antiseptics.

Chloraseptic Liquid
(phenol, sodium phenolate)
Hurricaine Topical Anesthetic
(benzocaine)

Diagnostics

WITHOUT REACTIVATION RISK: All diagnostic medications are without reactivation risk for recovering alcoholics/addicts since they pose no risk to continued abstinence.

Certain diagnostic medications are ingested. These include drugs that stimulate or inhibit the adrenal cortex to test for adrenal corticosteroid production. Commonly used medications of this kind include Metopirone and Acthar. Among other diagnostics that are swallowed or injected are sera for allergy skin tests, radiographic contrast media for special x-rays such as angiography, and drugs that are used to test renal function.

Diuretics ("Water Pills")

WITHOUT REACTIVATION RISK: Diuretics pose no risk to the continued sobriety of recovering alcoholics/addicts. They are used to decrease the amount of salt and water in the tissues, which when excessive is called *edema*. They accomplish this in part by increasing urinary output. Diuretics are used to reduce edema arising in connection with such conditions as congestive heart failure, hepatic cirrhosis, and the after effects of corticosteroid and estrogen therapy. They are also used by women to treat excess water retention prior to menstruation and are commonly used to treat high blood pressure.

Among widely used diuretics are hydrochlorothiazide (often called HCTZ), Lasix (furosimide), and Maxzide (triamterene, hydrochlorothiazide).

Gastrointestinal System Medications

This section covers medications of five broad types that are used to treat gastrointestinal system difficulties:

Antacids, Antiflatulents, Digestants
Antidiarrheal Agents, Oral Electrolyte Solutions
Antinauseants (Antiemetics; Anti–Motion Sickness Agents)
Antiulcer-Antisecretory Agents; Antispamodics
Laxatives

ANTACIDS, ANTIFLATULENTS, DIGESTANTS

Antacids, antiflatulents, and digestants are gastrointestinal medications used to treat conditions such as acid indigestion, heartburn, upset stomach, and gastritis.

Antacids, Antiflatulents, Digestants: Prescription Medication That Calls for CAUTION

CAUTION: One medication of these three related kinds calls for CAUTION by recovering alcoholics/addicts. The prescription drug listed here has as its active ingredients phenobarbital, a potentially habit-forming barbiturate; simethicone, an antiflatulent; and pancreatic enzymes (provided as digestants, for persons whose pancreas produces insufficient enzymes).

Phazyme-PB
(phenobarbital, simethicone, pancreatic enzymes)

Antacids, Antiflatulents, Digestants: Prescription and Nonprescription Medications That Are WITHOUT REACTIVATION RISK

WITHOUT REACTIVATION RISK: The antacid, anti–digestive gas, and digestion-promoting active ingredients of these drugs are WITHOUT REACTIVATION RISK for recovering alcoholics/addicts, in the sense that such ingredients do not endanger continued abstinence. Most medications of these kinds are nonprescription drugs, but a few are available only by prescription. Among them are combination drugs; some, for example, contain both antacid and antiflatulent active ingredients.

Among examples of widely used antacids are Alka-Seltzer (sodium bicarbonate, potassium bicarbonate), Maalox (magnesium hydroxide, aluminum hydroxide), and Tums (calcium carbonate). Combination antacids/antiflatulents include Gelusil (aluminum hydroxide, magnesium hydroxide, simethicone) and Rioplan Plus (magaldrate, simethicone). Digestants include the prescription drug Cotazym (pancrelipase), and the nonprescription drug Phazyme (simethicone, pancreatic enzymes).

ANTIDIARRHEAL AGENTS; ORAL ELECTROLYTE SOLUTIONS

Antidiarrheal agents are used to treat diarrhea. Patients may need oral electrolyte solutions as adjuncts to diarrheal treatment to offset ill effects of excessive fluid and electrolyte loss.

Antidiarrheal Agents: Prescription Medications That Call for CAUTION

CAUTION: Antidiarrheal agents containing active ingredients that are narcotic controlled substances call for CAUTION by recovering alcoholics/addicts. Those ingredients include diphenoxylate and opium.

Donnagel-PG
    (opium, kaolin, pectin, hyoscyamine sulfate, atropine sulfate, scopolamine hydrobromide)
Lomotil
    (diphenoxylate hydrochloride, atropine sulfate)
paregoric
    (camphorated tincture of opium)

Parepectolin
(paregoric, pectin, kaolin)

Antidiarrheal Agents: Prescription Medications That Are WITHOUT REACTIVATION RISK

WITHOUT REACTIVATION RISK: The following drugs are prescription drugs that are WITHOUT REACTIVATION RISK for the recovering alcoholic/addict with respect to continued abstinence. These medications work by a number of different mechanisms. For example, loperamide hydrochloride acts by slowing intestinal motility and by decreasing loss of water and electrolytes.

Arco-Lase Plus (NOTE: FOLLOW PRECAUTIONS)
(trizyme, lipase, hyoscyamine sulfate, atropine sulfate, phenobarbitol) (Precautions to observe to avoid risk of reactivating addiction are as follows: [1] use only when medically prescribed for diarrhea; [2] use exactly as prescribed; and [3] stop taking at the end of the prescribed period.)
Imodium
(loperamide hydrochloride)
loperamide hydrochloride

Antidiarrheal Agents: Nonprescription Medications That Are WITHOUT REACTIVATION RISK

WITHOUT REACTIVATION RISK: Medications in this group are nonprescription drugs that are WITHOUT REACTIVATION RISK for recovering alcoholics/addicts with respect to continued abstinence. Active ingredients range from digestive enzymes to bacterial flora which aid in digestion.

Arco-Lase
(trizyme, lipase)
Charcocaps
(activated vegetable charcoal)
Diasorb
(attapulgite)
Donnagel
(kaolin, pectin, hyoscyamine, atropine, scopolamine)
Enterodophilus
(strains of *Lactobacillus acidophilus* and *Lactobacillus casei* subsp. *rhamnosus*)
Kaopectate

(kaolin and pectin)
Lactinex
(strains of *Lactobacillus acidophilus* and *L. bulgaricus*)
Mitrolan
(calcium polycarbofil)
Pepto-Bismol
(bismuth subsalicylate)
Rheaban Maximum Strength Tablets
(attapulgite)

Oral Electrolyte Solutions

WITHOUT REACTIVATION RISK: Oral electrolyte solutions pose no risk to continued abstinence for recovering alcoholics/addicts. Their main purpose is to serve as adjuncts to the treatment of diarrhea. During the course of mild to severe diarrhea, excessive amounts of water and electrolytes may be lost. Oral electrolyte solutions are designed to replace these, and they usually contain carbohydrates and ions of various kinds—potassium, calcium, magnesium, sodium, and others. Infalyte, Lytren, and Pedialyte are commonly used oral electrolyte solutions.

ANTINAUSEANTS (ANTIEMETICS; ANTI–MOTION SICKNESS AGENTS)

Antinauseants are generally used for relief from nausea, vomiting, motion sickness, and morning sickness. They are accordingly also called *antiemetics* and *anti–motion sickness agents*.

Antinauseants: Prescription Medications that Call for CAUTION

CAUTION: The drugs in this group call for CAUTION on the part of recovering alcoholics/addicts. Some consist of or contain dronabinol, a controlled substance. Also termed delta-9-THC, dronabinol is one of the major ingredients in marijuana. Its street name is "THC" or "tea." Other medications in this group have as an active ingredient pentobarbitol, which is also a narcotic controlled substance.

dronabinol
Marinol

(dronabinol)
"THC"
"tea"
Wans
(pyrilamine maleate, pentobarbital)

Antinauseants: Prescription Medications that call for PRECAUTIONS

FOLLOW PRECAUTIONS: For recovering alcoholics/addicts, the medications in this group are without risk of reactivating addiction if used WITH PRECAUTIONS. Some, such as Atarax and Vistaril, are used to alleviate nausea and itching. Others, such as Benadryl, are antihistamines. Still others are antidepressants or tranquilizers. Some of these medications have noneuphoric mood-altering effects.

As a result, recovering individuals should observe the following precautions if they find it necessary to take any medications in this group: (1) tell their doctor with complete honesty about their alcoholism/addiction; (2) ask their doctor whether the medication can be avoided; and (3) if the medication is necessary, discontinue taking it and discard any remaining supply of it as soon as possible.

Atarax
    (hydroxyzine hydrochloride)
Benadryl
    (diphenhydramine hydrochloride)
Bucladin-S Softab
    (buclizine hydrochloride)
buclizine
chlorpromazine
Compazine
    (prochlorperazine)
cyclizine
diphenhydramine hydrochloride
Emete-Con
    (benzquinamide hydrochloride)
Marezine
    (cyclizine)
metoclopramide hydrochloride
perphenazine
Phenergan
    (promethazine hydrochloride)

promethazine hydrochloride
Reglan
    (metoclopramide hydrochloride)
Thorazine
    (chlorpromazine hydrochloride)
Tigan
    (trimethobenzamide hydrochloride)
Torecan
    (thiethylperazine maleate)
triflupromazine
Trilafon
    (perphenazine)
trimethobenzamide
Vesprin
    (trimethobenzamide)
Vistaril
    (hydroxyzine pamoate)

Antinauseants: Nonprescription Drugs That Are WITHOUT REACTIVATION RISK

WITHOUT REACTIVATION RISK: These nonprescription antinau-seants are WITHOUT REACTIVATION RISK for recovering alcoholics/addicts, inasmuch as they pose no danger to continued abstinence. However, Dramamine and drugs containing meclizine can cause drowsiness.

Bonine
    (meclizine hydrochloride)
Dramamine
    (dimethylhydrinate)
Emetrol
    (dextrose, levulose, phosphoric acid)
meclizine
Pepto-Bismol
    (bismuth subsalicylate)

ANTIULCER-ANTISECRETORY AGENTS; ANTISPASMODICS

The drugs listed in this group are used in treating problems associ-ated with ulcers of the gastrointestinal tract. Active ingredients in some *antiulcer drugs*, such as sucralfate, in effect coat the ulcer site and protect it from digestive acids. *Antisecretory agents*, such as cimetidine, inhibit the release or secretion of stomach acids, pepsin, and other secretions into the stomach. *Antispasmodics* relieve irritable bowel syndrome and spasm associated with ulcers (as with the use of belladonna alkaloids such as atropine, hyoscyamine, belladonna, and scopolamine which act as smooth muscle relaxants to relieve spasms of the gastrointestinal tract).

Antiulcer-Antisecretory-Antispasmodics: Prescription Drugs That CALL FOR CAUTION

CAUTION: The medications in this group call for CAUTION on the part of recovering alcoholics/addicts because they contain addictive barbiturates (such as butabarbital) or other possibly addictive ingredients (for example, the antianxiety drug chlordiazepoxide or the tranquilizer meprobamate).

Butibel
(belladonna extract, butabarbital sodium)
Librax
(chlordiazepoxide hydrochloride, clidinium bromide)
Milpath
(meprobamate, tridihexethyl chloride)
Pathibamate
(meprobamate, tridihexethyl chloride)

Antiulcer-Antisecretory-Antispasmodics: Prescription Drugs That CALL FOR PRECAUTIONS

FOLLOW PRECAUTIONS: The antiulcer drugs in this group can be taken by recovering alcoholics/addicts without reactivation risk provided that they observe precautions: (1) use only when medically prescribed for one or more of these purposes (antiulcer, antisecretory, or antispasmodic); (2) take precisely as prescribed; and (3) stop taking at the end of the prescribed period. Caution is needed mainly because one ingredient is phenobarbital, a barbiturate that may be habit-forming but that has no euphoric effects at these dosages.

Antrocol
(atropine sulfate, phenobarbital)
Barbidonna

(phenobarbital, hyoscyamine sulfate, atropine sulfate, scopolamine hydrobromide)
Belap
(phenobarbital, belladonna extract)
Belladenal and Belladenal-S
(belladonna alkaloids, phenobarbital)
Bellergal and Bellergal-S
(phenobarbitol, ergotamine tartrate, belladonna alkaloids)
Daricon PB
(oxyphencyclimine hydrochloride, phenobarbital)
Donnatal
(phenobarbital, hyoscyamine sulfate, atropine sulfate, scopolamine hydrobromide
Hybephen
(atropine sulfate, scopolamine hydrobromide, hyoscyamine sulfate, phenobarbital)
Kinesed
(phenobarbital, hyoscyamine sulfate, atropine sulfate, scopolamine hydrobromide)

Antiulcer-Antisecretory-Antispasmodic: Prescription Drugs That Are WITHOUT REACTIVATION RISK

WITHOUT REACTIVATION RISK: For recovering alcoholics/addicts, the drugs listed in this group are WITHOUT REACTIVATION RISK, in that they contain no addictive ingredients. The antispasmodic ingredients used in these medications are belladonna alkaloids, which are nonaddictive.

A-Spas
(dicyclomine hydrochloride)
Antispas
(dicyclomine hydrochloride)
Antrenyl
(oxyphenonium bromide)
atropine sulfate
Banthine
(methantheline bromide)
Baycyclomine
(dicyclomine hydrochloride)
belladonna tincture
Bellafoline

(levorotatory alkaloids of belladonna)
Bentyl
(dicyclomine hydrochloride)
Byclomine
(dicyclomine hydrochloride)
Cantil
(mepenzolate bromide)
Carafate
(sucralfate)
Combid
(prochlorperazine maleate, isopropamide iodide)
Cyclocen
(dicyclomine hydrochloride)
Darbid
(isopropamide iodide)
Daricon
(oxyphencyclimine hydrochloride)
Dibent
(dicyclomine hydrochloride)
Dicen
(dicyclomine hydrochloride)
Dilomine
(dicyclomine hydrochloride)
Di-Spaz
(dicyclomine hydrochloride)
Enarax
(oxyphencyclimine hydrochloride, hydroxyzine hydrochloride)
Festalan
(lipase, amylase, protease, atropine, methyl sulfate)
Kutrase Capsules
(amylase, protease, lipase, cellulase, phenyltoloxamine sulfate, hyoscyamine sulfate)
Levsin and Levsinex
(hyoscyamine sulfate)
Neoquess
(dicyclomine hydrochloride)
Nospaz
(dicyclomine hydrochloride)
Or-Tyl
(dicyclomine hydrochloride)
Pamine

(methscopolamine bromide)
Pathilon
(tridihexethyl chloride)
Pro-Banthīne
(propantheline bromide)
Quarzan
(clidinium bromide)
Robinul and Robinul Forte
(glycopyrrolate)
scopolamine hydrobromide
Spasmoject
(dicyclomine hydrochloride)
Tagamet
(cimetidine)
Tral
(hexocyclium methylsulfate)
Valpin
(anisotropine methylbromide)
Vistrax
(oxyphencyclimine hydrochloride, hydroxyzine hydrochloride)
Zantac
(ranitidine hydrochloride)

LAXATIVES; STOOL SOFTENERS

WITHOUT REACTIVATION RISK: Laxatives and stool softeners
are generally WITHOUT REACTIVATION RISK for recovering alco-
holics/addicts. They do not include addictive or habit-forming ingredients. Most are available without prescription. Active ingredients in
laxatives usually stimulate the peristaltic activity of the intestine. Ex-
Lax (yellow phenolphthalein) is a commonly used laxative. Stool
softeners such as Colace (docusate potassium) and Dialose (docusate
potassium) act as surfactants which promote the absorption of water
into the stool. With laxatives in capsule or liquid forms, it might be
wise to check the ingredients for possible alcohol content.

Geriatric Medications

WITHOUT REACTIVITION RISK: Geriatric medications are prescription drugs used to help relieve a wide variety of medical

problems characteristic of old age. Since none contains mood-altering drugs, they are without reactivation risk for the recovering alcoholic/addict.

A few examples of widely used types of geriatric drugs include Arlidin (nylidrin hydrochloride), which is used to dilate blood vessels especially in the extremities to improve blood circulation; Pavabid (papaverine hydrochloride), also for dilating blood vessels; and Hydergine (ergoloid mesylates), for the treatment of a decline in mental capacity when the cause of such decline is unknown.

Heart Disease Medications

WITHOUT REACTIVATION RISK: Medications for heart disease are prescription drugs that are WITHOUT REACTIVATION RISK for recovering alcoholics/addicts. They consist largely of four broad types of medications: antianginal agents, antiarrhythmics, cardiac preload and afterload reducers, and cardiac glycosides. Among examples of widely used heart disease drugs are antianginal agents Nitrostat (nitroglycerine), Inderal (propranolol hydrochloride), Isordil (isosorbide dinitrate), and Procardia (nifedipine); antiarrhythmics Norpace (disopyramide phosphate) and Tonocard (tocainide hydrochloride); and the cardiac glycoside Lanoxin (digoxin).

Hemorrhoidal Medications

WITHOUT REACTIVATION RISK: For recovering alcoholics/addicts, drugs to treat hemorrhoidal problems are without reactivation risk with respect to continued abstinence. Such medications are used to relieve not only the pain and itching associated with hemorrhoids, but discomfort resulting from proctitis, rectal surgery, cryptitis, fissures, and incomplete fistulas. Their active ingredients usually include lubricants, anti-inflammatory agents, antipruritic (anti-itch) agents, and vasoconstrictive agents. These drugs are applied locally to the affected area. Among commonly used hemorrhoidal medications are Anusol-HC Rectal Cream (hydrocortisone acetate, bismuth subgallate, resorcin compound, benzyl benzoate, Peruvian balsam, zinc oxide; available only by prescription), Preparation H

Ointment (live yeast cell derivative, shark liver oil), and Nupercainal Ointment (dibucaine).

Hormones

WITHOUT REACTIVATION RISK: Hormones are the natural substances produced by glands in the body. As medications they represent a broad range of natural and synthetic drugs that are used to treat wide varieties of physical disorders. They contain no habit-forming nor addictive ingredients and are therefore without reactivation risk for recovering alcoholics/addicts insofar as continued abstinence is concerned. Major broad types of hormonal medications include androgens, estrogens, progestins, fertility inducers, prolactin inducers, and thyroid hormones. (Corticosteroids, another major type, are treated in a separate section in this chapter.) Most are prescription drugs.

Commonly prescribed androgens (used to treat such conditions in men as impotence and eunuchism) include Danocrine (danazol) and DEPO-Testosterone (testosterone cypionate). Examples of other widely used hormonal medications are: estrogens (used for menopausal symptoms, ovarian insufficiency, and certain cancer therapies) including Premarin (conjugated estrogens) and Estrace (estradiol); progesterins (used for abnormal uterine bleeding or lack of menstrual discharge), which include Norulate (norethindrone acetate) and Provera (medroxyprogesterone acetate); fertility inducer Clomid (clomiphene citrate); prolactin inhibitor (used in some applications to treat infertility) Parlodel (bromocriptine mesylate); and thyroid hormones Cytomel (liothyronine) and Synthroid (levothyroxine sodium).

Muscle Relaxants

Medications in this section are used for the treatment of muscle strain due to injury, muscle pains or cramps, and muscular tension due to stress. (They are used for muscles attached to the skeleton, rather than the muscles of internal organs.)

MUSCLE RELAXANTS: PRESCRIPTION DRUGS THAT CALL FOR CAUTION

CAUTION: Addictive ingredients in the medications listed in this group call for CAUTION by recovering alcoholics/addicts from the standpoint of continued abstinence. Diazepam, the active ingredient in the antianxiety drugs Valium and Valrelease, is an addictive controlled substance. Another active ingredient, carisoprodol, acts by blocking intraneural activity in the spinal chord. Some cases of psychological dependence and abuse with this drug have been reported. It hence seems possibly addictive.

carisoprodol
Rela
    (carisoprodol)
Soma
    (carisoprodol)
Soma Compound
    (carisoprodol, aspirin)
Soma Compound with Codeine
    (carisoprodol, aspirin, codeine phosphate)
Soprodol
    (carisoprodol)
Valium
    (diazepam)
Valrelease
    (diazepam)

MUSCLE RELAXANTS: PRESCRIPTION DRUGS THAT ARE WITHOUT REACTIVATION RISK

WITHOUT REACTIVATION RISK: The drugs in this group are WITHOUT REACTIVATION RISK for recovering alcoholics/addicts in that they contain no ingredients endangering reactivation of addiction. Ingredients in these drugs act in a number of different ways. For example, dantrolene controls spasticity by relaxing the contractile response of the muscle directly at the muscle itself. Cyclobenzaprine has its site of action at the brain stem to reduce muscle spasm. Orphenadrine is thought to act by analgesic properties in the brain stem.

Banflex
  (orphenadrine)
chlorzoxazone
Dantrium
  (dantrolene sodium)
Delaxin
  (methocarbamol)
Disipal
  (orphenadrine)
Flexeril
  (cyclobenzaprine hydrochloride)
Flexoject
  (orphenadrine)
Flexon
  (orphenadrine)
K-Flex
  (orphenadrine)
Lioresal
  (baclofen)
Maolate
  (chlorphenesin carbomate)
Marbaxin
  (methocarbamol)
methocarbamol
Myolin
  (orphenadrine)
Neocyten
  (orphenadrine)
Norflex
  (orphenadrine citrate)
Norgesic
  (orphenadrine citrate, aspirin, caffeine)
Norgesic Forte
  (orphenadrine citrate, aspirin, caffeine)
O-Flex
  (orphenadrine)
Orflagen
  (orphenadrine)
orphenadrine
Orphenate
  (orphenadrine)
Paraflex

(chlorzoxazone)
Parafon Forte
(chlorzoxazone and acetaminophen)
Quinamm
(quinine sulfate)
Robaxin
(methocarbamol)
Robaxisal
(methocarbamol, aspirin)
Skelaxin
(metaxalone)
Urispas
(flavoxate hydrochloride)
X-Otag
(orphenadrine)
X-Otag S.R.
(orphenadrine)

Parasitic Disease Medications

WITHOUT REACTIVATION RISK: All of these drugs are WITH-
OUT REACTIVATION RISK for recovering alcoholics/addicts, since
they contain no ingredients likely to reactivate acute substance
abuse. They are of two main types—antihelminthics and scabicides/
pediculicides. Antihelminthics are used to treat infestations by various types of worms (including roundworms, pinworms, thread-
worms, hookworms, and whipworms). They are most often
prescription drugs in tablet form. Widely used antihelminthics include Antiminth (pyrantel pamoate) and Povan (pyrvinium).

Scabicides/pediculites are used to treat scabies (mange), head lice,
and crab lice. These parasite-killing drugs are applied topically in
the form of shampoos, liquids, or creams. Some are prescription
drugs. Medications of this type in wide use include Kwell (lindane)
and Rid (pyrethrins, piperonyl butoxide, petroleum distillate, benzyl
alcohol).

Potassium Supplements

WITHOUT REACTIVATION RISK: Potassium supplements are
WITHOUT REACTIVATION RISK for recovering alcoholics/addicts.

Their primary active ingredient—a potassium salt—is not addictive and poses no risk to the continued abstinence of recoverees. Other amino acids or vitamins may be secondary ingredients. These drugs are used to offset actual or potential potassium depletion, usually through losses in the urine or stool. They are available only by prescription. Widely used potassium supplements include Kaon Tablets (potassium gluconate), K-Lyte/DS Effervescent Tablets (potassium bicarbonate, potassium citrate), and Slow-K (potassium chloride).

Psychoactive Agents

Psychoactive agents or psychiatric drugs are medications usually given for emotional disorders or psychotic conditions—states of lesser and greater degrees of mental illness. All are available only by prescription. The major kinds are:

Antianxiety Agents (Minor Tranquilizers)
Antidepressants/Antimanic Agents
Major Tranquilizers (Antipsychotics)
Central Nervous System (CNS) Stimulants

IMPORTANT NOTE 1: The authors think it especially important to emphasize here that the designation "WITHOUT REACTIVATION RISK" means the following with these medications: Any medication so designated does not endanger the continued abstinence of recovering alcoholics/addicts only *if* medically required. No drug is without reactivation risk when taken for relaxation, tranquilization, or sleep unless prescribed by an M.D. familiar with the dynamics of addiction. Any drug taken for the purpose of effecting a change in mood is dangerous to the continued abstinence of a recovering alcoholic/addict, whether that drug be an analgesic, an antihistamine, a sedative, or a tranquilizer.

IMPORTANT NOTE 2: The authors are aware of the controversy in some circles of recovering alcoholics/addicts concerning these psychoactive medications. At issue in the controversy is whether or not a recovering alcoholic/addict who takes these medications is as "sober" (that is, as free of addictive substances) as other recoverees who use no psychoactive medications. The authors' view is that a recovering alcoholic/addict who takes psychoactive medications that are identified below as "WITHOUT REACTIVATION RISK" is completely "sober" in this sense if the medications taken are prescribed by a psychiatrist thoroughly familiar with addiction.

ANTIANXIETY AGENTS (MINOR TRANQUILIZERS)

Antianxiety medications are prescribed to reduce nervous tension or anxiety that continues and that troubles the patient beyond normal and objectively justified levels. They are commonly called *tranquilizers;* in psychiatry they are sometimes termed *minor tranquilizers.*

Antianxiety Agents: Prescription Drugs That Call for CAUTION

CAUTION: The medications listed call for CAUTION on the part of recovering alcoholics/addicts. Indeed, these drugs are often abused by many cross-addicted alcoholics or addicts.

These medications in effect reduce excess activity of the brain that results in tension or fear. This action of theirs is not unlike some actions of alcohol or drugs of abuse on the central nervous system (CNS).

Most of these medications are in the chemical family called *benzodiazepines*—of which perhaps the best known is Valium (diazepam). The benzodiazepines are the most highly addictive of the medications listed here. Meprobamate, a major active ingredient in other medications listed, has a comparatively lesser addictive quality.

Ativan
(lorazepam)
Centrax
(prazepam)
chlordiazepoxide
Clonopin
(clonozepam)
Dalmane
(flurazepam)
diazepam
Deprol
(meprobamate, benactyzine hydrochloride)

Equanil
  (meprobamate)
Halcion
  (triazolam)
Libritabs
  (chlordiazepoxide hydrochloride)
Librium
  (chlordiazepoxide hydrochloride)
Limbitrol DS Tablets
  (chlordiazepoxide, amitriptyline)
Lipoxide
  (chlordiazepoxide hydrochloride)
lorazepam
Menrium
  (chlordiazepoxide, esterified estrogens)
Meprospan
  (meprobamate)
Miltown
  (meprobamate)
Miltown 600
  (meprobamate)
Murcil
  (chlordiazepoxide)
Pathibamate
  (tridihexethyl chloride, meprobamate)
Paxipam
  (halazepam)
PMB 200 and PMB 400
  (premarin, meprobate)
Reposans
  (chlordiazepoxide hydrocholoride)
Restoril
  (temazepam)
Serax
  (oxazepam)
Sereen
  (chlordiazepoxide)
SK-Lygen
  (chlordiazepoxide)
Tranxene
  (clorazepate dipotassium)
Tranxene-SD

(clorazepate dipotassium)
Valium
(diazepam)
Valrelease
(diazepam)
Xanax
(alprazolam)

Antianxiety Agents: Prescription Drugs That Call for PRECAUTIONS

FOLLOW PRECAUTIONS: These medications are without reactivation risk for recovering alcoholics/addicts (1) *if* they are prescribed and taken for a purpose *other than anxiety.* Such purposes for which they are medically recognized include nausea, and sedation in conjunction with general anesthesia before and after surgery. Other precautions are that the recovering alcoholic/addict (2) take them only for the limited length of time prescribed and (3) discontinue them and discard any remaining supply by the end of the time for which they are prescribed.

Atarax
(hydroxyzine hydrochloride)
Atarax 100
(hydroxyzine hydrochloride)
Durrax Tablets
(hydroxyzine hydrochloride)
Vistaril
(hydroxyzine pamoate)

ANTIDEPRESSANTS/ANTIMANIC AGENTS

Antidepressants are medications used to treat conditions in which patients not only feel hopeless, despairing, and fearful without objective cause, but may also have intense apathy, thoughts of suicide, and little or no appetite or sexual interest. Antimanic agents are medications used to treat manic depressive illness, in which periods of intense depression alternate with periods of intense elation and hyperactivity.

Antidepressants: Prescription Drugs that call for CAUTION

CAUTION: The following antidepressants call for CAUTION by recovering by alcoholics/addicts, inasmuch as they contain potentially addictive ingredients that might endanger continued abstinence.

Deprol
    (meprobamate, benactyzine hydrochloride)
Limbitrol (also used as an antianxiety agent)
    (chlordiazepoxide, amitriptylene hydrochloride)

Antidepressants: Prescription Drugs that are WITHOUT REACTIVATION RISK WHEN MEDICALLY REQUIRED

WITHOUT REACTIVATION RISK WHEN MEDICALLY REQUIRED: Antidepressants in this group are WITHOUT REACTIVATION RISK for recovering alcoholics/addicts because they have no active ingredients known to be addictive. In addition, they are WITHOUT REACTIVATION RISK only when medically required and prescribed by a physician thoroughly informed about the dynamics of addiction.

Adapin
    (doxepin hydrochloride)
Amitril
    (amitriptyline hydrochloride)
amitriptyline
Asendin
    (amoxapine)
Aventyl
    (nortriptyline hydrochloride)
Desyrel
    (trazodone hydrochloride)
Elavil
    (amitriptyline hydrochloride)
Emitrip
    (amitriptyline hydrochloride)
Endep
    (amitriptyline hydrochloride)
Enovil

(amitriptyline hydrochloride)
Etrafon
(perphenazine, amitriptyline hydrochloride)
imipramine
Janimine
(imipramine hydrochloride)
Ludiomil
(maprotiline hydrochloride)
Marplan
(isocarboxazid)
Nardil
(phenelzine sulfate)
Norpramine
(desipramine hydrochloride)
Pamelor
(nortriptyline hydrochloride)
Parnate
(tranylcypromine sulfate)
Pertofrane
(desipramine hydrochloride)
Sinequan
(doxepin hydrochloride)
SK-Amitriptyline
(amitriptyline hydrochloride)
SK-Pramine
(imipramine hydrochloride)
Surmontil
(trimipramine hydrochloride)
Tipramine
(imipramine hydrochloride)
Tofranil
(imipramine hydrochloride)
Tofranil-PM
(imipramine pamoate)
Triavil
(perphenazine, amitriptyline hydrochloride
Vivactil
(protriptyline hydrochloride)

Antimanic Agents—Prescription Drugs That Are WITHOUT REACTIVATION RISK

WITHOUT REACTIVATION RISK: Antimanic agents in this group are WITHOUT REACTIVATION RISK for recovering alcoholics/-addicts because they have no active ingredients known to be addictive.

Cibalith-S
(lithium citrate)
Eskalith
(lithium carbonate)
Eskalith-CR
(lithium carbonate)
Lithane
(lithium carbonate)
lithium carbonate
lithium citrate
Lithobid
(lithium carbonate)
Lithonate
(lithium carbonate)
Lithotabs
(lithium carbonate)

MAJOR TRANQUILIZERS (ANTIPSYCHOTICS): PRESCRIPTION DRUGS THAT ARE WITHOUT REACTIVATION RISK

WITHOUT REACTIVATION RISK: Medications in this group are used to treat severe mental illnesses that block the patient's rational thinking, understanding of reality, and normal functioning. Common types of such illness include paranoia and schizophrenia.

When medically prescribed for appropriate psychiatric illness, these medications are WITHOUT REACTIVATION RISK, inasmuch as they do not contain habit-forming ingredients. In addition, they are not involved in drug abuse or cross-addiction and do not prove attractive for abuse by individuals practicing active addiction to varieties of other drugs.

Chlorazine
(prochlorperazine)
Clorazine

(chlorpromazine)
Compazine
(prochlorperazine)
Eskalith-CR
(lithium carbonate)
Etrafon Tablets
(perphenazine and amitriptyline HC1)
Haldol
(haloperidol)
Loxitane
(loxapine succinate)
Loxitane C
(loxapine hydrochloride)
Loxitane IM
(loxapine hydrochloride)
Mellaril
(thioridazine)
Mellaril-S
(thioridazine)
Millazine
(thioridazine)
Moban
(molindone hydrochloride)
Navane
(thiothixene)
Orap
(pimozide)
Ormazine
(chlorpromazine)
Permitil
(fluphenazine hydrochloride)
Prolixin
(fluphenazine hydrochloride)
Prolixin Decanoate
(fluphenazine decanoate)
Prolixin Enanthate
(fluphenazine enanthate)
Promapar
(chlorpromazine)
Promaz
(chlorpromazine)
Prozine

(promazine)
Quide
(piperacetazine)
Raudixin
(rauwolfia serpentina)
Serentil
(mesoridazine besylate)
Sparine
(promazine hydrochloride)
Stelazine
(trifluoperazine hydrochloride)
Suprazine
(trifluoperazine)
Taractan
(chlorprothixene)
Thorazine
(chlorpromazine hydrochloride)
Thor-Prom
(chlorpromazine)
Tindal
(acetophenazine maleate)
Triavil
(perphenazine and amitriptyline hydrochloride)
Trilafon
(perphenazine)
Vesprin
(triflupromazine hydrochloride)

CENTRAL NERVOUS SYSTEM (CNS) STIMULANTS

Central nervous system (CNS) stimulants are prescribed mainly for *narcolepsy*—a tendency to fall asleep involuntarily when well rested—and for pathological hyperactivity in children.

CNS Stimulants: Prescription Drugs That Call for CAUTION

CAUTION: The medications in this group call for CAUTION on the part of recovering alcoholics/addicts, mainly because of their inclusion of a chemical of the amphetamine family as an active ingredient. Amphetamines are also prescribed for weight-reduction purposes but are issued with warnings that they have a high potential for abuse. In illegal use, they are known by such street names as "speed" and "uppers." Another common name is "diet pills."

In the authors' view, there is no medical situation in which these medications are appropriate for a recovering alcoholic/addict. The only possible exception to this might be a well-established diagnosis of narcolepsy.

"bennies" (street name for illegally distributed amphetamines)
Cylert Tablets
    (pemoline)
Desoxyn
    (methamphetamine hydrochloride)
Dexosyn Gradumet Tablets
    (methamphetamine hydrochloride)
Dexedrine
    (dextroamphetamine sulfate)
dextroamphetamine sulfate
methamphetamine hydrochloride
Ritalin Hydrochloride Tablets
    (methylphenidate hydrochloride)
Ritalin-SR Tablets
    (methylphenidate hydrochloride)
"speed" (street name for illegally distributed amphetamines)
"uppers" (street name for illegally distributed amphetamines)

Sedatives/Hypnotics

A number of medications that are widely employed as tranquilizers are also sometimes prescribed as sedatives. These are grouped in the section on tranquilizers, rather than being listed here. Similarly, some of the sedatives listed here are sometimes prescribed as antianxiety agents.

Sedatives are used to quiet the system; *hypnotics* are used to produce sleep. Most of the medications listed here can be used as either sedatives or hypnotics, depending on dosage.

SEDATIVES: PRESCRIPTION MEDICATIONS THAT CALL FOR CAUTION

CAUTION: Sedatives of the kinds listed in this group might be recommended mainly to relieve serious insomnia and/or severe nervous apprehension or anxiety. Most of them act as central nervous system depressants, dulling the brain and bringing on drowsiness. For almost any one of these sedatives available only by prescription, a large dose can make one unconscious; an overdose can be fatal.

In addition, for recovering alcoholics/addicts, even light dosages of these sedative medications call for SPECIAL CAUTION, from the standpoint of reactivating either addictive behavior or addiction. (See the discussion of dual addiction in Chapter 1.) Almost every one is habit-forming—addictive—to an extremely strong degree. The addictive active ingredient (ingredients) is (are) indicated by an indented entry in parentheses directly under the trade name of the medication (when entries are trade names). In generic name entries, that addictive active ingredient is the medication identified in the generic name itself.

If you are recovering from alcohol or drug abuse, DO NOT TAKE ANY OF THESE SEDATIVES IF YOU CAN POSSIBLY AVOID TAKING THEM—with the one exception of phenobarbital used for seizure control as described in the section on barbiturates directly below.

Should you need relief from insomnia or anxiety, do all you can to use other means recommended in this book instead of these prescription sedatives.

Barbiturates: Prescription Drugs That Call for CAUTION

DANGEROUS: Barbiturates (such as the ones identified in this subsection) have been considered classically addictive drugs for a great many years. Although varying somewhat in effects, most barbiturates are markedly sedating and some also have euphoric qualities. They therefore call for SPECIAL CAUTION by recovering alcoholics/ addicts because of their high potential for reactivating an acute addiction or dual addiction.

Since barbiturates like these are present in common headache and pain medications, as well as in many anesthetics, you should take special care to guard against taking them by accident.

Phenobarbital—when prescribed for seizure control in alcoholics—is the one exception to this warning against all other barbiturates. The most common two-drug combination prescribed for seizure control consists of phenytoin (Dilantin) and phenobarbital. Phenobarbital has unique properties that give it very little of the sedating qualities of other barbiturates, and none of the euphoric effects.

Because of these unique characteristics, recovering alcoholics can usually use phenobarbital without risking reactivation of their addiction when it is necessary for seizure control. Some recovering alcoholics who seem subject to chronic seizures or convulsions are accordingly prescribed it on a continuing basis through life. Phenobartital is also often given with phenytoin (Dilantin) for only a number of days as part of detoxification from alcohol. This is also to prevent alcohol withdrawal seizures. When it is taken exactly as prescribed for this purpose of seizure control, phenobarbital does not seem to have a reactivation risk.

However, a recovering alcoholic/addict should avoid taking phenobarbital for any purpose other than such seizure control.

Alurate Elixir
   (aprobarbital; 20 percent alcohol)
amobarbital
Amytal Sodium
   (amobarbital sodium)
B-A-C Tablets
   (butalbital)
butabarbital
Buticaps; Butisol Sodium Tablets, Elixir
   (sodium butabarbital; Elixir, sodium butabarbital, 7 percent
   alcohol)
Lotusate
   (talbutal)
Luminal
   (phenobarbital)
   (Note: See special exception and warnings about phenobar-
      bital in the text headed "Barbiturates" directly above.)
Mebaral Tablets
   (mephobarbital)
Nembutal Elixir Ampuls, Vials (for injection)
   (pentobarbital, 10 percent alcohol)
Nembutal Sodium Capsules, Solution, Suppositories
   (pentobarbital sodium)
pentobarbital
phenobarbital, phenobarbital sodium
   (Note: See special exception and warnings about phenobar-
      bital in the text headed "Barbiturates") directly above.
"reds" (stree name for Seconal capsules)
secobarbital

Seconal Sodium Capsules, Injection, Suppositories
    (secobarbital sodium)
Tuinal
    (secobarbital sodium, amobarbital sodium)
"yellows" (street name for Nembutal capsules above)

Other Sedatives: Prescription Drugs That Call for CAUTION

CAUTION: Like the barbiturate sedatives these other prescription sedatives call for CAUTION by recoverees. If you are recovering from alcohol or drug abuse, DO NOT TAKE ANY OF THESE SEDA-TIVES—without exception. Go without sleep instead, if necessary.

chloral hydrate capsules, elixir, syrup, suppositories
Dalmane
    (flurazepam hydrochloride)
Doriden
    (glutethimide)
glutethimide
Halcion
    (triazolam)
Largon
    (propiomazine hydrochloride)
" 'ludes" (a street name for methaquaalone)
"Mickey Finn" (a street name for chloral hydrate capsules, when
    dissolved in a high-proof alcohol drink)
Noctec
    (chloral hydrate)
Noludar, Noludar 300
    (methyprylon)
methaquaalone (formerly marketed with brand names that in-
    cluded Quaalude, Mequin, and Parest, but no longer on the
    market; had been widely used addictively in recent decades and
    is illegally made and sold as a street drug to some extent)
Placidyl
    (ethchlorvynol)
Restoril
    (temazepam)
"soapers" (a street name for methaquaalone)
Valmid
    (ethinamate)

SEDATIVES: NONPRESCRIPTION DRUGS THAT CALL FOR CAUTION

CAUTION: For the nonprescription sleep preparations listed here, the sedative properties of antihistamines are applied to produce their effectiveness. Antihistamines have a dulling or drowsiness-inducing effect. But they seem to have little or no habit-forming effect. (See the introductory text in the "Antiallergy Medications" section in this chapter.)

Nevertheless, in the authors' judgment, the act of taking antihistamines to change one's state of consciousness (from wakefulness to sleep) can bring reactivation risk for any recovering alcoholic/addict. Such an act risks reactivating acute addiction because it tends to revive old patterns of addictive behavior for the purpose of changing mood (or conscious state).

Accordingly, the authors deem the taking of these antihistamine preparations as sedatives to call for CAUTION by recovering alcoholics/addicts. (It should be noted, though, that using antihistamines for other purposes—to combat allergies or upper respiratory congestion, for instance—is deemed WITHOUT REACTIVATION RISK, because the purpose does not involve mood changing and the active ingredients are not habit-forming.)

Nervine Night-Time Sleep Aid
    (diphenhydramine)
Nytol Tablets
    (diphenhydramine hydrochloride)
Sleep-Eze Tablets
    (diphenhydramine hydrochloride)
Sominex 2
    (diphenhydramine hydrochloride)
Unisom Nighttime Sleep-Aid
    (doxylamine succinate)

Serum Cholesterol and Fat Lowering Medications (Hypolipidemics)

WITHOUT REACTIVATION RISK: Medications of this type are used to reduce the levels of cholesterol and triglycerides in the blood. Cholesterol and triglycerides are fats that are thought to contribute to the development of atherosclerosis and related cardiovascular disease (e.g., heart attacks and strokes). These medications are WITHOUT REACTIVATION RISK for recovering alcoholics/addicts.

Among widely used drugs of this type are Lopid (gemfibrozil), Mevacor (lovastatin), and Questran (cholestyramine).

Urinary Tract Agents

Urinary tract agents include medications to combat infections (anti-infectives), relieve pain (analgesics), relax constriction (antispasmodics), and improve urinary retention (parasympathomimetics). They are generally prescription drugs.

URINARY TRACT AGENTS: PRESCRIPTION DRUG THAT CALLS FOR CAUTION

CAUTION: The urinary analgesic listed here calls for CAUTION on the part of recovering alcoholics addicts. It contains butabarbital, a barbiturate that is an addictive controlled substance.

Pyridium Plus
(phenazopyridine hydrochloride, hyoscyamine hydrobromide, butabarbital)

URINARY TRACT AGENTS: PRESCRIPTION DRUGS THAT ARE WITHOUT REACTIVATION RISK

WITHOUT REACTIVATION RISK: Urinary tract medications are WITHOUT REACTIVATION RISK for the recovering alcoholic/addict with respect to continued abstinence when they contain no mood-altering ingredients. Urinary anti-infectives generally have bacteriacidal ingredients such as sulfonamides for the treatment of uncomplicated urinary infections. Commonly prescribed anti-infectives include Bactrim (trimethoprim, sulfamethoxazole) and Macrodantin (nitrofurantoin macrocrystals).

Other widely used urinary medications include analgesics, such as Pyridium (phenazopyridine hydrochloride); antispasmodics, such as Urispas (flavoxate hydrochloride); and parasympathomimetics, such as Urecholine (bethanechol chloride).

Vitamins and Mineral Supplements: Nutritionals

WITHOUT REACTIVATION RISK: Vitamins, minerals, and other special nutritional preparations are WITHOUT REACTIVATION RISK for recovering alcoholics/addicts, in that they pose no risk to continued abstinence. This holds true whether they be taken as therapy or for health maintenance. The only precautions to observe with them are wise for all medications: take them on the basis of competent medical advice, and check their ingredients to protect against the possibility that they may have some alcohol content (an unlikely possibility, in the case of these supplements).

Contraceptives

WITHOUT REACTIVATION RISK: Oral contraceptives for women, popularly called birth control pills, prevent pregnancy primarily by inhibiting ovulation. They are WITHOUT REACTIVATION RISK for recovering alcoholics/addicts, inasmuch as none of the three major types currently used tend to reactivate chemical dependence. Widely used birth control pills contain a progestin, a synthetic version of the female sex hormone, progesterone. They include those of the combined type that also contain a natural or synthetic estrogen (such as Brevicon, Enovid, and Ortho Novum 2), the progestin-only type (such as Micronor and Ovrette), and the phased-type (these contain varying proportions of a progestin and a natural or synthetic estrogen; examples include Ortho Novum 10/11 + 7/7/7 and Tri-Phasil).

Also safe for recovering alcoholics/addicts from the standpoint of continued recovery are various types of topical contraceptives applied locally within the vagina (such as spermacidal contraceptives in the form of creams, foams, and jellies); barrier contraceptives such as diaphragms to block the female cervix and condoms to encase the male penis; and intrauterine contraceptive devices implanted within the uterus.

CHAPTER 7

Women in Recovery and Their Special Needs

ALMOST EVERYTHING SAID ELSEWHERE IN THIS BOOK, OF COURSE, APPLIES equally to women and men. However, active alcoholism/addiction damages women in a number of special ways, and they accordingly enter recovery with certain special needs and questions in the area of health care. These typically concern physical appearance and attractiveness, menstrual periods, sexual desire and normal sexual functioning, fertility and pregnancy, risks of birth defects in a baby should they have one, and menopause.

For concerns in all these areas, it is particularly important that women have a comprehensive medical examination early in recovery. A medical checkup should reveal any conditions beyond the typical physiological consequences of active alcoholism/addiction that need to be treated for improved health.

An extremely important part of such a checkup early in recovery is a thorough gynecological examination. Studies indicate that women alcoholics seem to have a strikingly high incidence of difficulties with their reproductive systems. For instance, one such study found that 78 percent of the women alcoholics studied had suffered from obstetrical or gynecological problems; only 8 percent of the nonalcoholic women studied who were otherwise comparable to the alcoholic women had had such problems. [Wilsnack, Sharon, "The Impact of Sex Roles on Women's Alcohol Use and Abuse," in Greenblatt, M., and M. A. Schuckit, eds., *Alcoholism Problems in Women and Children* (New York: Grune & Stratton, 1976)].

Clinical findings and recommendations presented in this chapter have been developed largely on the basis of experience with alcoholics. They certainly apply with equal validity to recovering alcoholics who also abused other drugs. For persons in recovery who had abused only or mainly drugs—prescription drugs or illegal drugs—the findings and recommendations also have fair validity.

Physical Appearance and Attractiveness

During the time when their alcoholism/addiction is at its worst, in the period just before hitting bottom, many women suffer disturbing changes in their physical appearance. Some are appalled to see their hair falling out to leave bald patches on their heads. For others, the hair grows dull and brittle. Some become bloated and fat. Others waste away to skin and bones. Still others shudder to see veins on their nose disgustingly stand out ever more and more swollen and inflamed.

"I remember each day as I put on my makeup, I always examined my nose in the magnifying side of my mirror," Clara K. recalled. "There was a knot in my stomach and I tried to decide whether or not the veins stuck out more hideously than the day before." She adds, "I knew I was a lush and drinking too much. But I couldn't stop even though I realized that I'd soon look like that comedian in old movies, W. C. Fields. Then everybody would know what I was."

For the woman in mid-life, it's often worse. Muscles atrophy while more weight makes for a dumpy figure. There is loss of skin tone, skin may bruise easily, and be thinned out, dry, and scaly. Compounding the horror over looking awful can be feelings of physical illness that result from the effects of excess alcohol on the liver, the digestive system, and the whole circulatory system.

"I was thirty-seven years old when I stopped drinking," commented Melanie R., a recovering alcoholic who is now also an alcoholism counselor. "My stomach had rebelled for years." She paused reflectively. "You can tell the women who have been drinking for years," she said. "They have wrinkled skin."

Continuing, Melanie talked of others she had seen as a counselor. "In some of the worst cases, women alcoholics have very pouchy stomachs. One like that was a woman who had been a nurse and who went to AA meetings for a short time. It was so bad that she even looked six months pregnant! She couldn't quit, though, and started drinking again. Then one day she hemorrhaged. She bled to death." Melanie paused.

"Many are women who were once very beautiful," Melanie went on. "One who first came to me for counseling help several years ago was an old friend, then in her late forties. She had been beautiful as a young woman. But by then, her skin looked like parchment. She had wrinkles around her mouth and a fragile, elderly, transparent look.

"I ached that time I first saw her because she couldn't yet admit she was an alcoholic," Melanie declared. "But after her third drunk-driving arrest, she finally got started in AA. Thank heavens, she stuck with it. And after three years, what a change! The essence of her old loveliness came back, in her eyes, in the way she carried herself, in a certain glow about her. My friend—my sober friend, at fifty-three—is a beautiful woman again. Maybe she's even more beautiful than ever."

Physiologically, most women can very substantially reverse the damage to their appearance while recovering from alcoholism/addiction, as indicated in this case described by Melanie R. As vital organs such as the heart, liver, and digestive system return to normal function and restore healthy tissue metabolism, the entire system typically improves. Circulatory balance returns and restores healthy color and tone to the complexion. Some women feel that hair takes on a better quality. Muscles start firming up. Posture straightens. Bloodshot eyes grow clear.

Women in recovery from alcoholism/addiction can cultivate still greater improvement in their physical appearance and attractiveness by building habits for good health. As explained in Chapter 4, these involve sound nutrition, exercise and physical fitness, sleep, optimum health care, and avoidance of excessive stress.

Menstrual Cycles

Menstrual periods stop for many women in their childbearing years who drink heavily as active alcoholics/addicts. Such interruptions in their periods resemble similar cessations experienced by women who spend much time in strenuous exercise, such as athletes or dancers, or by women who are experiencing serious illnesses.

Women early in recovery from alcoholism/addiction who worry about such an interruption in their periods can feel reassured. In typical cases, menstrual periods that have thus stopped recover from interruption and irregularities after complete abstinence for some six months.

Some women whose periods have stopped may experience escessive vaginal bleeding while they are going through acute alcohol withdrawal. This usually occurs during the first five to seven days after they quit drinking. Hormone treatment can often clear up such bleeding, however.

Some women beginning in recovery also worry about what to take to relieve menstrual cramps, or *dysmenorrhea*. A number of them had used alcohol to help them through their periods. If the dysmenorrhea becomes quite painful, it's advisable to use one of a number of extremely effective prescription drugs that are also very safe for recovering alcoholics/addicts. Among these are Motrin, Anaprox, Naprosyn, and Ponstel. A woman typically finds that one of these medications works better for her than the others do. Accordingly, discuss and work out with your doctor which one would be most effective for you.

Sexual Desire and Normal Sexual Functioning

Women's sexual response tends to constitute a greater part of their total emotional life than is generally the case with men. As a result, the guilt, depression, and low self-esteem of active alcoholism/addiction may have an even more direct effect on suppressing sexual response for women than for men.

Moreover, active alcoholism/addiction has far-reaching physiological effects throughout the woman's body—including depressed functioning of the nervous system, abnormal hormonal kinetics, and metabolic disruptions. Such pathological developments as these unquestionably interfere with normal sexual response and functioning, even though the exact mechanisms of that interference are not yet known.

Once recovery starts, however, both the emotional and the physiological pathologies of the woman alcoholic/addict typically begin clearing up. The return of sexual normality is not a quick or simple matter, however. It unfolds quite gradually—for many women, over as long a time as one or two years in sobriety. But, over periods of time on this order, self-esteem grows, relationships flower, and, as the principles of the recovery program go on working, normal sexual function generally resumes.

You should realize that not all women embarking on recovery suffer from severely disrupted sexual desire and functioning. Women fortunate enough to start recovery before developing extensive emotional and physiological pathology often have near-normal sexual response and function.

On the other hand, a number of recovering women with decades-long histories of active alcoholism/addiction may have entered the postmenopausal phase of their lives beyond age forty or fifty without having adapted to it. For some, this can pose an especially difficult task of adjustment in sobriety. In time, though, they can successfully adapt to this new sexual phase of their lives.

Fertility and Pregnancy

Recovering women in their childbearing years are also often concerned about their fertility. Their concern has substantial justification. Just as active alcoholism/addiction increasingly suppresses normal sex drive and functioning the further it progresses, so does it suppress fertility.

For example, one study analyzed the fertility of groups of married couples who were trying to have children, couples in which the wives were active alcoholics. Overall, only one out of four of the couples was able to conceive. Study results indicated that the most heavily drinking women were unable to conceive at all (Wilsnack, Sharon, "Sex Role Identity in Female Alcoholism," *Journal of Abnormal Psychology* 82 (1973), pp. 253–261).

In typical premenopausal women who are recovering from alcoholism/addiction, fertility seems to return, as a general clinical observation, without any delays beyond the initial direct effects of the alcohol and/or drugs.

However, even if a woman happens to be fertile before the end of her first year in recovery, it would probably be advisable for her to round out at least a solid year of sobriety before becoming pregnant. With such a period of sustained progress in recovery, she should be better able to cope with the emotional strains of childbearing and child raising than if she were to become pregnant earlier.

Two other medical considerations may bear on a woman's decision to get pregnant in recovery. One is that, even after becoming well established in recovery, some women who wish to do so find themselves unable to conceive. In cases like this, the woman and her partner should consult a doctor, or a fertility specialist or clinic, in order to try to detect and possibly resolve other conditions that may be blocking conception.

The second medical consideration—one of potentially grave concern—is discussed in the next section.

BIRTH-DEFECT RISKS SHOULD PREGNANCY DEVELOP

Fetal alcohol syndrome (FAS) afflicts alarmingly large numbers of the babies born to mothers who are active alcoholics—and in dramatic, lifelong ways. Perhaps most seriously, FAS-affected babies are mentally retarded—to such an extent that the syndrome represents one of America's leading causes of mental retardation. These babies often display typical malformations of the head—disproportionately small diameter, underslung jaw, low-set ears, flattened bridge of the nose. Varying bones and joints are also often malformed. More than half of the FAS-affected babies who are girls have abnormalities of the genital organs as well. These infants also often have heart defects. And, according to some estimates, at least 40 percent of all infants born to actively alcoholic mothers are victims of FAS [Shapiro, Howard I., The Pregnancy Book for Today's Woman (New York: Harper & Row, 1983)].

Incidentally, even small amounts of alcohol consumed by mothers who are not alcoholics have been shown to increase risks of childbearing difficulties such as miscarriage, stillbirth, premature birth, or low birth weight. As a result, any woman who is trying to conceive or is pregnant is advised to consume no alcohol whatever by the surgeon general of the United States.

For a recovering woman, then, a crucial question may be, "How soon can I safely get pregnant and have a child without danger of birth defects from FAS?" To avoid producing an infant with FAS, one need wait only until all alcohol is cleared from the system. This should take only a matter of days. However, other health problems that result from the years of chronic alcohol intake can endanger a pregnancy as well. Thus, it would be wise to wait until total health returns before considering pregnancy. Again, for the emotional and psychological reasons mentioned previously, it may be preferable to delay pregnancy even longer, until after at least a full year of recovery.

Birth defects can arise from many other possible causes besides alcoholism/addiction. Guidance from your doctor on protection against conceiving a baby with birth defects due to any cause should be part of your agenda for sound prenatal medical care.

PRECAUTIONS AFTER A NORMAL BABY'S BIRTH

If need arises, women who have normal babies and who are recovering from alcoholism/addiction should be ready to take certain precautions. Measures may be needed to deal with a mild to severe depression that may appear for a few weeks after the birth. Termed *postpartum depression*, this condition is also experienced in some cases by normal women who have had completely normal babies.

In the event such a depression starts coming on, the new mother in recovery should take immediate countermeasures to protect her sobriety. Members of recovery groups like AA typically suggest that she should be especially careful to keep up or increase the number of recovery program meetings she regularly attends. They add that she should take the baby to the meetings if she cannot arrange for a sitter. Typically, others at the meeting will be glad to help her tend the baby and won't mind if the baby fusses or cries or needs to be taken outside the meeting-room. In addition, the mother should make sure to draw on all the emotional support the program offers, particularly by phoning her sponsor daily or more often, as well as calling other women members she finds friendly and helpful.

Another situation necessitating caution may arise if a relative or even a doctor advises the new mother in recovery to use some alcohol-content drink as a kind of old-fashioned or folk remedy. One report, for example, concerned a nursing mother in recovery who asked her obstetrician what she should to do overcome some difficulty she was having in breastfeeding her baby. She had even told the obstetrician that she was a recovering alcoholic. He advised her to drink some beer to improve her breastfeeding. As another example, scotch whisky rubbed with a finger on the baby's gums is sometimes recommended for a baby who is fussy. To any suggestions that either the mother or the baby should ingest alcohol in any form or amount, the mother should be prepared to say absolutely no.

Menopause

Menopause is a very disturbing and difficult experience for a number of women recovering from alcoholism/addiction—difficult for physiological as well as emotional reasons. It results from a decline in the functioning of the ovaries in maturing and releasing egg cells with subsequent menstruation about every twenty-eight days and commonly develops after age forty or fifty. There are both hormonal changes as well as changes in the menstrual cycle at this time. The decline in function occurs rather gradually and is due to a natural aging of the ovaries.

However, rate of decline in ovarian function varies from one woman to another. And the more rapid the decline, the more severely the woman feels the possible disturbances of menopause. Rapidity in decline is accompanied by instability of the autonomic nervous system. A woman suffering such rapid decline can be swept by sudden feelings of nervousness, like proverbial "hot flashes" (consisting of outbreaks of sweating and hot, flushed face), excitability or depression, headaches, dizziness, and nausea.

Such physical instability compounded by possibly extreme depression brought on by menopause leads some recovering women to slip or relapse. Women in recovery from alcoholism/addiction who are going through menopause should accordingly be especially active in their recovery program. In addition, they can watch for signs of danger resulting from physical and emotional discomfort. If they detect any possibility of a relapse or slip, they should immediately seek hormone therapy from their doctor to relieve the effects of menopause. The hormones taken in such therapy are quite safe for recovering alcoholics/addicts in the sense that they do not endanger continued abstinence.

On the other hand, experience varies among women recovering from alcoholism/addiction. For some, menopause proceeds gradually, and they suffer from little or no instability or depression.

CHAPTER 8

Dealing with Associated Diseases

CERTAIN DISEASES AND COMPULSIVE HABITS ARE FREQUENTLY ASSOCIATED with the disease of alcoholism. Some of the associated diseases or health problems result from the physical effects of alcohol, and some from the accompanying psychologic and emotional dysfunction.

Hypertension

One of the physiologic patterns that deserves mention is hypertension in the alcoholic. *Hypertension,* or high blood pressure, is medically important because, if left untreated, it hastens the development of atherosclerotic cardiovascular disease and associated sequelae. High blood pressure is directly linked to the incidence of strokes, heart attacks, and other medical problems related to blood vessel abnormalities.

Alcoholics have several problems related to hypertension. For one, alcohol itself affects the blood pressure. When one is actively drinking, intoxication and withdrawal constantly fluctuate. Both states stress the cardiovascular system and can produce hypertension.

Often, when alcoholics are seen medically during their years of active drinking, they are found to be hypertensive. They may receive medication for the high blood pressure and then, upon becoming sober, assume the medication is still necessary. Indeed, it might not be. In other words, a diagnosis of hypertension made during active drinking is unreliable. On getting sober, an alcoholic with a history of hypertension should consult a physician for a blood pressure reevaluation. Medications that were previously prescribed might not be needed after sobriety is established.

This evaluation should not be undertaken too soon, however, for blood pressure during withdrawal and detoxification is unstable and often elevated. This period of time is best monitored by a physician for a variety of reasons. However, an evaluation for hypertension should be repeated after the period of withdrawal is complete.

The history of Jim W. is illustrative. Jim was a school principal whose active drinking was a problem for more than twenty years. During that time he saw different physicians for various problems. At one point he was told he had high blood pressure, measured at 160/110.

Several medicines were tried in an attempt to treat his hypertension, and eventually he was stabilized on a drug called Inderal. After this medication had been started, Jim saw other physicians, all of whom legitimately kept him on the Inderal, assuming that to be the correct treatment.

Jim began sobriety in a well-known alcohol rehabilitation center and proceeded to do well. During his early sobriety, he came to the author's office for a problem of impotency. This condition had been bothering him for years, but during his active drinking, he neither cared enough nor was functional enough to engage in sexual activity.

After assessing the impotency problem, it seemed there were two issues at hand. One, the drug Inderal can cause impotency as a side effect. Two, Jim's blood pressure was now 130/70 on the medication. Since Jim was in good health otherwise, the author decided to test two hypotheses by stopping the Inderal. First, we would see whether Jim's impotency was related to the medication. Second, we would find out whether Jim's hypertension was only due to the effects of his drinking.

As it turned out, Jim's blood pressure remained normal with no medication. He had no underlying hypertension after all. Then, after a short time, sexual function returned.

The point here is that many medical patterns, especially hypertension, are brought on during active alcohol and drug use and may or may not continue after normalization of the body in sobriety.

Let us not forget that an alcoholic may also have real hypertension. One should not stop medication upon attaining sobriety without an evaluation by a doctor.

Sexual Disorders

Jim W.'s sexual problem brought his unnecessary treatment for blood pressure to light. In this situation, the medication was the major cause of his impotency. However, Jim's sexual problem was not only physical.

As we mentioned earlier, throughout the years of his active drinking, Jim had no active sexual functioning. The medication may have been part of the reason for a decreased libido (sexual desire), but other factors certainly played a role as well. Jim was married throughout his drinking years. His wife, over the last ten years of his drinking, had become angry and uncommunicative. She resented his unreliable, self-centered behavior. She felt no warmth toward him and had no desire to pursue a sexual relationship.

Jim's daily life involved a pattern of coming home from work, drinking himself into a stupor, and either passing out in front of the television or dragging himself to bed. He had no room for any relationship, sexual or personal. Alcoholism had filled every pore of his personality. When not intoxicated, Jim admitted to having felt disgusted with himself and sexually inadequate.

His sexual problem had many facets. There was lack of libido. There was a deteriorating, and ultimately disastrous, personal relationship with his wife due to his alcoholic behavior. There was in Jim a feeling of self-disgust and a total personality disintegration. Obviously, a sexual relationship could not survive.

His scenario is typical. Active alcoholics and drug addicts can rarely sustain healthy sexual relationships. Sexual problems run the gamut from physical to emotional and reflect the inability of interpersonal relationships to survive in a climate of active addiction.

Couples afflicted by active addiction of one or both members often stay together because of other needs, such as emotional dependency, financial support, family cohesion, religious compliance, or outward respectability. But the basis is seldom healthy sexual and personal fulfillment.

As a result, when recovery begins, sexual problems often need attention. As the alcoholic/addict develops in early recovery, he or she must face the destructive effect of the disease on interpersonal relationships. Certainly, normal sexual activity doesn't develop immediately on cessation of drinking.

Through the AA program, the recovering individual gradually learns to act in a responsible and mature manner with regard to close relationships. Intimate relationships such as marriage can often be restored to a fulfilling and healthy state, and a good sexual relationship can be part of this change. However, the process may take a long time—years, in some cases.

The specific sexual disorders that are reported by men and women in recovery usually relate to libido and male impotence. Another case history illustrates typical problems with libido and their resolution. Margaret T. was seen by the author during an outpatient, or "ambulatory," detoxification program. During this time, she expressed the sense of feeling "neuter." She had no desire for sexual contact. She also lived an isolated existence working as a private-duty nurse at night, and coming home to sleep in her apartment during the day.

As Margaret progressed in her sobriety, she became more concerned with her life-style. She saw the limitations of her isolation, and although she didn't feel any return of sexual desire, she did discover in herself a need for social contact. Soon it became apparent that her job was confining. She took a position as an office nurse working in the daytime. She gradually made friends but was afraid to date and was concerned about her lack of sexual desire.

Although AA helped her to grow as a person, she sought private counseling as well. She soon became aware that social life and interpersonal relationships were important to her and were missing from her life because of alcoholism. She took steps to change. After some months her life took on a more normal pattern. She began dating and, after eighteen months of sobriety, Margaret had a successful sexual relationship. Her life now has the usual ups and downs, but she has normal sexual function and a healthy social life.

The point here is that sexual problems are not isolated disorders, but are intricately related to the entire disease of alcoholism or addiction. As recovery progresses and the emotional ravages of the disease of addiction lift, sexual problems generally dissipate. There may be some problems that require more specific therapy, but, in general, patience will be rewarded.

Sexual disorders don't affect every alcoholic, but the prevalence of sexual problems among alcoholics/addicts is high. The emotional and psychological aspects of the disease combine with the physical effects of alcohol or drugs. Alcohol, for example, has effects on the blood vessels, the liver (which metabolizes many hormones), and the central nervous system, all of which are involved in the sexual response. Cocaine in particular has extremely debilitating effects on the sexual response. All drugs must be cleared from the system and a significant period of time must pass for the physiological component of the sexual response to normalize.

Men find their most frequent pattern of sexual difficulty to be indifference and impotence as the later stages of alcoholism are reached. Frank P., for instance, was married, and as his alcoholism progressed, his wife could not relate sexually to him. Frank sought relationships outside the marriage. After two years of promiscuity, though, he became less interested in sexual activity. On the few occasions where he had become involved sexually, he experienced impotency. This intensified his growing self-disgust and feelings of inadequacy. By the end of his active drinking, Frank gave up even trying to perform sexually. He had little desire and feared sexual failure.

This again is an example of the complex issues that develop in active addiction. A disintegrating marital relationship with a spouse, destructive promiscuity, sexual failures, and avoidance of sexual activity are all part of a common pattern. With the advent of sobriety, there is usually a restoration of a more normal sexual life. However, first the alcoholic/addict must begin recovery step by step, slowly healing wounds and reconstructing his or her personality, feelings, and relationships.

As this recovery matures, in varying time frames, sexual attitudes and function return to a more normal state. Recovery doesn't guarantee sexual health. For some, problems linger, and others need professional help—but so do nonalcoholics. As in most areas, honesty, proceeding with the basic AA principles of recovery, and patience will yield rewarding results.

It might be noted that many recovering alcoholics/addicts are also the children of alcoholics/addicts. This group has been shown to have suffered a higher than normal incidence of sexual abuse in childhood. Sexual dysfunction in recovery for persons with a history of such abuse might accordingly result in part from repressed painful experiences. In cases like this, normal sexual functioning might be restored if these experiences are dealt with in therapy conducted by a qualified professional.

Smoking

A smoke-filled room with a coffee urn somewhere close by is a familiar image to anyone who has attended an AA meeting. The message is strong and clear: alcoholics smoke a lot, and they drink a lot of coffee. Because they are addiction-prone, these predilections are not surprising. Nicotine and caffeine are drugs prevalent in our society. Of course, addicts will succumb in greater proportion than nonaddicts.

It has been a longtime principle among alcohol treatment programs to consider smoking a necessary evil for the nicotine-addicted recovering alcoholic. To ask the alcoholic who smokes to give up a second addiction is just too much. However, in recent years, the evidence demonstrating the ill effects of tobacco has been strong and widely publicized. Medical studies indicate that respiratory problems and illnesses, as well as cancer and heart disease, are more prevalent among smokers than nonsmokers.

Consequently, attitudes are changing. Many treatment programs, AA included, have nonsmoking meetings. The alcoholic might do well not to rely on the enabling principle that to cease smoking during early recovery causes too much stress and is too distracting. For some it may be, but the health issues at hand demand a new attitude. Smoking is too dangerous, perhaps even to people around the smoker, not to be confronted as unhealthy and worth stopping even for the recovering alcoholic.

On the other hand, sobriety still must come first. Alcoholism/ addiction represents the more urgently dangerous compulsion. Moreover, a recovering alcoholic/addict who slips is very unlikely to stop smoking. For reasons like these, sponsors in AA often advise a person who wants to stop smoking to wait until after about the first year of sobriety. Persons thus well established in abstinence frequently find that the practices and social support of AA that worked for their drink/drug compulsion also prove effective against their smoking compulsion.

Excessive Caffeine Intake

Overuse of caffeine in coffee (and in cola-type soft drinks) characterizes quite a few alcoholics/addicts recovering in AA, as noted earlier. Excess caffeine rarely poses a serious health hazard unless the individual suffers from a condition such as heart disease or hypoglycemia.

However, sensitivity to caffeine varies widely. Some individuals especially sensitive find it speeds their heartbeat uncomfortably (and irregularly), makes them feel overexcited and anxious, upsets their stomach by its acidity, and keeps them awake and tense through much of the night.

In general, and particularly for such persons, moderate to no caffeine intake seems preferable for sound health. Today, this viewpoint is commonly reflected at AA meetings by the customary presence of a decaffeinated coffee urn beside the traditional regular coffee urn—as well as the provision of regular and herbal teas.

It's generally an idea for good health to limit caffeine intake to no more than two or three cups of coffee a day (or two or three cans or bottles of caffeine-containing soft drinks). And it's probably wise for best health to have still less or no caffeine at all.

If you do cut off heavy caffeine consumption all at once, you'll probably feel some withdrawal symptoms. These typically include headaches, irritability, unaccustomed drowsiness, and sometimes aches in the legs or arms. Withdrawal symptoms gradually subside over a period of several days. (Severe reactions can be eased by drinking small amounts of coffee until your system adjusts to operating with less or no caffeine.)

Eating Disorders

The compulsive disorder that allows alcoholism or addiction to flourish may also be manifested by other unhealthy behavior. Smoking is one example; excessive coffee drinking is another. Eating disorders, as a group, also exemplify maladaptive behavior rooted in the same compulsive drives that fuel addiction.

We should not assume that these compulsive disorders overlap, but they are seen in the alcoholic population with more than average frequency. Certainly there are nonalcoholic smokers, overeaters, anorectics, and other types of compulsives, and certainly many alcoholics are spared these problems. Nevertheless, within the alcohol/ addict group, relatively few have been completely free of at least one of these associated compulsions.

When first entering recovery, individuals with these compulsions usually find them operating in full force. It is often advised that sobriety be stabilized before any attempt is made to discontinue other compulsive habits. This theory assumes that all energies are needed for efforts related to achieving comfortable sobriety. It is often suggested that one wait before attacking smoking, overeating, or other compulsions than alcohol/drug abuse. Such suggestions constructively counter the frequent but unwise eagerness of the newly sober person to cure everything at once. Putting "First Things First"—in the words of the familiar AA slogan—is instead commonly and properly advised.

Eating disorders constitute a group of complex compulsive patterns of behavior. Overeating with resulting obesity is probably the most common. Anorexia and bulimia are two other disorders. Many alcoholics begin recovery having neglected their health in general, but particularly in the realm of nutrition. Compulsive overeating can sometimes flare up in early recovery. The overweight person who is in early recovery and is a compulsive overeater has few tools to use in regard to his or her eating disorder.

Concentration is on the principles of recovery, and these principles are not integrated enough into the recovering individual's personality and behavior to be generalized to other areas of living. Compulsive overeaters often gain weight during early recovery. Although this is distressing, patience is advisable. Fad diets and extreme measures to deal with obesity are particularly unhealthy at this time. Eventually, as the anxieties of everyday living are more naturally handled using the principles of recovery programs, and as moods are somewhat stabilized, the compulsive eating is more easily controlled.

In dealing with drinking or drugs, abstinence is the foundation of recovery. The first drink or drug will ruin sobriety and trigger eventual relapse. With overeating, abstinence is obviously not the answer. However, one can correlate any "compulsive eating" with a first drink. If the alcoholic is powerless over alcohol, as an overeater he can think of himself as powerless over "compulsive eating." Thus, a three-meal-a-day, nutritionally balanced, moderate-calorie intake can be positively and safely established. The first time the overeater grabs a handful of cookies or otherwise lets go and eats because of a compulsive drive, he or she is probably in for a damaging "food-binge slip." Many obese compulsive overeaters who are recovering from alcoholism/addiction can use the principles of the recovery program to replace their other compulsions with healthy behavior.

However, this takes time. It seems to be after the second or third year of recovery that many overeaters or anorectics and bulemics begin to deal with their eating disorders successfully. These disorders have lifelong roots and emotionally charged associations. Therefore patience, honesty about one's feelings, and steady progress in sobriety usually produce success with eating disorders in recovering alcoholics/addicts. Some recovering alcoholics/addicts with deep-seated and stubborn cases of anorexia and bulemia in particular find that special medical and/or psychotherapeutic treatment also helps to deal with the disorders.

CHAPTER 9

Dealing with Mental Illness

AT LEAST IN PART, ALCOHOLISM ITSELF QUALIFIES AS A MENTAL ILLNESS. A classic view in the field is expressed in the core sourcebook of AA, *Alcoholics Anonymous*, which holds that alcoholism is a threefold disease having physical, mental, and spiritual components. (It also sets forth a second step of recovery involving action by alcoholics "to restore us to sanity.") Moreover, as noted in Chapter 1, a recent edition of the official diagnostic manual of the American Psychiatric Association defines the symptoms of alcohol or drug dependence as a mental illness.

Mental illness—or the possibility of mental illness—complicates alcoholism/addiction and recovery from it in two respects that have far-reaching implications.

First, what often masquerades as a separate mental illness (e.g., depression) before recovery, turns out in recovery to have been primarily the disease of alcoholism/addiction. The misdiagnosis is frequently made by the alcoholic/addict and by his or her psychiatrist as well. This is especially true with anxiety and depression. Anxiety, depression, and other psychiatric manifestations of alcoholism/addiction generally subside as the process of recovery strengthens.

Second, some persons who are alcoholics/addicts also suffer from an additional psychiatric disorder or mental illness. In such cases, their recovery (through total abstinence and progress in a recovery program such as AA or NA) does not alone relieve the second emotional disorder or mental illness. Guidelines based on experience can help you decide in the face of psychiatric symptoms of this kind on the most effective ways to assure safety and promote recovery from both afflictions.

Guidelines for Health with Mental Illnesses in Addition to Alcoholism/ Addiction

If you are a recovering alcoholic/addict and think you may have a mental illness in addition to alcoholism/addiction, you should follow a number of guidelines for health and safety. These guidelines reflect a consensus of wide clinical experience as well as experience gained by persons in recovery.

1. IF NECESSARY, TAKE IMMEDIATE EMERGENCY ACTION FOR SAFETY.

If you are a recovering alcoholic/addict and are feeling suicidal—or if an active or recovering alcoholic/addict close to you is talking about committing suicide—get immediate help from a psychiatrist, possibly by going to a hospital emergency room. Moreover, police respond to calls involving suicide attempts. Suicidal feelings and attempts are not uncommon among active alcoholics/addicts, especially when they become sickened and desperate because of their disease and are nearing their bottom.

If a family member with alcoholism/addiction has violent outbreaks, also seek immediate help. Call the police. They should take the family member to a psychiatric department of a hospital for diagnosis. This applies also if you yourself are an alcoholic/addict in recovery who is having uncontrollable outbreaks of violence that worry you after they've passed. If so, you should act immediately on the next guideline.

2. GET AND FOLLOW THE ADVICE OF A PSYCHIATRIST WELL INFORMED ABOUT ALCOHOLISM/ADDICTION.

When you first see in yourself as a recovering alcoholic/addict (or in a close family member who is a recovering alcoholic/addict) bothersome evidence of a severe disorder or mental illness besides alcoholism/addiction, seek a diagnosis and treatment recommendation from a psychiatrist well informed about alcoholism/addiction.

Above all, *don't act as a doctor yourself* in deciding what the condition is. Also, *don't let anyone else act as the doctor.* Get and follow the psychiatrist's diagnosis and recommendation for treatment.

If you are an alcoholic/addict and have begun recovery with active participation in a recovery program, talk over what you're doing and why with your sponsor (and possibly with other friends in the program whom you trust). They should approve of this course of yours if they're experienced and informed. For instance, the official AA booklet, *The AA Member—Medications and Other Drugs*, sets forth as a rule in areas like this: "No A.A. Member Plays Doctor."

Also be sure to follow this book's earlier stipulations about working with any doctors, including psychiatrists. Be especially sure to observe three stipulations: choose a psychiatrist thoroughly informed about alcoholics/addicts and recovery; be absolutely honest with the doctor about your alcoholism/addiction; and, if a medication is prescribed, make sure to take it precisely in the dosages and at the intervals prescribed—and no more.

In addition, be wary of recommendations that you use any minor tranquilizer, sedative, psychostimulant drug, or narcotic drug. As reported in Chapter 6, these are the drugs dangerous to recovering alcoholics/addicts because of risk of reactivating their acute alcohol or drug abuse. Should a drug of these types be proposed for you, ask the psychiatrist if a different medication safe for alcoholics/addicts might be substituted.

If a medication safe in this sense cannot be substituted, carry out all the precautions and safeguards recommended earlier for drugs dangerous to alcoholics/addicts—precautions discussed mainly in Chapters 3, 5, and 6. Also, keep reminding the psychiatrist to have the dosage lowered and the medication stopped if—and as soon as—taking these actions is feasible.

Getting and following competent psychiatric advice without delay can prove critically important. This is illustrated by a particularly unfortunate case. Stan B. felt the depression from which he had long suffered grow deeper and deeper after he had been sober and active in AA for seven months. The depression had lifted somewhat when he'd first started recovery and the depressant effects of alcohol had dissipated. But the depression had then returned worse than ever before. Neither at that time nor before had he obtained a psychiatric evaluation and recommendation for the depression.

Around the time of his seventh month in AA, Stan never admitted to his AA sponsor and friends that he felt much worse than before. As a result, he never learned that other members of his group had also felt hideously depressed and had found relief through psychiatric treatment. Some with clinical depressions had been helped by newer and nonaddictive types of antidepressant medications. Others who suffered extreme manic-depressive swings from far up to far down were on carefully worked-out doses of nonaddictive lithium, which had largely stabilized their mood swings. And in particular, Stan had never learned that, before getting medications, his fellow AA members who had suffered depressions had often also been tormented by thoughts of suicide.

One weekend Stan did phone his sponsor to say he was feeling terrible and was afraid of what he might do. His sponsor rushed to Stan's house but arrived too late. Stan had already left in his car and had driven at high speed on a local highway to ram into a tree, killing himself.

3. BEGIN RECOVERY FROM ALCOHOLISM/ ADDICTION IF YOU HAVEN'T YET BEGUN (OR GET YOUR FAMILY MEMBER STARTED).

It may be that you're already being treated for a mental illness diagnosed by a psychiatrist, and you also know that you suffer as well from alcoholism/addiction.

If this is true, make every effort to start recovery. Join an AA or NA group and go to meetings every night for three months, as is usually suggested. Follow all actions suggested to help you become an active and committed member. Or, if you need to begin as an inpatient or outpatient going through rehabilitation treatment (possibly preceded by detoxification), by all means do that and then become active in AA or NA.

Continue working hard at recovering as your group suggests after your first three months. You may find that the program helps substantially to relieve the mental illness or disorder you have in addition to your alcoholism/addiction.

In the case of a family member, try to persuade him or her to follow this advice. That is, if the family member has begun treatment for a mental illness but is also an alcoholic/addict, urge him or her to enter an alcoholism/addiction recovery program.

4. PROGRESS WITH THE SECOND MENTAL ILLNESS MAY BE IMPEDED UNLESS RECOVERY FROM ALCOHOLISM/ADDICTION IS BEGUN.

Progress in recovering from a second mental illness may be slowed or blocked entirely if you do not get started in recovery from alcoholism/addiction. Tom R., for instance, was a diagnosed schizophrenic who heard voices and at times thought he was the illegitimate son of God who could ask God to take all the nuclear bombs away from the earth on a spaceship and keep them safely in another galaxy. He was also multiple addicted, mainly abusing alcohol, marijuana, cocaine, and LSD.

Tom was treated by a psychiatrist for nine years and was kept sedated by heavy doses of Thorazine and Prolixin. They merely stabilized his second mental illness, with little or no improvement over the years, while his alcoholism/addiction continued unchecked. For most of those years he was completely unemployable and lived on welfare. Because of his alcoholism, he had three DWI convictions and was convicted as well for driving without a license. He was thus facing a felony sentence of up to four years in jail.

Tom's judge said that if he spent six months in an alcoholism recovery program he wouldn't have to go to jail (though he would serve an overall five-year suspended sentence under tight control of his parole officer). Tom entered a six-week inpatient alcoholism program at a state psychiatric hospital and continued in an outpatient day program for alcoholism over the rest of the six months. At the same time he was as active as he could be in AA. His schizophrenia improved markedly after he progressed in abstinence and sobriety. He could live independently and hold jobs while maintained on relatively light and decreasing doses of Thorazine.

A 1987 study made for the federal government found that alcohol or illegal drugs are abused by at least half of the nation's million and a half to two million persons with chronic mental illness. The study also reported that those abusing alcohol or drugs commit suicide at twice the rate of those who are abstinent. It strongly recommended that both substance abuse and mental illness be treated at the same time.

"Sometimes the chemical dependency is paramount, and you can't get to the psychiatric disorder until you come to grips with the addiction," was one professional comment on the report. It was made by Dr. Robert Morse, who heads the addictive-disorders services at the Mayo Clinic in Rochester, MN. (His statement appeared in the *Time* article on the study in the issue of August 3, 1987.)

Our opinion is that this is definitely true, not only for psychiatric disorders, but for problems of many other kinds. That is, persons suffering from alcoholism/addiction can make little or no progress on such other problems as marital relations, sexual dysfunction, weight, or even elevated blood-pressure problems until they begin a program of recovery from the alcoholism/addiction.

5. AFTER LONG PROGRESS IN RECOVERY, REASSESS THE DIAGNOSIS AND TREATMENT, AND ADJUST ACCORDINGLY.

Each year of very active participation in AA or NA with complete abstinence from alcohol and any other former drugs of choice, you and your psychiatrist should reassess the diagnosis and treatment plan for your second mental illness. On one of these annual reviews, you may find that the second mental illness has begun clearing up— possibly to the point of enabling you to plan with your psychiatrist a careful tryout sequence of reducing your medication. You may even find that treatment might be tentatively brought to an end in the near future.

For instance, Harriet L. had experienced episodes of intense rage and intense depression after starting to recover from her alcoholism in AA. After some eight months in the program, she found that these episodes had become much less frequent and upsetting. But then her mother died, and in a few weeks her depressions returned with their old intensity. She tried the AA methods that had worked before in easing her depression, such as phoning her sponsor when feeling troubled and attending more meetings. But most of the time they failed to bring relief. Some mornings she was so depressed that she couldn't get out of bed and couldn't even phone anyone.

Her sponsor stopped by on one of these occasions when the

depression was making Harriet feel completely helpless and hopeless. The sponsor suggested that Harriet should waste no time in seeing a psychiatrist who had helped some other members of their AA group with depression like hers.

She did and was soon put on a nonaddictive antidepressant medication and seeing the psychiatrist for therapy sessions twice a week. Harriet's mother had been extremely harsh, brutal, cold, and domineering. Harriet was able to bring her long-stifled and agonized feelings about her mother to light in the therapy sessions. And the medication seemed to lift that black, immobilizing despair of her depression.

After about eighteen months of therapy, Harriet no longer fell prey to the bouts of deep depression and felt far more at peace with and knowledgable about what had really happened between her and her mother all her life. She and the psychiatrist decided to try one therapy session a week and gradually reduced medication. After about another six months, Harriet felt even better. She and the psychiatrist decided on a trial ending of both therapy sessions and medication. Since then, she's found that depressions haven't developed anymore.

CHAPTER 10

Dealing with Chronic Illness

SOBRIETY GUARANTEES A QUALITY OF LIFE THAT GRADUALLY IMPROVES IN all dimensions. However, difficulties, tragedy, disease, and misfortune are part of any life, even a sober life. The alcoholic who had lost or failed to develop adequate coping skills while actively drinking learns in sobriety to deal with life's hardships without drinking. Recovery programs give to the alcoholic/addict tools to deal with the ups and the downs.

Chronic disease is difficult for anyone to handle. Most people when confronted with a chronic disease react first with disbelief and later with anger, depression, and acceptance. Recovering alcoholics/ addicts must go through the same emotions when they fall victim to chronic disease.

There are two major considerations that recovering alcoholics/ addicts afflicted with chronic disease must realize, however. One is that care must be exercised in dealing with pain (see the section "Pain" in Chapter 5). Second is the need to fully utilize the help offered by the programs and people of AA and related organizations.

Arthritis

Clark B., as an example, was sober for two years when he developed severe joint pains and a general sense of fatigue. His doctor made a number of tests and eventually found that Clark had rheumatoid arthritis. The doctor told Clark that his disease had a variable course but that he could expect to deal with chronic pain and stiffness.

At first Clark denied the reality of a long-term disability, but when his joints continued to hurt and his energy remained low, he became quite depressed. Fortunately, the physician involved knew the principles of recovery and did not offer pain medication to Clark. However, there was a need for chronic anti-inflammatory medication and a course of steroid therapy (see the section "Corticosteroids" in Chapter 6 for background information). This medicine caused an increase in energy and a decrease in pain, but when it was stopped, the pain remained.

Clark had to give up his job as a carpenter and became even more depressed. He stayed somewhat withdrawn for about three months, attending few AA meetings and never sharing his feelings. His mood gradually became more bleak.

One day, at the urging of his AA sponsor, Clark went to a meeting and discussed his fears and anxieties with his group. The outpouring of understanding and support made Clark feel better. He continued to participate more actively in his recovery program and gained strength steadily. Soon he accepted his illness and coped adequately. Eventually he obtained an appropriate office job in construction accounting work. Overall, he has been managing well though he has to cope with intermittent pain.

Clark is an example of the direct therapeutic effect of active participation in a recovery program on both of his diseases. His mood and his pain improved immediately when he used the tools of his recovery program. His type of arthritis is one of the most aggressive and painful. The more common osteoarthritis (typical age-associated arthritis) can be quite painful as well.

Medications safe for recovering alcoholics/addicts help to some extent with the arthritic pain, but strong analgesics must be avoided except in special circumstances (see the section "Pain" in Chapter 5). Among other methods of dealing with arthritic pain are physical therapy, low-impact exercise (swimming, as an example), and biofeedback.

Diabetes Mellitus

Another not uncommon chronic disease is diabetes mellitus. Probably its best-known feature is a relative lack of the body's naturally produced hormone insulin, and a resulting difficulty for the body to control the blood sugar level. As this disease progresses, there are other manifestations on the cardiovascular system, the kidneys, and other organs.

Dietary measures and careful control of blood sugar through insulin injections can minimize the progress of diabetes. But it remains a chronic disease that requires lifelong attention. Since life-style habits (such as eating, weight control, and exercise) must be modified for adequate diabetic control, the recovering alcoholic/addict has to deal with areas of difficulty (including impulse control, discipline, and giving up pleasures).

Again, there are no tricks to use as easy solutions. Careful dietary instructions should be obtained from persons experienced in diabetes counseling. These persons can be contacted through a doctor who is a diabetes specialist. Some doctors do this themselves.

The diabetic is dealing with a chronic disease requiring behavior modification. Therefore a recovering alcoholic/addict who is diabetic should fully utilize his or her recovery program. Again, fear, anger, depression, and anxiety are all part of dealing with a chronic disease—and this disease, as pointed out, has inherent problems. Recovery programs offer the alcoholic/addict means of dealing with these emotions, emotions which battle against sobriety. Recovering alcoholics/addicts with diabetes must exercise their greatest maturity and coping abilities to maintain a successful program in dealing with their two diseases concurrently.

Heart Disease

Heart disease is common in almost all populations. The most common form is *coronary artery disease,* a series of problems related to obstruction of the blood vessels feeding the heart muscle. Forms of heart disease that are related to coronary artery disease include *myocardial infarctions* (or heart attacks), congestive heart failure, certain cardiac rhythm disturbances, and angina.

For recovering alcoholics/addicts, the same principles apply to heart disease as to other chronic diseases they may develop. At the onset of heart disease, negative emotions are strong and, if sobriety is not strong as well, relapse into active addiction, or at least into "dry-drunk" emotional misery, can result.

With heart disease, a sense of vulnerability and doom typically begins a period of depression, fear, and a sense of inadequacy. These emotions are dangerous for the alcoholic/addict. Only recovery-program principles and the support of these programs can ensure adequate coping with a difficult time of life. Most heart medications are safe (without reactivation risk) for the alcoholic/addict.

Cancer

Cancer has an emotional impact unlike that of any other disease. Although, in reality, cancer is many different diseases with many different outcomes, when people learn they are victims of cancer, they usually react with fear and a sense of doom. Everyone, alcoholic or not, can use help and support when first coming to terms with having cancer. The recovering alcoholic/addict has to be particularly careful with some of the attitudes or reflexes that are part of his or her disease of addiction.

Negativism and projection (needless worry about future outcomes) are two tendencies that certainly might emerge here. To some degree, this is one time that such feelings might be normal. The alcoholic/addict, however, needs to guard against letting these attitudes and feelings become excessive and damaging. The best way to ensure against a flare-up of alcoholic attitudes is to intensify contact with the recovery program. Group support is particularly beneficial at times of crisis, offering a perspective that is most often extremely valuable. An alcoholic who deals with cancer alone is bound to experience much more pain than if he or she accepts the help offered by his fellow alcoholics/addicts.

By discussing their fears and projections with the recovery group, alcoholics/addicts are bound to find others who have had similar problems. They will learn that cancer has many potential outcomes, not just those they fearfully project. Expressing feelings is helpful in itself. Conversely, alcoholics/addicts who keep their problem to themselves and withdraw will probably see their alcoholic attitudes grow, giving them two active diseases to deal with. They may despair and face the danger of drinking or drugging—a course that would tragically undercut their most essential personal resources.

As stated, cancer has a variety of outcomes. Most often, treatment can prove effective, and, in many cases, a cure is likely. People need their coping skills more than ever during such times, and alcoholics/addicts can keep theirs in very adequate shape by taking advantage of the recovery program and its principles.

An alcoholic/addict afflicted with a type of cancer that leads to advanced disease faces one of the more difficult situations life has to offer. Numerous experiences have shown that the principles and support of one's alcoholism/addiction recovery program can also be valuable in situations like this. Here, alcoholics/addicts may confront the problem of dealing with narcotic pain relievers. There are no universally right answers in this difficult area. In our experience, however, alcoholics/addicts can safely take these medications for real pain arising in such situations.

Directory of Sources of Help and Further Information

THIS DIRECTORY GIVES ORGANIZATIONS AND THEIR PHONE NUMBERS AND addresses, as well as publications and details about them. These are the major organizations in the United States providing help with problems of alcoholism/addiction to afflicted individuals and their families. They are also sources of further information about recovering from alcoholism/addiction, as are the publications listed.

Sources of Help—National Offices of Organizations Consisting of Local Self-Help Groups Providing Aid Nationwide

These are the national offices in the United States of the major voluntary organizations consisting of self-help groups that aid alcoholics/addicts and their families. The organizations help individuals recover from the disease of alcoholism/addiction, or from its effects on persons close to the alcoholic/addict. These offices can also often help persons in other countries contact branches of the same organizations in their own countries.

ALCOHOLICS ANONYMOUS (AA)

World Services Office
P.O. Box 459, Grand Central Station
New York, NY 10163
Phone: 212-686-1100

Founded in 1935, Alcoholics Anonymous is the major organization through which individuals, who are primarily alcoholics, join with other alcoholics/addicts to safeguard and continue their recovery. It consists essentially of tens of thousands of relatively small, autonomous "AA groups" throughout the United States (and also in more than one hundred other countries). Increasing numbers of persons who are primarily drug addicts are joining AA groups today, some members observe.

This listing identifies the central services office of AA. From it, persons can find out about meetings of groups in their own locale, if they or someone they know may have a problem with alcohol.

Most treatment centers for alcoholism/addiction strongly recommend that alcoholics/addicts who have begun recovery as patients at the centers safeguard and augment continued recovery by joining and attending meetings of an AA group (or a group of the similar organizations primarily for drug addicts listed later). In addition, substantial numbers of AA members have succeeded in beginning their recovery simply by starting to attend meetings of a nearby AA group, without first going through a detoxification and rehabilitation program at a treatment center.

AA groups can also be located by phoning the local AA number listed in the telephone directories of many communities across the nation. Calls to these local numbers are answered by persons (usually volunteers) who tell where and when a group near the caller meets. Other helpful information and encouragement concerning an alcoholism/addiction problem may also be given in answer to such a call.

An example of a local AA information phone number is that of the

"New York Intergroup" office, which serves the New York City metropolitan area. That number, listed in New York phone directories
under "Alcoholics Anonymous, Central Office for Groups of Greater
New York," is 212-473-6200.

AL-ANON FAMILY GROUP HEADQUARTERS, INC.

World Service Office for Al-Anon and Alateen Groups (and for
more than 1,000 Adult Children of Alcoholics groups)
P.O.Box 862, Midtown Station
New York, NY 10018-0862
Phone: 212-302-7240; Toll-Free, 1-800-356-9996 (throughout
the United States, 24 hours a day)
Throughout Canada: 613-722-1830

This is the major organization through which the family members
and friends of persons who are primarily alcoholics can help each
other recover from the damaging effects of alcoholism. A basic Al-
Anon belief is that "alcoholism is a family illness and that changed
attitudes can aid recovery." Al-Anon is completely separate from AA,
but functions in many ways as a companion organization to it. Al-
Anon similarly consists of tens of thousands of relatively small,
autonomous groups in communities throughout the United States
and scores of other countries. Affiliated with Al-Anon are similar
Alateen groups, in which the teenage children of alcoholics obtain
help with the troubles caused by a parent's alcoholism.

New affiliates of Al-Anon that have developed almost entirely in
the 1980s consist of more than a thousand groups for adult children
of alcoholics.

This listing identifies the central services office of Al-Anon. From
it, persons can find out about meetings of groups in their own locale,
if someone close to them may have a problem with alcohol. Individuals can also reach Al-Anon or Alateen groups throughout the world
by consulting an Al-Anon pamphlet, *Getting in Touch with Al-Anon/
Alateen*.

Al-Anon and Alateen serve family members and close friends of
alcoholics/addicts. Persons can benefit from Al-Anon or Alateen
membership both while the alcoholic/addict relative is active in
substance abuse, and while such a relative is in early and ongoing
recovery.

Al-Anon groups can also be located by phoning the local Al-Anon number listed in the telephone directories of many communities. Calls to these local numbers are answered by persons (usually volunteers) who tell where and when a group near the caller meets.

NARCOTICS ANONYMOUS (NA)

World Services Office
P.O. Box 9999
16155 Wyandotte St.
Van Nuys, CA 91409
Phone: 818-780-3951

Narcotics Anonymous is a major national organization through which individuals, primarily drug addicts, join with other alcoholics/addicts to safeguard and continue their recovery. Similar to AA in a number of ways, it consists essentially of a great many relatively small, autonomous "NA groups" throughout the United States and other countries.

The preceding listing identifies the central services office of NA. From it, persons can locate meetings of groups in their own community, if they or someone they know has a problem with drugs.

NA groups can also be located by phoning a local NA number listed in the telephone directories of a number of communities. Calls to these local numbers are answered by persons (usually volunteers) who tell where and when a group near the caller meets.

An example of a local NA information phone number is that of the Greater New York Regional Service Office. That number, listed in New York phone directories under "Narcotics Anonymous Helpline," is 718-805-9835.

COCAINE ANONYMOUS (CA)

6125 Washington Blvd., Suite 202
Culver City, CA 90230
Phone: 213-839-1141

Cocaine Anonymous is a major national organization through which individuals, primarily cocaine addicts, join with other alcoholics/addicts to safeguard and continue their recovery. Similar to

AA in a number of ways, it consists essentially of a great many relatively small, autonomous "CA groups" across the nation.

The listing identifies the central services office of CA. From it, persons can find meetings of local groups if they are or someone they know is affected by cocaine addiction.

CA groups can also be located by phoning a local CA number listed in the directories of a number of cities. Calls to these local numbers are answered by persons (usually volunteers) who tell where and when a group near the caller meets.

ADULT CHILDREN OF ALCOHOLICS (A.C.O.A.)

Central Service Board; World Services Office
P.O. Box 3216; 2522 W. Sepulveda Blvd., Suite 200
Torrance, CA 90505
Phone: 213-534-1815

Adult Children of Alcoholics has more than 1,350 local, 12-step, self-help meetings of persons who grew up in households with alcoholic parents. This is a worldwide service office for such groups. From it, individuals who might find it helpful to participate in a local group can learn the time and place of meetings, and obtain other helpful information.

Other A.C.O.A. groups are Al-Anon-affiliated or independent.

Sources of Help—National Organizations Providing Aid Services Nationwide

NATIONAL COUNCIL ON ALCOHOLISM, INC.

12 W. 21st St.
New York, NY 10010
Phone: 212-206-6770

Information and referral services to families and individuals seeking help with a drinking or drug problem represent one of the main ways in which the National Council on Alcoholism aids alcoholics/ addicts. A voluntary, nonprofit organization, it has more than 180 state and local affiliates throughout the country. Offices of local affiliates of the Council can be contacted for help either by consulting local telephone directory listings or by obtaining information about them from the central office.

Founded in 1944 by Mrs. Marty Mann, the Council combats alcoholism, other drug addictions, and related problems. Among its major programs are prevention and education, public information, public policy advocacy, conferences, and publications.

NATIONAL INSTITUTE ON DRUG ABUSE

Hotline for Drug Abuse Treatment Referral and information:
1-800-662-HELP (toll-free throughout the United States)

Calls to this toll-free number by persons needing help with a drug abuse problem will bring them help and information about getting into treatment, and how and where to do it.

The hotline service is operated by the National Institute on Drug Abuse, an arm of the U.S. Department of Health and Human Services.

PSYCHIATRIC INSTITUTES OF AMERICA

Hotline for Cocaine Abuse Treatment Referral and Family Information:
1-800-COCAINE (toll-free throughout the United States)

Many news reports and a book have made this hotline service for cocaine addicts and their families well known throughout the country. From it, persons wanting treatment for cocaine abuse can obtain referrals to sources of treatment in their locale. Family members of such persons can obtain from it referrals to Nar-Anon groups operating in their vicinity, or to Al-Anon groups if no Nar-Anon groups are available nearby. Nar-Anon is for family members of narcotics addicts and is similar to Al-Anon (see Al-Anon entry).

Organizations that Are Sources of Further Information

CENTER OF ALCOHOL STUDIES, RUTGERS, THE STATE UNIVERSITY OF NEW JERSEY

Smithers Hall, Busch Campus
Piscataway, NJ 08854
Phone: 201-932-4442, Library
      201-932-2190, General Information and Publications

The Center conducts extensive programs in research, education, clinical services, and information services. It serves as an international source of information on alcohol studies through operation of the Center Library, which contains one of the world's largest and most comprehensive collections of alcohol-related literature. The Center also publishes a leading scholarly periodical, *Journal of Studies on Alcohol,* as well as books, monographs, and pamphlets. The staff operates the Summer School of Alcohol Studies, which more than twelve thousand students have attended for continuing professional education.

HAZELDEN EDUCATIONAL MATERIALS

Pleasant Valley Rd.
Box 176
Center City, MN 55012-0176
Phone: 1-800-328-900 (toll-free, United States, outside Minnesota)
      1-800-257-0070 (toll-free within Minnesota)
      612-257-4010 (Alaska, other countries)

This organization distributes and publishes a great many books, booklets, pamphlets, audio tapes, videotapes, and films concerned with recovery from alcoholism/addiction, especially through twelve-step programs. It functions as part of the Hazelden Foundation, which operates a leading treatment center (see the center's entry in Appendix 2), and serves as an alternate source for the major official publications of Alcoholics Anonymous, Al-Anon Family Groups, and Narcotics Anonymous. The staff sends catalogues on request.

NATIONAL CLEARINGHOUSE FOR ALCOHOLISM AND DRUG INFORMATION U.S. DEPARTMENT OF HEALTH AND HUMAN SERVICES

P.O. Box 2345
Rockville, MD 20852

The Clearinghouse publishes and distributes pamphlets, booklets, posters, and other materials concerned with treatment and prevention of alcoholism/addiction that are originated by the Alcohol, Drug Abuse, and Mental Health Administration of the Public Health Service. A catalogue and order form for its materials are available on request.

Publications

The following is a selective listing of a number of the publications that seem most helpful or interesting to recovering alcoholics/addicts and their families.

MAJOR OFFICIAL BOOKS PUBLISHED BY TWELVE-STEP ALCOHOLISM/ADDICTION RECOVERY GROUPS

The books most important to members that are published officially by Alcoholics Anonymous, Al-Anon Family Groups, and Narcotics Anonymous are identified by title. The organizations themselves are credited as the books' authors. Publishing dates are not given inasmuch as the books go through reprintings and minor revisions periodically.

Copies may be obtained from the organizations (see the addresses listed in this appendix) and at meetings of local groups of the organizations. They are also available from Hazelden Educational Materials (see listing above).

Each organization publishes other books and numerous booklets and pamphlets. Complete and current publications listings are available on request from the central offices.

Alcoholics Anonymous—Titles of Major Books

Alcoholics Anonymous. This book gave the organization its name. Traditionally it is called "The Big Book."
Twelve Steps and Twelve Traditions.

AL-ANON FAMILY GROUPS, ALATEEN—TITLES OF MAJOR BOOKS

Al-Anon Faces Alcoholism
Al-Anon's Twelve Steps and Twelve Traditions
Alateen: Hope for Children of Alcoholics

Narcotics Anonymous—Title of Major Book

Narcotics Anonymous

GENERAL REPORTS OR ANALYSES ON ALCOHOLISM/ADDICTION

Alcoholics Anonymous World Services, *The A.A. Member—Medications and Other Drugs; A Report from a Group of Physicians in A.A.* (eighteen-page pamphlet) (New York: AA World Services, Inc., 1984). A pioneering official AA statement on the dangers of sedatives, tranquilizers, and stimulants to recovering alcoholics; it also emphasizes that other psychoactive medications (such as those for depression, schizophrenia, and epilepsy) can be necessary to alleviate "disabling physical and/or emotional problems" of recoverees and do not compromise sobriety when properly prescribed and taken.

Black, Claudia, *"It Will Never Happen To Me!"; Children of Alcoholics, As Youngsters—Adolescents—Adults* (New York: Ballantine, 1987) (first published in 1981). A best-selling book that reports on the deep-seated neurotic difficulties developed by people who grew up with alcoholic parents and ways they can help resolve those difficulties as adults.

Beasley, M.D., Joseph D., *Wrong Diagnosis, Wrong Treatment: The Plight of the Alcoholic in America* (Durant, Okla.: Creative Informatics, 1987). An impassioned effort "to diminish the gruesome harvest of alcoholism now" by setting forth a very detailed case history exemplifying alcoholism as a basically biochemical disorder rather than a psychiatric one. Explains for alcoholics and families causes, intervention to start recovery, and treatment in the views of the author, who is medical director at Brunswick House, a treatment center in Amityville, New York.

Goodwin, Donald, *Is Alcoholism Hereditary?* (New York: Oxford University Press, 1976). A work for general readers summarizing extensive research evidence to indicate that a predisposition toward alcoholism is inherited genetically.

Jellinek, E. M., *The Disease Concept of Alcoholism* (Piscataway, N.J.: Center of Alcohol Studies at Rutgers, 1960). A classic, this scholarly work by the Center's first director traces the history of attitudes toward alcoholism and of the relatively recent conception of it as an illness.

Johnson, Verne. *I'll Quit Tomorrow* (New York: Harper & Row, 1973). Generally considered the pioneering work on intervention as a technique of influencing the alcoholic to begin recovery earlier than he or she might otherwise, by the chief originator of the technique.

Ketcham, Katherine, and L. Ann Mueller, M.D., *Eating Right to Live Sober* (New York: New American Library/Signet, 1983). Associates of James R. Milam, Ms. Ketcham and Dr. Mueller set forth explanations of the physiological basis of alcoholism similar to Milam's, especially emphasizing their theories of nutritional factors. The book makes detailed recommendations concerning diet, vitamins, and minerals that theoretically promote recovery from alcoholism.

Mann, Marty, *Marty Mann Answers Your Questions about Drinking and Alcoholism* rev. ed. (New York: Holt, Rinehart & Winston, 1981). Basic questions about alcoholism answered by one of the early members of Alcoholics Anonymous and a founder of the National Council on Alcoholism.

Milam, James R., and Katherine Ketcham, *Under the Influence: A Guide to the Myths and Realities of Alcoholism* (New York: Bantam, 1981). Explains for lay readers what the disease of alcoholism is and identifies the typical physiological and biochemical factors that lead some individuals and not others to become alcoholics. Emphasizes nutritional factors in both the onset and the cure of alcoholism and sets forth recommended methods of treatment. A clinical psychologist, Dr. Milam is cofounder of the Milam Recovery Centers in Bothell, Washington (see Appendix 2).

Moore, Jean, ed., *Roads to Recovery: A National Directory of Alcohol and Drug Addiction Treatment Centers* (New York: Macmillan/Collier Books, 1985). Informational entries for some five hundred treatment centers and programs, of the several thousand throughout America.

Mueller, L. Ann, and Katherine Ketcham, *Recovering: How to Get and Stay Sober* (New York: Bantam, 1987). Presents a further refined and extended statement of the approach to alcoholism causation and treatment developed by James R. Milam, by two of his associates.

O'Brien, Robert, and Morris Chafetz, *The Encyclopedia of Alcoholism* (New York: Facts on File, 1982). A one-volume encyclopedia with A-to-Z entries presenting a wealth of information.

O'Brien, Robert, and Sidny Cohen, *The Encyclopedia of Drug Abuse* (New York: Facts on File, 1984). A companion volume to O'Brien and Chafetz's alcoholism encyclopedia.

Robertson, Nan, *Getting Better: Inside A.A.* (New York: Morrow, 1988). A contemporary report on Alcoholics Anonymous by a Pulitzer Prize–winning reporter with *The New York Times* who is also a member of AA.

Seixas, Judith S., *Living With a Parent Who Drinks Too Much*. New York: Greenwillow (Morrow), 1979. A book for children living with parents who are active alcoholics; explains the disease of alcoholism and how it affects their parents and themselves, and largely through case-histories of other children gives them ways to make life more bearable and productive. Tells also where they can get help. A related book for adult children of alcoholics by Ms. Seixas with Geraldine Youcha is *Children of Alcoholism: A Survivor's Manual* (New York: Crown, 1985).

Vaillant, George E., *The Natural History of Alcoholism* (Cambridge, Mass.: Harvard University Press, 1983). Reports on a very large, pioneering study that followed the lives of more than six hundred individuals for more than forty years to investigate such questions as who developed alcoholism and why, who recovered and in what ways, and who did not and why not. Difficult but definitive within its scope. Dr. Vaillant is a professor of psychiatry at Dartmouth Medical School.

Wallace, John, *Alcoholism: New Light on the Disease* (Newport, R.I.: Edgehill Publications, 1985). Reports on recent research evidence indicating the basic physiological causes of the disease and treatment for it. The author is director of treatment at the Edgehill Newport treatment center (see Appendix 2).

Williams, Roger J., *Alcoholism: The Nutritional Approach* (Austin: University of Texas Press, 1959). A short, early work on research investigations of possible disorders in nutrition as factors theoretically contributing to the onset of alcoholism.

Woititz, Janet Geringer, *Adult Children of Alcoholics* (Pompano Beach, Fla.: Health Communications, 1983). A paperback that became a best-seller in 1987, this book reports on the deep-seated neurotic difficulties developed by people who grew up with alcoholic parents and ways they can help resolve those difficulties as adults.

Youcha, Geraldine, *Women and Alcohol: A Dangerous Pleasure* (New York: Crown, 1978, 1986). An up-to-date report for lay readers on the effects of alcohol, drinking, and alcoholism on women; explains how to recognize and get treatment for alcoholism.

Youcha, Geraldine, and Judith S. Seixas, *Drugs, Alcohol, and Your Children; A Parent's Survival Manual.* New York: Crown, 1989. Written for parents of children who have abused drugs and/or alcohol, this book by prominent authors and professionals in the field explains how best to deal with active abuse, how to influence the child to stop abuse and begin recovery, and how to help the child and the whole family heal the psychological damage of the past.

Zimberg M.D., Sheldon, John Wallace, Ph.D., and Sheila B. Blume, M.D., eds., *Practical Approaches to Alcoholism Psychotherapy*, 2d ed. (New York: Plenum, 1985). A professional work for physicians, counselors, and treatment program administrators.

BIOGRAPHICAL ACCOUNTS OF ALCOHOLISM/ ADDICTION

Anonymous, *Dr. Bob and the Good Oldtimers: A Biography with Recollections of Early A.A. in the Midwest* (New York: Alcoholics Anonymous World Services, 1980). AA's official biography of one of its two cofounders, with an account of AA's origin in Akron, Ohio, and early growth chiefly in Ohio.

Anonymous, *"Pass It On": The Story of Bill Wilson and How the A.A. Message Reached the World* (New York: Alcoholics Anonymous World Services, 1984). AA's official biography of one of its two cofounders; a carefully balanced account giving especially full information about Bill W.'s role in AA.

Fisher, Carrie, *Postcards from the Edge* (New York: Simon and Schuster, 1987). An autobiographical novel by the heroine of the celebrated *Star Wars* movies, who is the daughter of actress Debbie Reynolds and actor Eddie Fisher, and a recovering addict. Written after Ms. Fisher began recovery from drug addiction, the novel chronicles the start in recovery of an obsessive young movie actress.

Ford, Betty, with Chris Chase, *Betty: A Glad Awakening* (New York: Doubleday, 1987). An account of her recovery from addiction to prescription drugs and alcohol by the wife of President Gerald Ford, written primarily to help active alcoholics/addicts and those close to them. In it, Mrs. Ford tells how her recovery began with an intervention by her family, two doctors, and her friends in 1978. She also recounts how she led the effort to establish in 1982 a now widely-renowned treatment center, the Betty Ford Center in Rancho Mirage, California (see page 234). As with her lecture fees for speaking on alcohol and drug addiction, her royalties on the book go to the Betty Ford Center and other treatment centers.

Gordon, Barbara, *I'm Dancing As Fast As I Can* (New York: Harper & Row, 1979). A TV producer's account of her addiction to Valium and her efforts to stop.

Jackson, Charles, *The Lost Weekend* (New York: Farrar & Rinehart, 1944). An early, classic novel made into a film still shown on network TV in the 1980s; reports very graphically on the horrors and desperation of an alcoholic nearing his bottom. The author was an alcoholic who died by suicide.

Kirkland, Gelsey, *Dancing on My Grave* (New York: Doubleday, 1986). An autobiographical account of her career, addiction, and recovery by a former star ballerina with the American Ballet Theater.

Mohoney, Barbara, *A Sensitive, Passionate Man* (New York: David McKay, 1974). Depicts the disintegrating life of an active alcoholic and especially the effect of his alcoholism on his family.

Meryman, Richard, *Broken Promises, Mended Dreams* (Boston: Little, Brown, 1984). A novel about a woman hitting bottom with alcoholism and what she experienced while starting recovery in a treatment center. Based on the author's detailed interviews of actual women going through treatment.

Molloy, Paul, *Where Did Everybody Go?* (New York: Warner Books, 1982). An autobiographical account by a syndicated newspaper columnist with the *Chicago Sun-Times* of his alcoholism and repeated efforts to start recovering.

Reilly M.D., Patrick, *A Private Practice* (New York: Macmillan, 1984). Written under a pseudonym by a pediatrician, this autobiographical book briefly recounts his addiction to tranquilizers and sedatives and describes at length how he began recovering at a treatment center.

Robe, Lucy Barry, *Co-Starring Famous Women and Alcohol: The Dramatic Truth behind the Tragedies and Triumphs of 200 Celebrities* (Minneapolis: CompCare Publications, 1986). Reports on the alcoholism/addiction of famous women of the present and recent past. Includes many recovering women who have made public declarations such as Elizabeth Taylor, Mary Tyler Moore, and Joan Kennedy. Discusses others whose probable or little-known addictions the author documents, among them Marilyn Monroe, Edith Piaf, Judy Garland, Janis Joplin, Vivian Leigh, and authors Lillian Hellman, Margaret Mitchell, Dorothy Parker, and Edna St. Vincent Millay.

Somers, Suzanne, *Keeping Secrets*. New York: Warner, 1988. A famed television and film actress tells of her life as the child of an alcoholic, and about her recovery as an adult.

Thomas, Caitlin, with George Tremlett, *Caitlin: Life with Dylan Thomas* (New York: Henry Holt & Co., 1987). Reports on the author's marriage to the Welsh poet much celebrated in the 1950s before his death from alcoholism, and on her subsequent addiction, suicide attempts, and ten years' sobriety in AA.

Welch, Bob, and George Vecsey, *Five O'Clock Comes Early* (New York: Morrow, 1982). A former star pitcher for the Los Angeles Dodgers recounts the story of his addiction, treatment, and recovery.

Wholey, Dennis, *The Courage to Change: Hope and Help for Alcoholics and Their Families* (New York: Warner Books, 1984). Accounts of alcoholism and recovery by many celebrities as told to the author, himself a recovering alcoholic and host of a recent popular PBS-TV series, "LateNight America." Among those who tell of themselves or persons close to them in the book are Sid Caesar, Billy and Sybil Carter, the Reverend Jerry Falwell, Elmore Leonard, Wilbur Mills, Don Newcombe, Jason and Lois Robards, Grace Slick, Rod Steiger, and Pete Townshend.

Directory of Leading Treatment Centers for Alcoholism/ Addiction in the United States and Canada

VITAL HELP CAN BE FOUND HERE BY EITHER ACTIVE ALCOHOLICS/ADDICTS who want to seek intensive treatment or persons close to them (possibly after those persons have persuaded the alcoholic/addict to accept the need for treatment and recovery through an intervention of the kind described in Chapter 2).

For family members or close friends of active alcoholics/addicts approaching a crisis, these treatment centers in many cases offer advisory services on planning and carrying out interventions.

Recovering alcoholics/addicts and members of their families may also obtain help with the problem of locating physicians knowledgable about the special precautions needed in providing general medical care for a recovering alcoholic/addict. Requests for referrals to such physicians might be made to a center in your area.

This directory includes centers in all parts of the United States and Canada that admit alcoholics/addicts for intensive professional treatment. Most have inpatient live-in programs in hospital or hospitallike facilities. Others have outpatient program offerings in addition to or instead of inpatient programs, as noted in the entries.

Centers offer one or both of two kinds of major programs:

1. *Detoxification programs* with a treatment duration of some five to seven days. Special medical treatment (of kinds discussed in Chapter 1) is provided in these "detox" programs. This treatment relieves much of the acute physical distress of withdrawal from addiction in the time right after the alcoholic/addict stops drinking and/or drug taking.

2. *Rehabilitation programs* with a treatment duration of at least two to four weeks up to as long as six months. Such "rehab" programs provide extensive, day-long counseling and group sessions designed to change alcoholic behavior patterns, along with continued medical treatment as needed to promote recovery from the physical damage of excessive alcohol/drugs.

This is a selective directory designed to include, insofar as possible, the leading treatment centers for alcoholism/addiction throughout the United States and Canada. Entries are given for approximately one hundred centers. Several thousand more with similar programs operate across the country. If you should need a center in your immediate vicinity and find none listed here, you might telephone a listed center nearby for a local recommendation.

Entries for the centers are presented first by country, and then in alphabetic order by the states or provinces in which they are located, and next within each state or province in alphabetic order by the treatment center's name. This organization enables you to find the centers near you conveniently simply by looking through the entries for your state/province or neighboring states/provinces. On the other hand, should you know a center's name, you can locate its entry by finding the name and entry page number in the Index.

Rates of recovery from alcoholism/addiction were requested from the centers for their entries and are reported in the entry if supplied by the center. Considerable controversy surrounds the use of such recovery rates in professional circles, centering essentially around what types of patients were included or excluded in calculating rates. In requesting recovery rate data, we suggested use of only the fairly loose criteria indicated in the following listing. Our recovery rate data are hence indicative and approximate rather than definitive and conclusive.

Because of the approximate nature of the recovery rate data given here, readers are cautioned not to compare treatment centers on this basis. That information is presented instead to document the heartening fact that recovery actually can be achieved by a great many victims of alcoholism/addiction under a great many different circumstances.

Explanations of special terms used in the entries and not explained elsewhere in the book are as follows:

> *Twelve-Step Program:* Refers to the "twelve steps" of recommended actions to take for recovery from alcoholism originated by Alcoholics Anonymous and used in adapted form by similar organizations including Narcotics Anonymous, Cocaine Anonymous, Al-Anon Family Groups, and Alateen.
>
> *Hazelden Model:* The type of professional treatment of alcoholism/addiction at a rehabilitation center that the Hazelden Foundation in Center City, Minnesota, is generally credited with originating in the 1940s. (See the Hazelden entry in this directory.) Most rehabilitation programs in the United States today are patterned on this approach. The approach is also widely called the "Minnesota Model." Some professionals in the field identify its chief characteristics as: abstinence, the AA group as the preferred modality, use of counselors who are recovering alcholics/addicts, education about alcoholism/addiction, and family involvement in treatment and recovery.

Information of the following kinds is given in each center's entry (if it supplied all information requested):

Name of the treatment center

Address
Telephone number

Headed by:
Direct inquiries to:
Capacity (no. of patients):
Types of patients admitted:
Detoxification program offered?:
Inpatient treatment program—usual duration:
Inpatient treatment program—main features:
Outpatient treatment program:
Family program or services—main features:
Charges for treatment: (in Canadian entries, given in terms of Canadian dollars)
Can health-care insurance pay for charges?:
Accredited by: Joint Commission on Accreditation of Hospitals (JCAH) (if applicable)
Aftercare programs:
Multiply addicted among entering patients:
Recovery rates: (For the first-time patients completing the center's usual rehabiliation program, gives the percentages of those continuously and completely abstinent through specified periods of from six months to several years after treatment.)
Comments:

Directory of Leading Treatment Centers in the United States

ALABAMA

Parkside Lodge of Birmingham
P.O. Box 128, 1189 Albritton Rd.
Warrior, AL 35180
Telephone number: 205-647-1945 (staffed 24 hours a day)

Headed by: Jerry W. Crowder, Executive Director.
Direct inquiries to: Lawrence Rives, Admission Specialist
Capacity (no. of patients): 82.
Types of patients admitted: Men and women, 18 years or older, who are physically and mentally able to participate in the pro-

gram, and who have failed to maintain sobriety in an outpatient treatment setting. (Ineligible applicants will be given appropriate referrals.)

Detoxification program: 2-day usual duration.

Inpatient treatment program—usual duration: Up to 30 days. Length of stay is determined on an individual basis and is dictated by the progress of the patient.

Inpatient treatment program—main features: "We treat the whole person. Staff works as an interdisciplinary team with each patient assigned a primary counselor. We emphasize the disease concept and abstinence. The program consists of lectures, films, group discussions, group and individual therapy and orientation and experience, with 12-step recovery process. We involve the family and offer an in-residence Family Week Program. We have a 2-year Continuing Care Program."

Outpatient treatment program: 16-day usual duration. Main features include complete physical examination, psychological testing, evaluation for appropriateness, individual and group therapy, lectures, films and discussion groups, family involvement 2 nights a week.

Family program or services—main features: Contact by primary counselor, in-residence week-long program, conjoint therapy and participation in Continuing Care.

Charges for treatment: Inpatient—approximately $250/day, $8,500 total. Outpatient, $100/day, $2,300 total. Family program, $250/family member.

Can health-care insurance pay for charges?: Yes.

Accredited by: JCAH; State of Alabama, Department of Mental Health.

Aftercare programs: 2-year duration, no charge. "Recharge Weekends" at Parkside, offered at posttreatment intervals of 3, 6, 12, and 18 months, charge of $100/person.

Multiply addicted among entering in-patients: 58 percent; substances include cocaine, prescription drugs. Patients who suffer mainly from alcoholism are age 37 or older and are 68 percent male. Patients who suffer mainly from cocaine abuse are under age 37 and are 60 percent male.

Recovery rates: 81 percent, 6 months; 63 percent, 1 year; 58 percent, 3 years; 54 percent, 5 years. (Based on previous studies conducted by independent researchers. Now conducting in-house studies systemwide in the Parkside Medical Services Corporation.)

Comments: Brookwood Recovery Center was the institution's former name.

ALASKA

Charter North Hospital
2530 DeBarr Rd.
Anchorage, AK 99508-2996
907-258-7575

Direct inquiries to: Intake office.
Capacity (no. of patients): 80.
Types of patients admitted: Adult Unit, Adolescent Unit.
Detoxification program offered?: Only as part of treatment; duration, 1 to 5 days.
Inpatient treatment program—usual duration: 9 to 30 days.
Inpatient treatment program—main features: "AA/NA and Hazelden model."
Outpatient treatment program: Usual duration, 65 hours (aggregate time).
Family program or services—main features: Required as part of rehabilitation program.
Can health-care insurance pay for charges?: Yes. Approved for payment by Medicare.
Accredited by: JCAH; State of Alaska.
Aftercare programs: 3 to 12 months' duration.

ARIZONA

ARC/The Meadows
P.O. Box 197
Wickenburg, AZ 85358
602-684-2815

Headed by: James Patrick Mellody, Executive Director.
Direct inquiries to: James Patrick Mellody.
Capacity (no. of patients): 70.
Types of patients admitted: Men and women; patients under age 18 need Executive Director's approval.
Detoxification program offered?: As part of inpatient treatment; usual duration, 3 days.

Inpatient treatment program—usual duration: Average, 37 days; "length of stay is open-ended."

Inpatient treatment program—main features: "We treat all compulsive behaviors, stressing early childhood and family-of-origin issues. Our program is based on the 12 steps of Alcoholics Anonymous."

Family program or services—main features: "All patients have a family week during which their family members participate, having a chance to address their own issues. We also offer Family Workshop to anyone interested in working on their own issues."

Charges for treatment: $325/day; $13,800 total for 37 days of treatment. Families with patients in treatment receive their therapy as part of the patient's treatment.

Can health-care insurance pay for charges?: Yes.

Accredited by: JCAH; State of Arizona, Department of Health Services.

Aftercare programs: 25 weeks of aftercare provided at $15 per week as part of the patient's treatment.

Multiply addicted among entering patients: 65 percent; substances include alcohol, cocaine, prescription drugs, street drugs.

St. Joseph's Hospital, O'Reilly Care Center
350 N. Wilmot Rd.
Tucson, AZ 85711
602-721-3833

Headed by: Frank A. Laraia, Jr., Administrative Director.

Direct Inquiries to: O'Reilly Care Center.

Capacity (no. of patients): 18-plus.

Types of patients admitted: Men and women age 18 and older with alcohol and/or drug addiction.

Detoxification program offered?: Yes; duration as needed.

Inpatient treatment program—usual duration: 21 days; includes family program and followed by 6 months' Continuing Care.

Inpatient treatment program—main features: "Our primary treatment philosophy is one of individualized treatment within the context of a structured program that integrates a 12-Step approach to recovery. We offer a regimen of educational and therapeutic groups to help individuals and their significant others understand addictive processes. A unique aspect of our treatment approach includes an emphasis upon helping the individual to identify and work on those emotional factors that surround his/her chemical dependency. . . . Achievements in the therapeutic milieu are predicated on the willingness of the individual to abstain from the use of drugs and/or alcohol while in treatment. . . .

"Recovery is viewed as an ongoing process that begins with an evaluation and safe detoxification. Continued recovery is based on an effective continuum of care that includes outpatient programming and self-help groups (AA, Al-Anon, CA, ACOA, etc.)."

Outpatient treatment program: Medically managed; an intensive alcohol/drug abuse program offered as an alternative to inpatient treatment for those who cannot be absent from work and who do not require hospitalization. Patients attend 4 evenings a week for a minimum of 5 weeks.

Family program or services—main features: Offered as part of the inpatient program and of the outpatient program, and also offered separately. Includes 6 months' Continuing Care.

Charges for treatment: Inpatient program, total $8,500. Outpatient program, total $3,000. Family program, $1,300/family.

Can health-care insurance pay for charges?: Yes.

Accredited by: JCAH.

Aftercare programs: Continuing Care for first 6 months (cost included in program cost); Continuing Care after the first 6 months, $15/visit.

Multiply addicted among entering patients: 41 percent, for the inpatient program; 50 percent, for the out-patient program.

CALIFORNIA

Betty Ford Center at Eisenhower
Eisenhower Medical Center
39000 Bob Hope Dr.
Rancho Mirage, CA 92270
619-340-0033, ext. 1720
Toll-free, 1-800-392-7450 (in Cal.)
1-800-854-9211 (outside Cal.)

Headed by: John Schwarzlose, Executive Director/Vice President.

Direct Inquiries to: Susan Stevens, External Relations.

Capacity (no. of patients): Inpatient, 80. Outpatient, 25. Family program, 25.

Types of patients admitted: Men and women over age 17 with no major medical problems or psychiatric disorders. Center does not admit heroin patients.

Detoxification program offered?: Limited program; ambulatory patients only.

Inpatient treatment program— usual duration: At least 28 days.

Inpatient treatment program—main features: Program based on the 12 steps of Alcoholics Anonymous.

Outpatient treatment program: Two-phase, 12-month program: primary care phase consists of 4 evening sessions per week for 6 weeks attended by patient and family member(s); aftercare phase consists of a 1.5-hour meeting each week for 12 months. Offered for patients unwilling or unable to leave work/home responsibilities for treatment.

Family program or services—main features: 5-day to 10-day intensive process in the inpatient program; integral part of outpatient program.

Charges for treatment: Inpatient, $180/day. Outpatient, $2,600 for 6 weeks. Family program, $95/day for 5 days.

Can health-care insurance pay for charges?: Yes.

Accredited by: JCAH.

Aftercare programs: Aftercare offerings include individual and group counseling, weekly support group meetings, and monitoring and reporting system when authorized by the patient.

Comments: Founded in 1983 by the wife of the thirty-eighth President of the United States, Gerald Ford, this is one of the most famous treatment centers in the country. Mrs. Ford led in establishing the center after her own recovery from alcoholism/addiction. She serves as president of the center and frequently lectures there.

Beverly Hills Medical Center, Glen Recovery Center
1177 S. Beverly Dr.
Los Angeles, CA 90035
213-551-7900, Adult Program
213-551-7973, Adolescent Center

Headed by: Nancy Hafner, M.S., M.F.C.C., Program Director.

Direct inquiries to: Adult Program, Shawn Pechette, Intake Coordinator; Adolescent Center, Lilyah Lin, Intake Coordinator.

Capacity (no. of patients): Adults, 30; Adolescents, 31.

Types of patients admitted: Men and women; adults, ages 18 and over; adolescents, ages 10 to 18.

Detoxification program offered?: 3 to 7 days' average duration; additional for methadone.

Inpatient treatment program—usual duration: 28-day average.

Inpatient treatment program—main features: For adults: 12-step approach; heavy family/"significant other" involvement; children's group. For adolescents: 30 to 45-day program duration; help from other recovering adolescents; 1-year aftercare.

Outpatient treatment program: 6-week intensive program for adults meeting 5 days/week plus weekends; up to 2 years of aftercare.

Family program or services—main features: Meetings 3 times a week, children's group meets 2 times a week; "Couples in Recovery" group sessions; panel sessions.

Charges for treatment: Inpatient adult program, total $12,000 to $14,000. Adolescent inpatient program, $500/day inclusive. Adult outpatient program, total $3,500.

Can health-care insurance pay for charges?: Yes. Approved for Medicare payment.

Accredited by: JCAH.

Aftercare programs: For inpatient programs, meetings 2 times a week for one year. For outpatient program, 2-year aftercare. No charge for aftercare.

Multiply addicted among entering patients: More than 50 percent; substances include alcohol, cocaine, heroin.

Recovery rates: Adult program founded only in 1986, and adolescent program founded only in 1987. Recovery rate data hence not currently available.

CareUnit Hospital of Orange
401 S. Tustin Ave.
Orange, CA 92666
714-633-9582

Headed by: Joe Hunt, Administrator.

Direct inquiries to: Crisis Response Office.

Capacity (no. of patients): 104.

Types of patients admitted: Men and women, ages 12 to 75. All admissions considered on an individual basis.

Detoxification program offered?: Yes; duration varies.

Inpatient treatment program—usual duration: Varies from patient to patient.

Inpatient treatment program—main features: Adolescent program; 12-step-based program; family participation program; special cocaine program.

Family program or services—main features: Family program for adults, held usually during last week of inpatient treatment.

Can health-care insurance pay for charges?: Yes.

Accredited by: State of California Health Department.

Aftercare programs: Upon completion of program, lifelong participation free of charge.

Merritt Peralta Chemical Dependency Recovery Hospital, Treatment Division

435 Hawthorne Ave.
Oakland, CA 94609-3081
415-652-7000
TTD-TTY phone for hearing-impaired: 415-658-2604

Headed by: Barbara Stern, Division Director.

Direct inquiries to: Barbara Stern.

Capacity (no. of patients): 44 inpatient beds.

Types of patients admitted: Men and women between the ages of 18 and 65 inclusive.

Detoxification program offered?: usual duration, 3 to 5 days; offers only nonacute detoxification followed by rehabilitation treatment.

Inpatient treatment program—usual duration: Treatment is considered to include a 28-day inpatient component and to extend for a full year.

Inpatient treatment program—main features: Medical/social model; emphasis on 12-step recovery programs; drug-free; treatment components include group process, counseling, education, exercise, and nutrition.

Outpatient treatment program: 56 days, usual duration; main features include meetings 4 times per week; philosophy and approach are the same as for inpatient program (medical/social model, 12-step recovery programs, etc.)

Family program or services—main features: Adjunct to the inpatient and outpatient offerings; included in cost of treatment; offers counseling and education specific to the needs of the family.

Charges for treatment: Inpatient, $267/day, $7,500 total. Outpatient, $2,700 total. Family program, no charge.

Can health-care insurance pay for charges?: Yes.

Accredited by: Licensed by the State of California as a Chemical Dependency Recovery Hospital (CDRH).

Aftercare programs: Features include group counseling, relapse groups, group process, social events. (Cost included in previous treatment charges.)

Multiply addicted among entering patients: 85 percent; substances include alcohol, cocaine, prescription drugs, marijuana. Multiphy addicted patients are approximately two-thirds male and one-third female; their background "crosses all socioeconomic classes."

Recovery-rates: 65 percent, 2 years (on a self-reporting basis). "Current efficacy rates are being studied by the University of California San Francisco."

Comments: "MPI CDRH is unique in the breadth of programs offered, including a Monitoring and Reentry Program, an inpatient treatment program for adult children of alcoholics and codependents ("Step Ahead"), a program for young children of alcoholics (ages 8 to 12, called "Kid's Connection")." High quality of treatment is augmented by the Research Department headed by David E. Smith, M.D., Donald R. Wesson, M.D., and Stephanie Brown, Ph.D., and the in-house Institute for Addiction Studies.

Sequoia Hospital, Alcohol and Drug Recovery Center
Whipple and Alamdea
Redwood City, CA 94062
415-367-5504 (answered 24 hours/day)

Headed by: Barry M. Rosen, M.D., Medical Director; Dori J. Dysland, Program Director.

Direct inquiries to: Inpatient, Martha Crowell, Admissions Coordinator. Outpatient, Sheila Alvarez, Outpatient Secretary.

Capacity (no. of patients): Inpatient, 27. Outpatient, 50.

Types of patients admitted: Men and women over age 17. Inpatient, must be chemically dependent. Outpatient, must be chemically dependent in the early to middle stages of dependence.

Detoxification program offered?: 5 to 7 days, usual duration.

Inpatient treatment program—usual duration: 3 to 5 weeks.

Treatment programs—main features: "Treatment individualized by combining modalities of inpatient treatment, day treatment, and outpatient treatment. Relapse Prevention included in all modalities and aftercare. Family treatment emphasis (including the Children's Program and Outpatient Codependency Program) is on addressing the physical, mental, emotional, and spiritual manifestations of disease and recovery. Out-Patient Relapse Group offered for people who have been through a treatment program or who have been working a 12-step program for a significant time period and have returned to drinking/drug use."

Outpatient treatment program: 3 to 6 months, usual duration.

Charges for treatment: Inpatient, $330/day, plus approximately $15/day in ancillary charges.

Can health-care insurance pay for charges?: Yes.

Accredited by: JCAH.

Aftercare programs: Aftercare Counselor appointments given for periodic progress review through first 9 months after treatment. Alumni welcomed to attend Monday night alumni meeting and many other regular Center meetings.

Comments: "Central to the Sequoia approach are the disease concept of addiction and the 12 steps of AA, NA, and CA. Patients become involved in frequent AA, NA, or CA meetings as a crucial part of their recovery."

Scripps Memorial Hospital, McDonald Center
9904 Genesee Ave.
La Jolla, CA 92037
619-458-4300

Headed by: Carl P. Bergstrom, Assistant Administrator/Program Director.

Direct inquiries to: Carl Bergstrom.

Capacity (no. of patients): 88.

Types of patients admitted: Men and women. Adults, any age. Adolescents, 11 to 18.

Detoxification program offered?: Yes.

Inpatient treatment program—usual duration: 32 days, approximate average.

Inpatient treatment program—main features: "6-day primary phase to address key detoxification and denial issues. Staff of 40-plus attending physicians. Adolescent program with school state-licensed for instruction."

Outpatient treatment program: 6-week program offered, with 4-hour meetings per evening. "The significant other attends the entire 6-week program. Some activities for family members are separate."

Family program or services—main features: Intensive 1-week program for families of adult patients. Adolescent patients—intensive 1-week program plus ongoing participation throughout the 6 weeks of treatment. Family members of outpatients attend sessions the same number of hours as the patient.

Charges for treatment: Inpatient, average $330/day, total $10,500. Outpatient, $80/day, total $2,400. Family programs, $810 all-inclusive charge for entire family for 5-day program.

Can health-care insurance pay for charges?: Yes. Approved for payment by Medicare.

Accredited by: JCAH. State of California, Department of Health Services.

Aftercare programs: 3 months of structured aftercare (cost included in treatment fees).

Recovery rates: Follow-up studies being implemented in 1988.

St. Helena Hospital and Health Center, Alcohol and Chemical Recovery Program

650 Sanitarium Rd.
Deer Park, CA 94576
707-963-6204

Headed by: Lee A. Hamilton, Program Director.
Direct inquiries to: Admissions staff.
Capacity (no. of patients): 22.
Types of patients admitted: Men and women ages 18 and older.
Detoxification program offered?: 1 to 5 days, usual duration.
Inpatient treatment program—usual duration: 28 days.
Inpatient treatment program—main features: "Disease model of chemical dependency . . . family disease model . . . based on philosophy of the 12-step programs of AA and NA."

Outpatient treatment program: Phase I: attendance for 6 weeks at sessions held 4 times per week. Phase II: 12 months of ongoing treatment.

Family program or services—main features: Education, group, and family therapy. 5 days, usual duration.

Charges for treatment: Inpatient, $280/day, $8,200 total. Outpatient, $90/day, $2,450 total. Family program, no cost.

Can health-care insurance pay for charges?: Yes. Approved for payment by Medicare.

Accredited by: JCAH. State of California.

Aftercare programs: Group therapy once a week for 12 months. (Cost included in prior treatment fees.)

Multiply addicted among entering patients: 40 to 50 percent; substances include alcohol, cocaine, marijuana; multiply addicted tend to be "younger, single, white."

Recovery rates: 72 percent, 1 year (based on self-report of those former patients who responded to 12-month surveys).

COLORADO

AMI Saint Luke's Hospital, ARU (Addiction Recovery Unit)
601 E. 19th Ave.
Denver, CO 80203
303-869-2280

Headed by: William P. Kent, Director of Addiction Recovery Units.

Direct inquiries to: William P. Kent.

Types of patients admitted: Men and women; adults, in Adult ARU; adolescents of ages 13 to 18, in Adolescent ARU.

Detoxification program offered?: Yes.

Inpatient treatment program—main features: Includes medical assessment and evaluation, individual and group therapy, personalized family therapy program, employer-employee back-to-work conference, introduction to AA-NA-CA support groups.

Outpatient treatment program: 6-week program with four 3-hour evening meetings on weeknights and support-group meetings on weekends. Features similar to that of the inpatient program. Day outpatient programs for adults or adolescents also offered.

Additional offerings of the Evening Outpatient Program are provided at an alternative location in Englewood, Colorado (Healthcare Plaza-Centennial, 14200 E. Arapahoe Rd., Englewood). This is an 8-week program with three 3-hour evening meetings on weeknights.

Family program or services—main features: For inpatient programs, offers Monday through Friday family program offerings; features of family program include individual and group therapy, lectures, introduction to Al-Anon and Adult Children of Alcoholics.

Charges for treatment: Inpatient adult unit, $338/day; detox additional $136/day; family week, $320 up to two people. Inpatient adolescent unit, $360/day; other fees same as adults'. Evening outpatient program, $65 per 3-hour session.

Can health-care insurance pay for charges?: Yes.

Accredited by: JCAH. State of Colorado, Department of Health, Drug and Alcohol Abuse Division.

Aftercare programs: Relapse Prevention Support Program, 12-month recommended length; offers weekly meetings open to adults and adolescents. Designed to complement participation in AA, NA, and CA.

Comments: AMI Saint Luke's Hospital ARU is part of the AMI Rocky Mountain Healthcare System. Additional AMI-run Addiction Recovery Units are in other Colorado locations as follows:

Aspen—ARU Aspen, P.O. Box 7917, Aspen, CO 81612, phone 303-920-2107.

Durango—ARU Durango, 3801 N. Main Ave., Durango, CO 81301, phone 303-259-6151.

Grand Junction—ARU Grand Junction, 436 S. Seventh St., Grand Junction, CO 81501, phone 303-245-4213.

CONNECTICUT

Greenwich Hospital, Alcoholism Recovery Center
Perryridge Rd., Rm. 587 North
Greenwich, CT 06830
203-863-3278

Headed by: Philip Hurley, Director.

Direct inquiries to: Philip Hurley.

Capacity (no. of patients): 16.

Types of patients admitted: Men and women, ages 18 and up.

Detoxification program offered?: Yes, as part of inpatient program.

Inpatient treatment program—usual duration: 28 days (including detoxification, if necessary).

Inpatient treatment program—main features: "1. Individualized treatment plan; 2. group therapy daily; 3. family sessions with counselor."

Outpatient treatment program: Being developed; features one-on-one therapy for patients and weekly family and group therapy.

Family program or services—main features: Individual and family sessions with counselor and group meetings twice a week.

Charges for treatment: Inpatient, $8,800 total. Outpatient, $42.50/hr. visit. Family program—inpatients, no charge; outpatients, $11/group.

Can health-care insurance pay for charges?: Yes. Approved for payment by Medicare and Medicaid.

Accredited by: JCAH. State of Connecticut.

Aftercare programs: Weekly group meetings with 24-week commitment; cost, $11/visit.

Multiply addicted among entering patients: 33 percent; substances include cocaine, marijuana, tranquilizers.

Recovery rates: "We have been able to follow up about 50 percent of our patients. About 75 percent of these patients are sober at 2 years following discharge. Three-fourths of these patients have maintained complete abstinence; one-fourth have had one to three short relapses followed by abstinence."

Comments: Founded in 1981; has treated 1,500 patients since it began.

High Watch Farm

P.O. Box 206, Carter Rd.
Kent, CT 06757
203-927-3772

Headed by: J. Thompson Steel, Executive Director.

Direct inquiries to: J. Thompson Steel.

Capacity (no. of patients): Approximately 42.

Types of patients admitted: Men and women age 18 and over who are physically able to participate in all activities. New guests must have an AA sponsor, and sponsors are asked to recommend only guests serious about the AA program and not under the influence of alcohol or drugs.

Detoxification program offered?: No.

In-residence program—usual duration: Minimum of 2 weeks; "all are encouraged to stay longer."

In-residence program—main features: "Total orientation in the AA program, either as an introduction or renewal. . . . High Watch is neither a hospital nor a sanitorium; it does not accept guests who require hospitalization. . . . The fundamental program of High Watch is to provide a secluded atmosphere, essential to complete mental and physical relaxation and repose; to offer real help in forming a new philosophy and planning a new and more productive way of life—without dependence on alcohol. . . . A total of six AA meetings are held at the Farm each week. . . . Members of the permanent staff are qualified by experience and training to assist in the solution of alcohol-related problems and are available to guests at all times. . . ."

Charges for residence: $40/day, $250/week.

Can health-care insurance pay for charges?: No.

Accredited by: Licensed by State of Connecticut Department of Health Services.

Aftercare programs: AA participation.

Multiply addicted among entering guests: 50 percent; substances include alcohol, pot, cocaine, pills, heroin.

Comments: High Watch was established in 1939 by very early leading members of AA, with the aid and encouragement of Bill W., A.A. cofounder. From the start it has been operated as a retreat for anyone who feels he or she might have a problem with alcohol, and thousands of men and women from all walks of life have found help there. It is located on a 200-acre tract of high, wooded hills. Organized as a nonprofit corporation, its official name is The Ministry of the High Watch, Inc.

Silver Hill Foundation, Inc., Alcohol and Substance Abuse Service

P.O. Box 1177, 208 Valley Rd.
New Canaan, CT 06840
203-966-3561, ext. 308, 309

Headed by: Michael Sheehy, M.D., Medical and Executive Director. Carlotta Schuster, M.D., Chief, Alcohol and Substance Abuse Service.

Direct inquiries to: Carol Fahn, Admissions Office.

Capacity (no. of patients): 22, Substance Abuse Unit; 77, entire hospital.

Types of patients admitted: Equal numbers of men and women patients, ages 22 to 100. Adolescents admitted for substance abuse treatment in the Adolescent and Young Adult Service. "Patients referred from all over the world."

Detoxification program offered?: Yes; usual duration, by substance abused: alcohol, 3 to 10 days; sedatives, 2 to 4 weeks; cocaine, no detoxification; opoids, 21 days.

Inpatient treatment program—usual duration: 28 days; patients involved in rehabilitation while detoxifying. Advise 2 weeks drug-free prior to discharge.

Inpatient treatment program—main features: Psychiatric and 12-step orientation. Patients treated by physicians, psychologists, and counselors in team approach. Dual diagnoses treated when present.

Family program or services—main features: Education in groups and individual family counseling; 4-day program.

Charges for treatment: $12,000 total (4 weeks). Family program, $25/session.

Can health-care insurance pay for charges?: Yes. Approved for payment by Medicare.

Accredited by: JCAH. State of Connecticut.

Aftercare programs: 3-month aftercare program offered, for a charge of $588.

Multiply addicted among entering patients: 50 percent; substances abused include alcohol, cocaine, heroin, prescription benzodiazepines (tranquilizers), prescription narcotics. Dually addicted patients are of both sexes, in an age range of about 22 to 35. Singly addicted have an age range of about 20 to 100.

Comments: Silver Hill is a nonprofit psychiatric hospital established in 1931. It maintains a ratio of six patients to each physician. The cost of individual psychotherapy 3 times each week is included in weekly charges.

University of Connecticut Health Center, Alcohol and Drug Abuse Treatment Center

263 Farmington Ave.
Farmington, CT 06032
203-679-3422

Headed by: Dr. Ronald Kadden, Director.

Direct inquiries to: Admissions Director.

Capacity (no. of patients): 20.

Types of patients admitted: Men and women over age 17 who are addicted to any substances except heroin/methadone.

Detoxification program offered?: Only as part of rehabilitation.

Inpatient treatment program—usual duration: 21 days (including detoxification).

Inpatient treatment program—main features: "(a) Treatment of medical and psychiatric complications; (b) development of coping skills required for abstinence; (c) aftercare planning."

Outpatient treatment program: 38 days of aftercare following inpatient program; emphasizes continued development of coping skills.

Family program or services—main features: One day, during inpatient stay; weekly, in outpatient phase.

Charges for treatment: inpatient, $320/day, $8,000 to $10,000 total. Outpatient, $110/day, $4,180 total. Family program, no charge.

Can health-care insurance pay for charges?: Yes. Approved for payment by Medicare and Medicaid.

Accredited by: JCAH; State of Connecticut Department of Health.

Aftercare programs: 38 days' outpatient care, or group therapy available at $25 per group.

Multiply addicted among entering patients: 40 percent; substances include alcohol, cocaine, marijuana. Younger patients tend to be more often dually addicted or cocaine-addicted; older patients more often tend to be only alcohol-addicted. No differences in multiply addicted patterns between men and women patients.

Recovery rates: Emphasize percentages *completely abstinent*— 45 percent, 6 months; 30 percent, 1 year. "75 to 80 percent report improvements in psychosocial functioning. Additional 45 percent report *improvement* in drinking/drug problems. Total abstinent + improved = 30% + 45% = 75%."

DELAWARE

Recovery Center of Delaware
P.O. Box 546
Delaware City, DE 19706
302-836-1200

Headed by: John W. Moody, Project Director.
Direct inquiries to: Beverly Lynch; Cathy Flanders.
Capacity (no. of patients): 60.
Types of patients admitted: Men and women over age 17 who have substance abuse problems.
Detoxification program offered?: Duration, 3 to 7 days; for opiates, 7 to 10 days.
Inpatient treatment program—usual duration: 28 days.

Charges for treatment: $135/day; $3,780 total

Can health-care insurance pay for charges?: Yes.

Accredited by: JCAH; State of Delaware Division of Alcohol, Drug Abuse, and Mental Health.

Multiply addicted among entering patients: 90 percent; substances include cocaine, marijuana, speed.

Recovery rates: 67 percent, 6 months.

DISTRICT OF COLUMBIA METROPOLITAN AREA

Arlington Hospital Addiction Treatment Programs
1701 North George Mason Dr.
Arlington, VA 22205
703-558-6536

Headed by: Kitty Harold, M.S.W., R.N., C.S.A.C., Program Director.

Direct inquiries to: Eileen Barker.

Capacity (no. of patients): 65 beds.

Types of patients admitted: Men and women ages 12 and up.

Detoxification program offered?: 3 to 5 days, duration.

Inpatient treatment program—usual duration: 21 days.

Inpatient treatment program—main features: "Chronic disease rehabilitation model of addiction treatment with emphasis upon intensive education about physiogenetic nature of illness"; includes "strong self-diagnosis, task-group, and therapeutic-community components, AA/NA."

Outpatient treatment program: aggregate 21 days, usual duration; main features include Monday, Wednesday, Friday sessions, abstinence criteria, other features same as those of inpatient program.

Family program or services—main features: "Strong educational emphasis with combined group counseling."

Charges for treatment: Inpatient, $340/day, $8,500 to $9,500 total. Outpatient, $52/day, $1,207 total. Family program, no charge.

Can health-care insurance pay for charges?: Yes. Approved for payment by Medicare, Medicaid.

Accredited by: JCAH; State of Virginia.

Aftercare programs: Two sessions/week for 15 weeks; no charge.

Multiply addicted among entering patients: 70 percent; substances include sedatives, cocaine, marijuana. Multiple addiction most frequent among younger adult addicts, ages 19 to 30. Of outpatient program entrants, most are multiply addicted.

Recovery rates: Among patients completing both the inpatient program and aftercare: 88 percent, 1 year; 82 percent, 2 years.

Comments: "This program uses the National Council on Alcoholism definition of addiction with a firm philosophy rooted in the physiogenetic basis of the disease with psychosocial contributants of causation." It has "treatment focuses of intensive education, self-diagnosis, self-responsibility for treatment, and use of 12-step recovery plans."

Seton House at Providence Hospital
1053 Buchanan St., N.E.
Washington, DC 20017
202-269-7777

Types of patients admitted: Men and women.

Types of treatment offered: Inpatient detoxification and rehabilitation program. Outpatient rehabilitation program. Aftercare and follow-up services.

Accredited by: JCAH.

FLORIDA

Hanley-Hazelden Center at St. Mary's
1043 45th St.
West Palm Beach, FL 33407
305-848-1666

Direct inquiries to: Admissions Office.

Types of patients admitted: Men and women.

Detoxification program offered?: Yes.

Inpatient treatment program—usual duration: Approximately 28 days. Optional assessment services offer initial evaluation by a diagnostic team for 5 to 7 days, followed by referral to most appropriate type of treatment.

Treatment programs—main features: Modeled after the renowned Hazelden Primary Rehabilitation Center in Minnesota and operated by the Hazelden Rehabilitation Services. Offers a full range of assessment, treatment, aftercare, and family services. "Treatment based on AA and Al-Anon philosophy. Each person works with a multidisciplinary treatment team to develop an individualized treatment plan."

Outpatient treatment program: Duration, approximately 5 weeks.

Can health-care insurance pay for charges?: Yes.

Accredited by: JCAH.

GEORGIA

Charter Peachford Hospital, Addictive Disease Services
2151 Peachford Rd.
Atlanta, GA 30338
404-455-3200

Headed by: Larry Ashley, Administrator.

Direct inquiries to: Addictive Disease Services Service Director.

Capacity (no. of patients): 63, rehabilitation; 12, detoxification.

Types of patients admitted: Men and women over age 17.

Detoxification program offered?: 2½ days, usual duration.

Inpatient treatment program—usual duration: 28 days.

Inpatient treatment program—main features: 12-step program emphasis, educational component, group therapy, aftercare.

Outpatient treatment program: Aggregate 24 days, usual duration; same features as inpatient program.

Family program or services—main features: Twelve-step program emphasis, educational component.

Can health-care insurance pay for charges?: Yes. Approved for payment by Medicare.

Accredited by: JCAH; State of Georgia Department of Human Resources.

Aftercare programs: Approximately 2 years' duration; no charge.

Ridgeview Institute; Adult Chemical Dependence Program, Adolescent Chemical Dependence Program, Health-Care Professionals Program
3995 S. Cobb Dr.

Smyrna, GA 30080
404-434-4567

Headed by: Robert Fink, Chief Executive Officer.
Direct inquiries to: Dean Harrell, M.D., Program Coordinator.
Capacity (no. of patients): 62.

Types of patients admitted: Men and women adults (about seven of ten inpatients are men); men and women adolescents. Majority of patients in its specialized program for health professionals are M.D.s, R.N.s, D.D.s, and pharmacists.

Detoxification program offered?: Typical duration, 5 days. Each patient assessed; duration varies individually.

Inpatient treatment program—usual duration: Approximately 30 days in regular adult program, depending on severity of the disease.

Inpatient treatment program—main features: "Essentially, our goal is detox and stabilization during the first 2 weeks. We concentrate heavily on group therapy and AA/NA 12-step programs. We have a strong activity therapy program."

Outpatient treatment program: Follows inpatient treatment for 1 month; features "good continuity of care from inpatient to outpatient treatment."

Family program or services—main features: Family involved with the patient's treatment from day 1; includes a 5-day Family Workshop and Co-Dependence Program.

Charges for treatment: Inpatient, $325/day (plus possible fees for physician services, tests, etc.). Outpatient, approximately $92/day (being reduced). Family program, $125/family member.

Can health-care insurance pay for charges?: Yes. Approved for payment by Medicare.

Accredited by: JCAH; State of Georgia Department of Human Resources.

Aftercare programs: Offerings available without charge: (1) two aftercare group meetings per week for 2 years; (2) two couples aftercare meetings per week for 2 years; (3) Alumni Association sponsoring many activities with an annual 4-day retreat in May; (4) special individual liaison with staff members.

Health-Care Professionals Program—main features: Under way for the past 11 years. Minimum stay, 4 months. Phase I, 29-day inpatient treatment. Phase II, 30-day outpatient day program with residence and activities in halfway house system. Phase III, "mirror-imaging phase," 2-month assignment to one of the twenty-one

Atlanta metropolitan area Alcohol and Drug Treatment Centers counseling other alcoholics/addicts in their first few days of recovery. Follow-up for minimum of 2 years by the impaired professionals programs in the various states.

Multiply addicted among entering patients: 90 percent. Among patients in health-care professionals program, main substances abused include the following: for physicians, prescription medications, alcohol, various other substances; for nurses, Demerol, alcohol; for pharmacists, Percodan, alcohol.

Recovery rates: Results achieved improve "the longer a patient remains in treatment, and the greater the family support."

HAWAII

Castle Medical Center, Castle Alcohol and Addictions Program
640 Ulukahiki St.
Kailua, HI 96734-9982
808-263-4429

Headed by: Tina Dameron, Director.
Direct inquiries to: Karen Tam (phone 263-5326).
Capacity (no. of patients): 20.
Types of patients admitted: Men and women over age 12.
Detoxification program offered?: Average duration, 3½ days.
Inpatient treatment program—usual duration: 21 to 28 days.

Inpatient treatment program—main features: "Social therapeutic model; includes groups, lectures, individual counseling, marriage and family counseling, family program, daily AA or NA meetings, exercise program, nutrition counseling."

Outpatient treatment program: Duration, meetings 3 nights per week for 8 weeks plus aftercare. Main features include individual and group counseling, educational experiences about addiction and related topics. Permits patient to continue school or work and still attend treatment.

Family program or services—main features: 5-day duration, educational and supportive sessions, family therapy. Followed by 2-year family aftercare.

Charges for treatment: Inpatient, $300/day. Outpatient, $225/week. Family program, $100/family member (for 5-day sessions).
Can health-care insurance pay for charges?: Yes.
Accredited by: JCAH.

Aftercare programs: Weekly meeting for a minimum of 3 months.

Multiply addicted among entering patients: 70 percent; substances include alcohol, cocaine, heroin, marijuana, prescription drugs, plus addictions to eating disorders.

Recovery-rates: 66 percent, 1 year.

ILLINOIS

Addiction Recovery of Chicago
1776 Moon Lake Blvd.
Hoffman Estates, IL 60194
312-882-0070

Headed by: Carole J. Chandler, Executive Director.

Direct inquiries to: Ann F. Hamblet, Marketing Director.

Capacity (no. of patients): 85.

Types of patients admitted: Adult men and women over age 18; adolescent men and women, ages 12 to 18.

Detoxification program offered?: Duration, 1 to 5 days.

Inpatient treatment program—usual duration: Adults, 28 to 35 days. Adolescents, 42 to 56 days.

Inpatient treatment program—main features: "Focus on recovery from the disease of addiction through involvement in a 12-step program and life-style change. Group, individual, and family therapy as well as lectures, 12-step meetings, and therapeutic workshops are utilized."

Outpatient treatment program: Duration varies. Main features include Continuing Care for 6 months, codependency groups, ACOA groups, individual and family therapy, evening outpatient and day outpatient sessions.

Family program or services—main features: 4-day family recovery program; offers sessions of various types, including multi-family group sessions, "significant other" group sessions, and educational sessions.

Accredited by: JCAH; State of Illinois, Department of Alcoholism and Substance Abuse, Department of Public Health.

Aftercare programs: Cost, $30/group session, $45/individual session.

Multiply addicted among entering patients: 75 percent; substances include "primarily cocaine, alcohol, and marijuana" and various other mood-altering chemicals.

Recovery rates: Outcome studies currently being conducted.

Parkside Lodge of Champaign/Urbana, Women's Program
809-A West Church St.
Champaign, IL 61820
217-398-8616

Headed by: Sandra K. Benfield, Program Director.
Direct inquiries to: Sandra K. Benfield.
Capacity (no. of patients): 20.
Types of patients admitted: Women over age 18 suffering from alcohol and/or substance abuse, dual diagnoses, eating disorders.
Detoxification program offered?: No.
Inpatient treatment program—usual duration: 90 days.
Inpatient treatment program—main features: "Abstinence from addictive substances, AA/NA/Overeaters Anonymous foundation, practice follows primary focus on women's issues."
Family program or services—main features: No family program.
Charges for treatment: Inpatient, $155/day, total $13,950.
Can health-care insurance pay for charges?: Yes.
Accredited by: JCAH; State of Illinois Department of Public Health, Department of Alcohol and Substance Abuse.
Multiply addicted among entering patients: 98 percent; addictions include alcohol, multiple-drug, eating disorders (women patients with average age 32).
Recovery rates: 72 percent, 1 year.

INDIANA

Fairbanks Hospital
8102 Clearvista Parkway
Indianapolis, IN 46256
317-849-8222

Headed by: Thomas W. Brink, President/Administrator.
Direct inquiries to: Admissions Office.
Capacity (no. of patients): 96.
Types of patients admitted: Men and women age 12 and up

(children under age 12 admitted on acceptance by adolescent treatment team); separate twenty-eight-bed unit for inpatient adolescents.

Detoxification program offered?: Duration, 1 to 5 days.

Inpatient treatment program—usual duration: 1 to 24 days' rehabilitation for adults.

Inpatient treatment program—main features: "Flexcare" offered each patient, in which detoxification, inpatient, and outpatient care are tailored to individual needs with concurrence of the clinical staff. Inpatient rehabilitation program features include introduction to early steps of 12-step programs, AA, NA; AA/NA meetings attendance; group process meetings; activity therapy and diet therapy as appropriate; family week program; planning discharge/continuing care for patient and family. For adolescents, full-time teacher on staff for continued schooling.

Outpatient treatment program: Features include addiction, psychiatric, and social evaluation; individual, group, family, and marital therapy.

Family program or services—main features: Family week, addiction education in inpatient program; family and marital therapy in outpatient program.

Charges for treatment: Adults—detoxification, $197/day plus miscellaneous fees (average total $1,310); inpatient rehabilitation, $180/day plus miscellaneous fees (average total $4,370). Adolescents—detoxification and inpatient rehabilitation, $199/day plus miscellaneous fees (average total $8,200). Outpatient—group therapy sessions, $25/hour; individual counseling, $50/hour; family or marital therapy, $60/hour; psychiatric evaluation, $90/hour.

Can health-care insurance pay for charges?: Yes. Approved for payment by Medicare.

Accredited by: JCAH; State of Indiana, licensed by Department of Mental Health, certified by Division of Addiction Services.

Aftercare programs: Weekly meetings each at least 90 minutes long for $5/session cost, carried out according to individual treatment plans.

Multiply addicted among entering patients: 60 percent, inpatient entrants; substances abused "too many to list"; 30 %, outpatient entrants.

Recovery rates: 54 percent, 6 months; 48 percent, 1 year. Statistics represent "preliminary data from outcome studies conducted in 1986 and 1987 on 600 patients."

IOWA

Iowa Methodist Medical Center, Powell III Chemical Dependency Center

1200 Pleasant St.
Des Moines, IA 50308
515-283-6454; toll-free, 1-800-443-SOBR (inside Iowa),
1-800-523-SOBR (outside Iowa)

Headed by: Kathy Stone, Director.
Direct inquiries to: Kathy Stone.
Capacity (no. of patients): 40 beds inpatient, average 30 patients outpatient, 20 men in extended care facility residence.
Types of patients admitted: Men and women over age 18.
Detoxification program offered?: Duration up to 5 days, as part of total program.
Inpatient treatment program—usual duration: 28 to 30 days.
Inpatient treatment program—main features: Abstinence model, 12-step base, interdisciplinary treatment team, strong family involvement.
Outpatient treatment program: Aggregate duration, 25 days; main features include fully structured sessions, concurrent family involvement, philosophy same as for inpatient program.
Family program or services—main features: Integrated into treatment. Also offer free addiction education and intervention training; codependency program; adult children of alcoholics treatment.
Charges for treatment: Inpatient, $300/day, $8,400 total. Outpatient, $108/day, $2,700 total. Family program, no charge.
Can health-care insurance pay for charges?: Yes.
Accredited by: JCAH.
Aftercare programs: Continuing care offerings include post-treatment counseling, growth groups, ongoing follow-up, structured residential extended-care program for men. Also offer Relapse Treatment Program, an outpatient program for those with a history of relapse; includes 24 hours of structured therapy, one-on-one counseling, growth-group participation.
Multiply addicted among entering patients: 60 percent; substances include alcohol, marijuana, cocaine, amphetamines, benzodiazepines, opiates.

Recovery rates: 70 percent, 1 year.

Comments: This is the first private program of its kind in Iowa, opened in 1973. It offers a full range of chemical dependency services and is frequently a model for new programs in the state.

KANSAS

Atchison Valley Hope, Alcoholism and Drug Treatment Center
Box 312
Atchison, KS 66002
913-367-1618

Headed by: David Ketter, Program Director.

Direct inquiries to: David Ketter.

Capacity (no. of patients): 65.

Types of patients admitted: Men and women ages 15 and older; facilities are handicapped-accessible.

Detoxification program offered?: Usual duration, 3 days.

Inpatient treatment program—usual duration: 27 days.

Inpatient treatment program—main features: AA orientation, psychological adjustment, physical health, spirituality.

Outpatient treatment program: Ten sessions spread over a 2-month period.

Family program or services—main features: Marital and family therapy included in inpatient treatment.

Charges for treatment: Inpatient, $112/day, total $3,500.

Can health-care insurance pay for charges?: Yes.

Accredited by: JCAH; State of Kansas, Alcohol and Drug Abuse Services.

Aftercare programs: Twenty-seven sessions in 12 months; cost, $420; includes individual and group therapy, family therapy.

Multiply addicted among entering patients: 25 prcent; substances include cocaine, pot, speed, narcotics, sedatives.

Recovery rates: Alcoholic admissions, 66 percent, 1 year; drug-dependent admissions, 58 percent, 1 year; combined, 62 percent, 1 year.

Comments: Atchison Valley Hope is part of the nonprofit Valley Hope Association, which began with its center in Norton, Kansas (see following entry) in 1967 and now operates a total of seven inpatient treatment facilities and four outpatient centers in Kansas, Nebraska, Missouri, Oklahoma, and Arizona.

Norton Valley Hope, Alcoholism and Drug Treatment Center
Box 510
Norton, KS 67654
913-877-5101

Headed by: Kenneth C. Gregoire, Ph.D., Program Director.
Direct inquiries to: Kenneth C. Gregoire.
Capacity (no. of patients): 72.
Types of patients admitted: Men and women ages 15 and older.
Detoxification program offered?: Usual duration, 3 days.
Inpatient treatment program—usual duration: 27 days.
Inpatient treatment program—main features: "Abstinence-oriented; spiritually based; warm, caring environment; special emphasis on marital counseling; open, trusting treatment environment."
Family program or services—main features: "Marital group therapy, family group therapy, family participation during 30 days of treatment, and a family program on weekends."
Charges for treatment: Inpatient, $112/day.
Can health-care insurance pay for charges?: Yes.
Accredited by: JCAH; State of Kansas.
Aftercare programs: Support group sessions ($17.50/session single, $25.00/session couples), individual counseling ($50.00/hour).
Multiply addicted among entering patients: 50 percent.
Comments: Norton Valley Hope is part of the nonprofit Valley Hope Association, which began with this center in 1967 and now operates a total of seven inpatient treatment facilities and four outpatient centers in Kansas, Nebraska, Missouri, Oklahoma, and Arizona.

St. John's Hospital, Chemical Dependency Treatment Center
139 N. Penn
Salina, KS 67401
Toll-free, 1-800-432-0678 (in Kansas)
1-800-251-0026 (outside Kansas)

Other Program Locations: Kansas: Arkansas City, Beloit, Concordia, Dodge City, Ellsworth, Garden City, Great Bend, Hays, Junction City, Kansas City, Larned, Manhattan, Wichita (two locations). *Oklahoma:* Lawton, Norman, Oklahoma City.
Phone toll-free numbers listed for details of adult programs at

the Salina and other locations. Entry information for the St. John's Hospital Center Adolescent Treatment Unit follows.

Adolescent Treatment Unit, St. John's Hospital Chemical Dependency Treatment Center
1646 N. Ninth St.
Salina, KS 67401
913-825-7103

Headed by: Judy J. Arpin, C.A.D.C., Program Coordinator.
Direct inquiries to: Judy J. Arpin.
Capacity (no. of patients): 30.
Types of patients admitted: Men and women ages 12 to 18 and age 19 if appropriate for adolescent treatment.
Detoxification program offered?: No.
Inpatient treatment program—usual duration: 10-day evaluation, 35-day rehabilitation.
Inpatient treatment program—main features: "Family-oriented program with focus on 12-step recovery program."
Family program or services—main features: 5-day family-week program, which includes education and family therapy (for family members as well as patients).
Charges for treatment: Inpatient, $215/day, $9,800 total.
Can health-care insurance pay for charges?: Yes.
Accredited by: JCAH; State of Kansas.
Aftercare programs: 12-week aftercare at no cost to patients or families upon completion of treatment.

LOUISIANA

Silkworth Center
2414 Bunker Hill Dr.
Baton Rouge, LA 70808
504-928-6633

Headed by: David James, C.S.A.C., Service Director.
Direct inquiries to: David James.
Capacity (no. of patients): 30 inpatient.
Types of patients admitted: Men and women ages 17 and above who are chemically dependent.
Detoxification program offered?: Usual duration, 3 to 5 days.

Inpatient treatment program—usual duration: Individualized.

Inpatient treatment program—main features: "Comprehensive evaluation, education, and detoxification; utilization of 12-step self-help programs; multidisciplinary staff involvement; combination inpatient and outpatient treatment structure; aftercare."

Outpatient treatment program: Aggregate duration, 20 days. Main features include individualized treatment planning; specialized relapse focus; flexible inpatient and outpatient modalities.

Family program or services—main features: Family support group, family week, aftercare recommendations.

Can health-care insurance pay for charges?: Yes. Approved for payment by Medicare.

Accredited by: JCAH; State of Louisiana.

Aftercare programs: Special focus groups, counselor-led.

Multiply addicted among entering patients: 65 percent among inpatient entrants, 50 percent among outpatient entrants; substances include alcohol, cocaine, amphetamines, barbiturates, narcotics, hallucinogens.

MAINE

Eastern Maine Medical Center, Chemical Dependency Institute
489 State St.
Bangor, ME 04401
207-945-7272

Types of patients admitted: Adult and adolescent men and women.

Types of treatment offered: Detoxification/evaluation, 1 to 5 days' duration. Inpatient rehabilitation program running approximately 21 days. Family and children's counseling. Aftercare services. Nonresidential rehabilitation program.

Accredited by: JCAH; licensed by State of Maine Office of Alcoholism and Drug Abuse Prevention.

MARYLAND

Sheppard Pratt Hospital, Alcoholism/Chemical Dependency Unit
6501 N. Charles St., P.O. Box 6815
Baltimore, MD 21285-6815

301-823-8200, ext. 2589

Headed by: Penelope Ziegler, M.D.
Direct inquiries to: John Beemer, Program Coordinator.
Capacity (no. of patients): 15.
Types of patients admitted: Men and women ages 18 and up.
Detoxification program offered?: Yes.
Inpatient treatment program—usual duration: 30 days.

Inpatient treatment program—main features: "Emphasis on self-detoxification; addiction as a disease model; family treatment, addiction education; group living/work; individual counseling; full-time M.D., social worker, certified counselors on staff; tenets of AA/NA followed; relapse prevention planning; relaxation treatment; communication training."

Outpatient treatment program: Duration open-ended; main features include intake assessment and evaluation; group and individual treatment; family treatment available; addiction education.

Family program or services—main features: Group and individual sessions.

Charges for treatment: $291/day, total $11,730 and up.

Can health-care insurance pay for charges?: Yes. Approved for payment by Medicare.

Accredited by: JCAH.

Aftercare programs: Transition group sessions, 8 weeks (no charge). Outpatient addiction group sessions, led by cotherapists; $50/group.

Multiply addicted among entering patients: Inpatient entrants: 90 percent; substances include cocaine, heroin, marijuana, PCP (phencyclidine hydrochloride, an illegal street drug), benzodiazepines, narcotics, hallucinogens; patients of ages 18 to 60 have high percentages dually addicted, patients of ages 60 to 86 have high percentages singly addicted to alcohol or prescription drugs.

Recovery rates: 78 percent, 6 months; 68 percent, 1 year; 40 percent, 3 years ("no firm data").

MASSACHUSETTS

AdCare Hospital of Worcester
107 Lincoln St.
Worcester, MA 01605

617-799-9000, ext. 294

Headed by: David W. Hillis, President.
Direct inquiries to: Patrice M. Muchowski, Sc.D.
Capacity (no. of patients): 88 beds (soon will be 114).
Types of patients admitted: Men and women ages 18 and up.
Detoxification program offered?: Yes.
Inpatient treatment program—usual duration: Varies according to individual needs.
Inpatient treatment program—main features: "Inpatient treatment is designed by multidisciplinary treatment team. Program is based on AA. Patients participate in individual and group counseling; AA, NA, or CA meetings; and educational and skills training groups."
Outpatient treatment program: Day treatment option. Eating disorders program.
Family program or services—main features: Individual family sessions, family support group, family educational day; family program is free.
Charges for treatment: Inpatient, $308.06/day. Outpatient, $40/session. Family program, no charge.
Can health-care insurance pay for charges?: Yes.
Accredited by: JCAH.

McLean Hospital, Alcohol and Drug Abuse Treatment Center
115 Mill St.
Belmont, MA 02178
617-855-2781

Headed by: Roger D. Weiss, M.D., Director.
Direct inquiries to: Phone 855-2781.
Capacity (no. of patients): 22.
Types of patients admitted: Men and women ages 18 and over, voluntarily admitted, abusing alcohol or prescription or illicit drugs.
Detoxification program offered?: Yes.
Inpatient treatment program—usual duration: Combined detoxification/rehabilitation; approximately 28 days.
Inpatient treatment program—main features: "Comprehensive, individualized treatment program. Primary substance abusers and dual-diagnosis patients are welcome. Each patient gets individual, medical, psychiatric, family, and vocational evaluations in addi-

tion to an abstinence-oriented, 12-step disease-model program. Posthospital residential treatment available on the grounds and nearby."

Outpatient treatment program: Indefinite duration. Main features include "assessment, intervention, short-term educational and treatment program followed by longer-term group program. Groups available for A.C.O.A.s and relatives or friends of substance abusers."

Family program or services—main features: "Family program available for both inpatients and outpatients. For outpatients, program available whether or not the addicted relative is interested in treatment."

Charges for treatment: Inpatient, $406/day. Outpatient, charges vary by outpatient group. Family program, $80/family member for four sessions of 4 hours each.

Can health-care insurance pay for charges?: Yes. Approved for payment by Medicare.

Accredited by: JCAH; licensed by Commonwealth of Massachusetts, Departments of Mental Health, Public Health.

Aftercare programs: "Transitional program followed by long-term group program; drop-in center and residential treatment also available." Cost, transitional group, $33.

Multiply addicted among entering patients: Inpatient entrants, 60 percent (approximate percentages of patients abusing each substance are 40 percent, alcohol; 30 percent, cocaine; 20 percent, opiates; 10 percent, sedatives/hypnotics). Multiply addicted among outpatient entrants, percentage "varies greatly."

Recovery rates: 83 percent, 6 months; 72 percent, 1 year.

Comments: "McLean is a teaching hospital of Harvard Medical School and affiliated with Massachusetts General Hospital. Therefore, the hospital is able to deliver state-of-the-art treatment, with access to great resources. A great deal of research has emanated from McLean as well."

MICHIGAN

Brighton Hospital
12851 East Grand River
Brighton, MI 48116
313-227-1211

Headed by: Ivan C. Harner, President.
Direct inquiries to: Community Relations Department.
Capacity (no. of patients): 63.
Types of patients admitted: Men and women ages 18 and up. ("A unit for young adults, ages 13 to 23, will open in 1990.")
Detoxification program offered?: Usual duration, 1 to 3 days.
Inpatient treatment program—usual duration: 21 days ("Typical hospitalization is 21 days, which includes detox.").

Inpatient treatment program—main features: "Detoxification; individual counseling; group therapy; intensive patient education; introduction to AA, NA, and/or CA; family and friends counseling. Special groups offered for women, older adults, relapse patients, and cocaine patients. A special program is available for health-care professionals."

Outpatient treatment program: Usual duration, 6 months. Main features include "Emphasis on group therapy; individual counseling available. Special groups for Adult Children of Alcoholics, spouses, and patients needing introductory help."

Family program or services—main features: "Family therapists work exclusively with inpatients' family/friends; special programs on Wednesdays and Saturdays" (including programs for children ages 4 to 7, ages 8 to 12, and teens 13 and up; family group; and Al-Anon).

Charges for treatment: Inpatient: $235/day typical; typical total (including physician fees) for regular program (detoxification plus 21 rehabilitation days) $4,935, for relapse program (detoxification plus 14 rehabilitation days) $3,760; length of stay and charges vary with each patient's needs. Outpatient: individual or family therapy session fees, full $60/session, half $30/session, group therapy or lecture $35/session; miscellaneous fees for medical services, tests.

Can health-care insurance pay for charges?: Yes.

Accredited by: JCAH; State of Michigan, Department of Public Health, Office of Substance Abuse Services.

Aftercare programs: Provided by referrals to appropriate Out-Patient Department services in addition to participation in AA, NA, and/or CA.

Health-Care Professionals Program—main features: For physicians, dentists, nurses, pharmacists, psychiatrists, and other licensed professionals providing direct health care to the public; inpatient phase, detoxification plus 28-day rehabilitation, final week includes individual meeting with Brighton medical director for clinical orientation to addictive diseases physiology and medical rounds with the physician. Aftercare includes individualized 90-day contract between patient and his/her primary therapist requiring AA attendance, participation in a support group for health-care professionals, and other appropriate activities; after the 90 days, patient returns to Brighton for 5 days, accompanying medical director on daily rounds and participating in group meetings with other patients and individual therapist meetings; a second, less structured contract is developed at this time. Confidentiality of patients protected, with observation of rights to confidentiality of recipients of substance abuse services under state and federal laws and regulations.

International Doctors in Alcoholics Anonymous (IDAA), a voluntary fellowship for physicians, psychiatrists, dentists, nurses, pharmacists, veterinarians, and other health-care professionals, meets at Brighton the first Sunday of each month.

Multiply addicted among entering patients: 50 percent; substances abused vary from patient to patient.

Recovery rates: "After 2-year period, approximately 70 percent of first-time inpatients remain sober, based on 6-month follow-up surveys during this time."

Comments: "Founded in 1950, Brighton is the oldest treatment facility in Michigan and—along with Hazelden—one of the oldest in the United States. In the past 38 years we have helped more than 36,000 people from all walks of life and all areas of the United States and Canada begin their recovery from chemical dependence. We have even treated people from as far away as Australia, Singapore, and Colombia. As a pioneer in this field, Brighton Hospital has served as a model for many other centers and is widely respected and highly regarded for its innovative programs."

MINNESOTA

Hazelden Foundation
Box 11, 15245 Pleasant Valley Road
Center City, MN 55012
612-257-4010 (In Minnesota and outside continental United States)
1-800-262-5010 (toll-free, continental United States outside Minnesota)

(Phones answered 24 hours/day, 7 days/week).

Headed by: Harold A. Swift, President.

Direct inquiries to: The following, for the various Hazelden treatment offerings:

Residential Primary Rehabilitation Program (for inpatient assessment, detoxification/rehabilitation treatment), ext. 3307.

Hazelden Family Center (for relatives and close friends of any chemically dependent persons), ext. 2804.

Hazelden Pioneer House (for adolescents/young adults of ages 14 and up, inpatient detoxification/rehabilitation treatment), phone 612-559-2022 (located at 11505 36th Avenue North, Plymouth, MN 55441).

Hazelden Women's Program (for women able to maintain home, work, and family schedules while undergoing outpatient, nonresidential rehabilitation treatment), 612-349-9445 (located at 1400 Park Ave., Minneapolis, MN 55404).

Capacity (no. of patients): 198.

Types of patients admitted: Men and women ages 14 and up.

Detoxification program offered?: Usual duration, approximately 24 hours.

Inpatient treatment program—usual duration: Approximately 28 days; varies according to individual needs.

Inpatient treatment program—main features: "Treatment based on AA philosophy. Each person works with a multidisciplinary treatment team to develop an individualized treatment plan." Primary rehabilitation program includes daily group therapy, individual counseling sessions, AA participation, family care through Hazelden Family Center. Optional 5 to 7-day assessment program to identify and evaluate chemically dependent behavior and other problems and, as needed, develop specific treatment plan and refer patient to best treatment resources.

Outpatient treatment program: For women, through Hazelden Women's Program. First phase, 5-week intensive program with 3-hour meetings three times/week, individual counseling sessions. Aftercare, Living Skills Program with one 3-hour session/week for 10 weeks. Family Program with one 3-hour session/week, based on Al-Anon, strongly encouraged.

Family program or services—main features: 7-day Family Center program includes community meetings, group discussions, lectures, films, conferences with family counselors and clergy on staff.

Charges for treatment: Inpatient, adult: $139/day plus miscellaneous fees; total $5,200 (primary rehabilitation with 30-day stay, including miscellaneous fees). Family Program: residential at Family Center, $116/day; nonresidential, $83/day. Inpatient, adolescent/young adult: $139/day plus miscellaneous fees, total for average 38-day stay, $5,900 (at Hazelden Pioneer House; includes miscellaneous fees). Outpatient women: $1,536 total cost (includes primary treatment, aftercare, family program).

Can health-care insurance pay for charges?: Yes.

Accredited by: JCAH; State of Minnesota, Departments of Human Services, Health.

Aftercare programs: Aftercare plan developed with counselor and Hazelden aftercare staff by each inpatient; typical plans include participation in 12-step groups like AA and NA and might include marital counseling, individual therapy, or family therapy. Aftercare programs offered in the Minnesota Twin Cities/Center City area (group therapy meetings, aftercare visits to Hazelden facilities, family or couples aftercare group sessions, and marital communications workshops). Aftercare referrals also made through the Hazelden nationwide referral network.

Also offered are the services of the *Hazelden Extended Care Program,* in which patients with unusually complicated recovery problems spend further stays averaging 4 months on the Center City campus; *Hazelden Fellowship Club,* a halfway house for recovering men and women (headquartered at 680 Stewart Ave., St. Paul, MN 55012); and *Hazelden Renewal Center,* for any persons and their families or friends who are enjoying sobriety or need to revitalize their recovery program at a comfortable lodgelike residence in wooded hills on a lake; for arrival any time and stays of any length (located at Hazelden's central site).

Comments: Founded in 1949, Hazelden pioneered in developing the general type of alcoholism/addiction inpatient treatment on which most treatment programs throughout the United States are patterned (often referred to as the "Minnesota Model" of treatment). It did so in substantial part under the leadership of Daniel J. Anderson, Ph.D., president emeritus of Hazelden. Today, people come to its 288-acre central site from all over the world, representing all age, social, occupational, and religious backgrounds.

Mayo Clinic/Rochester Methodist Hospital, Alcoholism and Drug Dependence Unit
201 W. Center St.
Rochester, MN 55902
507-286-7593

Headed by: Michael A. Palmen, M.D., Medical Director.
Direct inquiries to: Bill Walker or Nanci Bernard.
Capacity (no. of patients): 33.
Types of patients admitted: Men and women ages 18 and up. Also offered is an inpatient alcohol and drug dependence program for adolescents; phone 507-286-7592.
Detoxification program offered?: Yes; duration varies.
Inpatient treatment program—usual duration: 28-day average (7-day inpatient evaluation).
Inpatient treatment program—main features: Combines "proven treatment measures for addictive disorders with the psychiatric, medical, and surgical experience of our medical center"; multidisciplinary staff; structured treatment program designed to meet individual needs and may include 12-step group attendance (AA, NA, CA, Al-Anon), group therapy, family involvement, individual counseling, chronic pain management component, dietary consultation, physical exercise, spiritual counseling. Approximate one-to-one patient-staff ratio.
Outpatient treatment program: Duration varies; main features parallel those of the inpatient program.
Family program or services—main features: Designed to meet individual needs; typically includes family sessions 2 days per week.
Charges for treatment: Inpatient, 28-day total approximately $9,000. Outpatient, total varies individually. Family program, no charge for patient family members/close friends.
Can health-care insurance pay for charges?: Yes.
Accredited by: JCAH.
Aftercare programs: Planned individually before discharge; outpatient program with group and individual counseling; annual reunion of staff, former patients, and families.
Multiply addicted among entering patients: 40 percent; substances include prescribed drugs, street drugs, cocaine, marijuana, amphetamines, benzodiazepines, alcohol.

St. Mary's Chemical Dependency Services at Riverside Medical Center

Riverside at 25th Avenue South
Minneapolis, MN 55454
612-337-4400 (in Minneapolis/St. Paul)
Toll-free: 1-800-338-2234 (in Minnesota)
1-800-231-2234 (outside Minnesota)

Headed by: Jay Hauge, Executive Director.
Direct inquiries to: Intake/reservations, Mary Houff, ext. 4409. General information, Jim Bermel, ext. 4455.

Capacity (no. of patients): Inpatient, 86 beds; residential outpatient, 23.

Types of patients admitted: Men and women ages 18 and up. Also offered is an inpatient adolescent chemical dependency program for men and women ages 12 to 17; phone ext. 4408.

Detoxification program offered?: Usual duration 2 to 3 days.

Inpatient treatment program—usual duration: 22 to 24 days (average length of stay of patients who complete treatment as inpatients).

Inpatient treatment program—main features: "2 to 3-day evaluation program, medical-model treatment approach incorporating 12 steps of AA, specialized therapy groups, comprehensive family program, aftercare program available up to 2 years following treatment."

Outpatient treatment program: Aggregate 20 days, usual duration. "Residential outpatient, day outpatient, and evening outpatient (nonresidential), 12 steps of AA incorporated in program, family program, and aftercare as in inpatient program. Separate program for relapse treatment."

Family program or services—main features: "Outpatient program for family/other-concerned persons, utilizing educational and group therapy approaches."

Charges for treatment: Inpatient, $205/day. Outpatient, $76/day. Family program, cost included in patient charges (for up to three family members, 5-day participation).

Can health-care insurance pay for charges?: Yes. Approved for payment by Medicare, Medicaid.

Accredited by: JCAH; State of Minnesota, Department of Human Services.

Aftercare programs: "Growth Group" recovery support, $56/year, available up to 2 years; 3-day return visitor program for out-of-state patients at intervals of 3, 6, 12, and 24 months after completing treatment.

Multiply addicted among entering patients: 70 percent; substances include alcohol, marijuana, cocaine.

Recovery rates: 70 percent, 6 months; 70 percent, 1 year; 70 percent, 3 years.

Comments: "Now in its twentieth year, St. Mary's has established a strong reputation nationwide for excellence in patient care and programs; 40 percent of St. Mary's patients are from outside Minnesota." Founded in 1968 as one of the first private-hospital programs treating chemical dependency in adults, St. Mary's has served as a frequent model for other treatment centers. Through a related nonprofit subsidary, ChemQuest, St. Mary's professionals work with other hospitals to develop an entire chemical dependency program, enhance an existing program, or provide management services for a program.

MISSISSIPPI

Mississippi Baptist Chemical Dependency Center
Mississippi Baptist Medical Center
1225 N. State St.
Jackson, MS 39202
601-968-1102

Headed by: Mary B. Ross, Director.
Direct inquiries to: Mary B. Ross.
Capacity (no. of patients): 62.
Types of patients admitted: Men and women, adults and adolescents (adolescents are screened prior to admission).
Detoxification program offered?: Usual duration, 1 to 5 days.
Inpatient treatment program—usual duration: Average, 42 days.
Inpatient treatment program—main features: "Medical history/physical examination, psychological evaluation, individual counseling, group therapy, educational aspect concerning disease concept of alcoholism and drug addiction, program philosophy based on that of Alcoholics Anonymous."
Outpatient treatment program: Usual duration, 45 days. Main features include evening program which meets 3 nights per week

for 15 weeks. Psychological evaluation, individual counseling, group therapy, lectures, films, family conferences.

Family program or services—main features: Evening sessions meeting 3 nights/week for 4 weeks. Group therapy, individual counseling.

Charges for treatment: Inpatient, detoxification $310/day, rehabilitation $145/day, total approximately $7,000. Outpatient, $45/day, total approximately $1,450. Family program, $400/family member (one family member, no charge if relative is in the inpatient or outpatient program).

Accredited by: JCAH.

Aftercare programs: Available to inpatients, outpatients, family members. Also offered, participation in an alumni group, the Alpha Association.

MISSOURI

The Edgewood Program/St. John's Mercy Medical Center
615 S. New Ballas Rd.
Saint Louis, MO 63141
314-569-6500

Headed by: Lyle Cameron, Vice President.
Direct inquiries to: Jane Kniestedt.
Capacity (no.of patients): 52.
Types of patients admitted: Men and women, adults and adolescents.
Detoxification program offered?: Duration based on patient's needs.
Inpatient treatment program—usual duration: 28 days, average.
Inpatient treatment program—main features: Initial evaluation and assessment with "Prevention/Intervention" counselor and development of individualized treatment plan; individual and group counseling, lectures, recreation therapy, family involvement, 12-step program orientation.
Outpatient treatment program: Duration, about 3 months; main features include evaluation and assessment with development of individualized treatment plan, individual counseling, lectures, films, group therapy, family involvement.
Family program or services—main features: "Available to codependents whether or not a chemically dependent person is still

present in their daily lives"; initial individual interviews; primary group sessions held 9 A.M. to 4 P.M. weekdays for 2 weeks with small group meetings, lectures, films for the purpose of helping "the patient to accept chemical dependency as a family disease and to begin living a recovery program based on the 12 steps of AA/Al-Anon."

Charges for treatment: Inpatient, $260/day detoxification, $240/day rehabilitation, total $7,000. Outpatient, $30/hour. Family program, $970/family member for 10-day program.

Can health-care insurance pay for charges?: Yes. Approved for payment by Medicare.

Accredited by: JCAH; State of Missouri, Department of Health.

Aftercare programs: Minimum 14-week aftercare at no additional cost; includes group sessions, individual counseling, family involvement. Follow-up care available beyond aftercare. Edgewood Program Alumni group aids Edgewood and current patients, holds meetings.

Multiply addicted among entering patients: 51 percent; substances include alcohol and other drugs. (Data are for male patients with average age 31 years.)

Recovery rates: "Edgewood participates in a follow-up study by the Hazelden Foundation which includes abstinence from both alcohol and drugs; participation in AA; participation in Edgewood Aftercare; overall quality of life; self-image; relationship with higher power; relationship with spouse and employment. We will share figures with individuals upon request."

Comments: Edgewood was founded in 1971 to become the first private, nonprofit, inpatient hospital in the St. Louis area designed exclusively to treat alcoholism.

MONTANA

Rimrock Foundation
1231 N. 29th St.
Billings, MT 59101
406-248-3175
Toll-free: 1-800-841-2874 (in Montana)
1-800-227-3953 (outside Montana)

Headed by: David W. Cunningham, Executive Director.
Direct inquiries to: Mona Sumner, Associate Director.

Capacity (no. of patients): 61 residential patients, 8 detoxification program patients.

Types of patients admitted: Men and women, ages 13 and over, who suffer from dependency disorders including chemical dependency (alcohol/drug addiction), codependency (the sick relationship of one person to another, usually another who is dependent on chemicals, food, or gambling); eating disorders; compulsive gambling; and dual dependencies (dual addiction or a dependency disorder complicated by a psychiatric disorder or symptom, such as depression).

Detoxification program offered?: Usual duration, 2½ days.

Inpatient treatment program—usual duration: Adult patients stay 28 days on average. Adolescent and eating-disordered patients stay an average of 35 days.

Inpatient treatment program—main features: "Treatment program is based on the essentials of dependency disorders and the healing principles of 12-step programs. That framework allows us to work effectively with patients having any compulsive disorder: chemical dependency, eating disorders, compulsive gambling, and codependency, in a progressive and flexible program tailored to meet individual needs."

Adult treatment program includes medical evaluation; 24-hour medical care/nursing services; individual and group therapy; books and study materials; lectures and films; recreational and leisure skill training; family therapy and comprehensive family education program; codependency program for two family members; assistance in becoming involved with support groups such as AA or Gamblers Anonymous (G.A.); aftercare and follow-up.

Adolescent treatment program also includes adolescent issues groups; adolescent and family recreation; academic program; parenting program; aftercare planning that includes parents and concerned school personnel.

Outpatient treatment program: Services include assessment and diagnosis, aftercare, and family program.

Family program or services—main features: Outpatient family program includes weekly sessions for 8 weeks: 8 Tuesday evening sessions that feature lectures and peer therapy group/counselor meetings; 4 Wednesday day-long Family Treatment Day sessions with educational and group therapy; involvement with support groups that include Al-Anon, Alateen, OA, with Saturday night Open Speaker's Meeting featuring talk by an AA member on working within the 12-step program.

Charges for treatment: Inpatient program, $80/day detoxification; adults, $6,200 for 28-day average length of treatment; adolescents, $7,800 for 35-day average length of treatment; eating-disordered patients, $8,500 for 35-day average length of treatment; per diem rate for additional treatment days; additional fees for miscellaneous services.

Can health-care insurance pay for charges?: Yes.

Accredited by: JCAH; State of Montana Department of Institutions, Alcohol and Drug Abuse Division.

Aftercare programs: Adults, weekly meetings for 3 months; Adolescents, weekly meetings for up to one year. Cost is covered by residential program rates.

Multiply addicted among entering patients: Inpatient program: 71.4 percent among male patients, 28.6 percent among female patients; the multiply addicted are concentrated in age group 13 to 30; age group 30 to 60+ mainly abuse alcohol; substances abused include alcohol and marijuana.

Recovery rates: "We have not yet conducted nonparametric statistical studies on recovery rates; however, medical record reviews suggest recovery rates above 80 percent."

Comments: Foundation policy is to provide "leading quality treatment in the Northern Rockies."

NEBRASKA

Eppley Treatment Center
Methodist Midtown—The Nebraska Methodist Hospital
3612 Cuming St.
Omaha, NE 68131
402-554-4700

Headed by: Christopher Eiel, Director.

Direct inquiries to: Christopher Eiel.

Capacity (no. of patients): 86 beds.

Types of patients admitted: Men and women; adults ages 18 and up; adolescents ages 13 to 17.

Detoxification program offered?: Yes; duration varies.

Inpatient treatment program—usual duration: Average detoxification and rehabilitation, 31 days; varies by individual needs.

Inpatient treatment program—main features: "12-step AA

model; strong family involvement; strong spirituality component." Also offers eating disorders program.

Outpatient treatment program: Usual duration, thirty-two sessions over an 8-week period. Main features same as those of inpatient program.

Family program or services—main features: Fifteen sessions over a 3-week period; stresses 12-step program support groups. Children's program also available; offers sessions for ages 16 to 18, 13 to 15, 10 to 12, 6 to 9; consists of twelve evening sessions over a 3-week period.

Charges for treatment: Inpatient, adults $177/day for 30 days, $5,900 all-inclusive total fee; adolescents, $220/day for 45 days, $11,500 all-inclusive total fee. Outpatient, $56/session (for thirty-two sessions), total $2,036 with ancillary fees. Family program, $540/family member (for fifteen-session 3-week program).

Can health-care insurance pay for charges?: Yes. Approved for payment by Medicare.

Accredited by: JCAH.

Aftercare programs: Offerings include groups for relapse prevention, couples, men, women, adolescents, communication; one-year aftercare provided at no additional charge.

Multiply addicted among entering patients: Inpatient programs: adolescents, 82 percent; adults, 58 percent. Substances abused include the following: among adolescents, alcohol, a variety of street drugs, some cocaine; among adults, alcohol, street drugs, tranquilizers.

Outpatient programs: alcohol only, 57 percent; alcohol and street drugs, 26 percent; cocaine, 11 percent; others, 6 percent.

Recovery rates: Eppley program completion rates: adult inpatients, 86 percent; adolescent inpatients, 81 percent; outpatients, 73 percent; family program, 90 percent. "Research programs are in place but not yet yielding sufficient data to warrant presentation" of recovery rates.

O'Neill Valley Hope
Box 918
O'Neill, NE 68763
402-336-3747
Toll-free, for admissions: 1-800-544-5101

Headed by: Kaye Scott, Program Director.
Direct inquiries to: Kaye Scott.

Capacity (no. of patients): 65.

Types of patients admitted: Men and women ages 13 and up with chemical dependency problems.

Detoxification program offered?: Yes.

Inpatient treatment program—usual duration: 30 days.

Inpatient treatment program—main features: "Physical, psychological, and spiritual aspects of recovery from chemical dependency and codependency."

Family program or services—main features: Addictive disease education, codependency therapy; 10-day program.

Charges for treatment: $112/day, approximately $3,400 total for 30 days. Family program, $950/family member, 10-day program.

Can health-care insurance pay for charges?: Yes.

Accredited by: JCAH; State of Nebraska.

Multiply addicted among entering patients: Inpatient program 75 percent; substances include alcohol, pot, cocaine.

Recovery rates: 67 percent, one year.

Comments: O'Neill Valley Hope is part of the nonprofit Valley Hope Associaton, which began with the Norton (Kansas) Valley Hope center (see entry) in 1967. The Association now operates seven inpatient treatment facilities and four outpatient centers in Kansas, Nebraska, Missouri, Oklahoma, and Arizona.

NEVADA

Truckee Meadows Hospital
1240 East Ninth St.
Reno, NV 89512
702-323-0478

Types of patients admitted: Adult and adolescent men and women with alcoholism and/or drug addiction.

Types of treatment offered: Detoxification and rehabilitation inpatient program, outpatient program, 1-year aftercare. Family treatment, occupational and recreational therapy. Programs are flexible to provide optimal care for each individual.

In addition, a residential program for adolescents is available at Willow Springs Center, a new sixty-four-bed freestanding facility. A Christ-centered treatment program is also part of the program offerings.

Accredited by: JCAH; State of Nevada.

NEW HAMPSHIRE

Spofford Hall
Route 9A, P.O. Box 225
Spofford, NH 03462
603-363-4545
Toll-free, 1-800-451-1717 (in New Hampshire)
1-800-451-1716 (outside New Hampshire)

Headed by: Rene Zimmerman, M.S., Executive Director.
Direct inquiries to: Admissions Department.
Capacity (no. of patients): 143.
Types of patients admitted: Men and women ages 13 and up.
Detoxification program offered?: Usual duration 3 days, depending on program.
Inpatient treatment program—usual duration: 28 days, according to individual need and program.
Inpatient treatment program—main features: "Five programs available—adult chemical dependence, chronic relapse, crisis intervention, cocaine, adolescent. Each program includes personal and group therapy, lectures, pastoral counseling, activity therapy, family counseling." Treatment program centered on "the principles and traditions of Alcoholics Anonymous and Narcotics Anonymous, which integrated into every aspect of therapy."
Outpatient treatment program: Offered through Spofford Hall Regional Service Offices throughout New England.
Family program or services—main features: 4-day program; educational and group therapy which involves the patient.
Charges for treatment: Inpatient, for various programs, $259/day, total $9,015; $309/day, total $10,625; $365/day, total $20,505. Family program, $300/family member (4-day program).
Can health-care insurance pay for charges?: Yes.
Accredited by: JCAH; State of New Hampshire, Department of Public Health.
Aftercare programs: Group therapy; one day per week for 6 weeks at Spofford Hall regional offices; no charge.
Recovery rates: Two-year follow-up study results (sample of 56 former patients discharged during a 2-month period in 1984): 55 percent had maintained complete abstinence since admission to Spofford two years before; 88 percent had been abstinent during the 30 days prior to study interviews (with former patients and

with relatives or other persons significant to the patient); 73 percent reported abstinence during the 6 months prior to study interviews.

Comments: Spofford Hall occupies a 16-acre wooded site on Spofford Lake. It is a treatment facility of the Mediplex Group, Inc., Alcohol and Substance Abuse Division. Locations, names, addresses, and phone numbers of other Mediplex alcohol and substance abuse treatment facilities are as follows:

Carmel, NY: Arms Acres, Seminary Hill Rd., Carmel, NY 10512, phone 914-225-3400.

Charlottesville, VA: Mountain Wood, 500 Old Lynchburg Rd., Charlottesville, VA 22905, phone 804-971-8245.

Scotia, NY: Conifer Park, 150 Glenridge Rd., Scotia, NY 12302, phone 518-399-6446.

Shawnee, KS: Cedar Ridge, 7405 Renner Rd., Shawnee, KS 66217, phone 913-631-1900.

NEW JERSEY

Little Hill—Alina Lodge
Box G, Squires Rd. and the Paulinskill River
Blairstown, NJ 07285
201-362-6114

Headed by: Geraldine O. Delaney, Chief Executive Officer.

Direct inquiries to: Admission by referral only, of men and women from 18 to 80; "we take no direct referrals from families." Referrals made by physicians, clergy, caseworkers, and members of AA and Alcoholism Information Centers. Entrants must be nonpsychotic, ambulatory, and alcohol-and-drug-free for 5 to 7 days. For alcoholics and those polyaddicted.

Capacity (no. of patients): 60.

Types of patients admitted: "we are limited to the 'Reluctant to Recover.' These are people who have tried many treatment places and can't make it without some special attention. The main things that we have that other places don't have is Tincture of Time, for our treatment is open-ended. We take people on referral only and very selectively, because our capacity is 60 and we are full. . . ."

Detoxification program offered?: No.

Inpatient treatment program—usual duration: "the length of stay is determined by the individual's progress, usually upwards of 3 months . . . although each is judged on an individual basis. . . ."

Inpatient treatment program—main features: "We have very highly structured living, including eating, sleeping, and education. We have a very dedicated and highly trained staff . . . We make no distinction between drugs, for alcohol is the oldest known drug of addiction. . . . We allow no smoking by students or visiting family (or visitors of any kind) on the grounds. . . ."

Outpatient treatment program: None.

Family program or services—main features: "We do have Family Programs, both for the students in residence and some special Pilot Programs for families who are still having problems and need to look at themselves. . . ."

Accredited by: JCAH; State of New Jersey.

Aftercare programs: "Aftercare and follow-up are of the utmost importance, and all students are urged to attend Alcoholics Anonymous and the family to attend Al-Anon and Alateen Family Groups, as well as to use other community resources."

Multiply addicted among entering patients: More than 50 percent, "using alcohol and some other substance, chiefly Librium and Valium and the sedative drugs both prescribed and over-the-counter, though many of the young prefer quaaludes, marijuana, cocaine, and alcohol."

Comments: The head of Little Hill—Alina Lodge has worked in the field of alcoholism treatment for more than 40 years, and her treatment center has a long-established and highly respected reputation.

Seabrook House

P.O. Box 5055, Polk Lane
Seabrook, NJ 08302-0655
609-455-7575
Toll-free (in New Jersey only): 1-800-582-5968

Headed by: Jerome J. Diehl, Administrator.

Direct inquuiries to: Supervisor of Admissions.

Capacity (no. of patients): 66.

Types of patients admitted: Men and women over age 18.

Detoxification program offered?: Usual duration, 5 to 7 days.

Inpatient treatment program—usual duration: 28 days (length depends on patient's needs).

Inpatient treatment program—main features: "Lectures, individual and group therapy, peer support, recreational therapy, counseling with family members, etc.; Seabrook believes in the philosophy of AA, NA, Al-Anon, and other 12-step programs."

Outpatient treatment program: Usual duration, 8 weeks with sessions 3 evenings per week; followed by transfer to regular aftercare program.

Family program or services—main features: One weekday session per week plus 4 Saturday sessions during a 12-week period, providing group counseling, lectures, films; also offer 8-week children's program, for children ages 8 to 14.

Charges for treatment: Inpatient, $225/day; outpatient, $90/session. Family program, $40/session.

Can health-care insurance pay for charges?: Yes.

Accredited by: JCAH; State of New Jersey, Department of Health.

Aftercare programs: Weekly sessions for 12 weeks, $40/session.

Multiply addicted among entering patients: 80 percent; substances include cocaine, marijuana, speed.

Comments: Located in southern New Jersey, on a 40-acre site.

Sunrise House

Intersection of Route 94 North and Route 15
Lafayette, NJ 07848
201-383-6300

Headed by: Frank L. Clisham, President/Chief Executive Officer.

Direct inquiries to: Admissions Department.

Capacity (no. of patients): 75 beds.

Types of patients admitted: Men and women ages 18 and up.

Detoxification program offered?: Usual duration, 3 to 5 days.

Inpatient treatment program—usual duration: 28 to 42 days.

Inpatient treatment program—main features: "Oriented to the treatment of the disease of alcoholism and other chemical dependencies. Committed to the principles, philosophy, and program of AA."

Outpatient treatment program: Usual duration, 15 to 75 sessions. Main features include group, individual, conjoint, marital, and family counseling sessions.

Family program or services—main features: 5-day residential family program; concurrent outpatient and aftercare programs.

Charges for treatment: Inpatient, $275/day detoxification; $225/

day rehabilitation. Outpatient, $50/session. Family program, $130/ family member per day for the 5-day residential program.

Can health-care insurance pay for charges?: Yes.

Accredited by: JCAH; State of New Jersey, Department of Alcoholism.

Multiply addicted among entering patients: 60 percent; substances include alcohol, cocaine, marijuana.

Recovery rates: 100 percent, 6 months; 80 percent, 1 year; 75 percent, 3 years.

NEW YORK

Bry-Lin Hospital, Rush Treatment Program
1263 Delaware Ave.
Buffalo, NY 14209
716-886-8200

Headed by: Leonard Pleskow, Chief Executive Officer.

Direct inquiries to: Brooks Cagle, Vice President, Chemical Dependency.

Capacity (no. of patients): 112.

Types of patients admitted: Men and women adults (ages 18 and up) and adolescents (ages 12 to 18).

Detoxification program offered?: Usual duration, 3 to 5 days; provided only when medically justified.

Inpatient treatment program—usual duration: Determined by individual patient need.

Inpatient treatment program—main features: "Special emphasis is given to individualized patient services based upon assessed need. Program strengths include major family therapy component. Patients are given extensive opportunity to confront dependency and abuse and are taught methods of alternative options."

Outpatient treatment program: Flexible duration. Main features: "Plan based upon individual patient need, which allows persons to progress through phases of treatment from intensive to supportive at individual pace."

Family program or services—main features: "Family members participate in treatment on weekly basis. Emphasis placed on relationships within family system and understanding dynamics of change resulting from treatment."

Charges for treatment: Inpatient, $285/day. Outpatient, $60/

visit. Family program, cost included in inpatient/outpatient charges.

Can health-care insurance pay for charges?: Yes.

Accredited by: JCAH; State of New York, Divisions of Alcoholism and Alcohol Abuse, Substance Abuse.

Aftercare programs: 16-week continuing care support following discharge; cost included within inpatient charges.

Multiply addicted among entering patients: Inpatient, 65 percent; substances include alcohol, cocaine, amphetamines.

Smithers Alcoholism Treatment and Training Center
St. Luke's–Roosevelt Hospital Center
428 W. 59th St.
New York, NY 10019
212-554-6491

Headed by: Anne Geller, M.D., Medical Director.

Direct inquiries to: Gerald Horowitz, Administrator.

Capacity (no. of patients): Inpatient: 43, rehabilitation; 17, detoxification. Outpatient: unlimited.

Types of patients admitted: Men and women over age 17 who abuse one or more than one substance.

Detoxification program offered?: Usual duration, 5 days.

Inpatient treatment program—usual duration: 28 days.

Inpatient treatment program—main features: "Intensive family program; AA-oriented philosophy; relapse-prevention services; health-care professionals groups."

Outpatient treatment program: Intensive evening outpatient program offered.

Charges for treatment: Inpatient, $450/day detoxification; $250/day rehabilitation. Outpatients, charged on a sliding scale.

Can health-care insurance pay for charges?: Yes.

Accredited by: JCAH; State of New York, Division of Alcohol Abuse and Alcoholism.

Aftercare programs: Twice-weekly group therapy plus family program, for up to one year.

Comments: Inpatient rehabilitation treatment conducted at a Manhattan mansion on 93d Street just off Park Avenue once owned by famed showman Billy Rose. It operates as part of a large treatment and training complex generously endowed by J. Brinkley Smithers. It opened in 1973. Its founding director was LeClair

Bissell, M.D., who today is one of the country's foremost authorities on treatment for alcoholism/addiction.

The Washton Institute, Outpatient Recovery Centers
Manhattan Office:
4 Park Ave.
New York, NY 10016
212-213-4900

Westchester Office:
933 Saw Mill River Rd.
Ardsley, NY 10502
914-693-1010

Headed by: Arnold M. Washton, Ph.D., Founder and Executive Director.

Direct inquiries to: Arnold M. Washton.

Capacity (no. of patients): 200.

Types of patients admitted: Men and women, employed adults, functional adolescents, and families.

Detoxification program offered?: No.

Outpatient treatment program: "6-month intensive outpatient evening program, offering individual and group counseling and education for patient and family."

Family program or services—main features: Family Education Program, 8 weeks.

Charges for treatment: $6,500 for 6-month program (all-inclusive charge). Family program charges included in cost of primary treatment.

Can health-care insurance pay for charges?: Yes (80 to 100 percent).

Accredited by: State of New York, Division of Substance Abuse Services.

Aftercare programs: Relapse Prevention Program; group and individual counseling; cost, $3,200.

Multiply addicted among entering patients: Majority addicted to cocaine and/or alcohol; approximately 10 percent opiate- or pill-dependent.

Recovery rates: 70 to 75 percent still drug-free, in 2-year follow-up.

NORTH CAROLINA

Charlotte Treatment Center
1715 Sharon Rd. West, P.O. Box 240197
Charlotte, NC 28224
704-554-8373

Headed by: Jack E. Harville, Executive Director.
Direct inquiries to: Brewster M. ("Robbie") Robertson, Director Outreach/Marketing.
Capacity (no. of patients): 64.
Types of patients admitted: Men and women ages 16 and up; must be ambulatory.
Detoxification program offered?: Usual duration, 2 to 3 days, depending on type of drug.
Inpatient treatment program—usual duration: 28 to 56 days, depending on each individual's needs.
Inpatient treatment program—main features: "We believe alcoholism/chemcial dependency is a treatable disease; model of treatment is based on principles of Alcoholics Anonymous."
Outpatient treatment program: Usual duration, 6 weeks with four sessions/week and 4 hours/session. Main features include "Required AA or NA meetings on Friday, Saturday, and Sunday of each week during the course of treatment. Treatment philosophy based on the 12 steps of AA."
Family program or services—main features: "Comprehensive 4-day program including individual and group counseling, informative lectures and video tapes, and joint sessions with the patient." Also offers "For Kids Only" program for patients' children ages 6 to 11 (also open to former patients' children); structured group program providing education, reinforcement, and support and guided by a trained professional; scheduled during family visiting hours Thursday evenings 5:45 to 7:15 P.M.; five sessions, total fee $25/child.
Charges for treatment: Inpatient, $165/day; outpatient, $1,980 total. Family program, $150/family member (if housing not needed; otherwise, $250/family member).
Can health-care insurance pay for charges?: Yes.
Accredited by: JCAH; State of North Carolina Department of Human Resources.

Aftercare programs: Minimum of twelve weekly sessions, 1½ hours/session; cost, $10/session.

Multiply addicted among entering patients: 43 percent; substances include alcohol and other drugs.

Recovery rates: Alcohol: 78 percent, 6 months; 69 percent, one year. Other drugs: 64 percent, 6 months; 61 percent, one year. (Data based on information collected on the Center's 1984 patients.)

Fellowship Hall
P.O. Box 13890
Greensboro, NC 27415
919-621-3381

Headed by: Ed F. Ward, Executive Director.

Direct inquiries to: Ms. Connye Post.

Capacity (no. of patients): 48 (Fellowship Hall uses the term guests rather than *patients).*

Types of patients admitted: Men and women ages 21 and up (and who are assessed as capable of participating in treatment as offered at Fellowship Hall).

Detoxification program offered?: Usual duration, 3 to 5 days (varies from individual to individual).

Inpatient treatment program—usual duration: 28 days (including detoxification).

Inpatient treatment program—main features: "Guests are taught and shown the problem and the solution, and are given a plan of action for recovery. This is done with films, lectures, and group therapy, all based on the ongoing recovery program outlined in the 12 steps of Alcoholics Anonymous."

Outpatient treatment program: Plans are to begin an outpatient program, possibly by late 1988.

Family program or services—main features: 4-day program featuring education as to addiction as a family disease, plus a recovery program for the entire family.

Charges for treatment: Inpatient, $130/day, total $3,650. Family program, one family member included in $3,650 total, $30/additional family member for 4-day program.

Can health-care insurance pay for charges?: Yes.

Accredited by: JCAH; State of North Carolina Department of Human Resources.

Aftercare programs: 1½-hour weekly group sessions for 12

weeks, attended by former guest and family members; cost, $90. Also carry out follow-up program, contacting former guests at posttreatment intervals of 30 days, 60 days, 90 days, 6 months, one year. Spring and Fall Conferences typically attended by some 550 former guests and their family members; several alumni groups in the Southeast United States hold regular meetings.

Multiply addicted among entering patients: 60 percent, approximately; substances include pot, prescription drugs, cocaine.

Recovery rates: 70 percent, 1 year (on the basis of results of follow-up program, "approximately 70 percent remain alcohol/drug-free at one year after treatment").

Comments: Continuously accredited by JCAH since 1975; founded in 1971, Fellowship Hall has treated more than 7,000 persons. In 1982, it was the first nonprofit facility to be given the Outstanding Program Award by the Alcoholism Professionals of North Carolina. Occupies a 78-acre site in rolling, wooded countryside a few miles north of Greensboro.

NORTH DAKOTA

Heartview Foundation
1406 Second St., NW
Mandan, ND 58554
701-663-2321
Toll-free (in North Dakota): 1-800-663-2000

Headed by: Edwin Gerhardt, Administrator/Chief Executive Officer.

Direct inquiries to: Dr. Mark Hanlon, Clinical Director.

Capacity (no. of patients): 91.

Types of patients admitted: Men and women of all ages (including adolescents 15 and younger); patients are admitted 24 hours a day.

Detoxification program offered?: Duration as needed; carried out at Heartview.

Inpatient treatment program—usual duration: Averages, 28 days for adults, 35 days for adolescents.

Inpatient treatment program—main features: "AA 12 steps; disease concept; 5-day family week program; medical and psychological evaluations available; adolescent treatment is age-specific (with groups for ages 15 and younger, and for ages 16 to 18) and with educational tutoring provided. Total abstinence is the goal. Adult women-only group therapy available."

Outpatient treatment program: Usual duration, twenty-four sessions. Main features: "evening program, family week, attendance at AA/NA/Al-Anon required. Adults and adolescents accepted. Women-only outpatient program offered." Also offer Adult Children of Alcoholics outpatient program.

Family program or services—main features: Sessions for 5 consecutive days; morning programming with other family members, afternoon sessions with patient and family members. In outpatient program, 5½-day family program.

Charges for treatment: Inpatient: adults, $145/day, total $4,300; adolescents, $170/day, total $6,300. Outpatient, $63/session, total $1,512. Family program, no charge; family housing available on-site at Heartview.

Can health-care insurance pay for charges?: Yes. Approved for payment by Medicare and Medicaid.

Accredited by: JCAH; State of North Dakota Department of Health.

Aftercare programs: Twenty counseling sessions at Heartview for adults or adolescents after treatment (out-of-area patients are referred to local aftercare professionals; cost, adults $25/session; adolescents $20/session).

Multiply addicted among entering patients: Inpatient: 52 percent; substances include alcohol, opioids, barbiturates, cocaine, marijuana, hallucinogens, amphetamines (for all inpatients, average age 30.8 years; 68 percent male, 32 percent female). Outpatient: 16 percent addicted to more than one chemical (for all outpatients, average age 32.7 years; 67 percent male, 33 percent female). 1987 calendar year for inpatient data; October 1987 through February 1988 for outpatient data.

Recovery rates: 75.7 percent, 6 months; 71.5 percent, one year. ("1985 continuing studies data. Percentages do not reflect entire population, but only those participating in continuing studies who returned their questionnaires.")

Comments: Founded in October 1964, Heartview is a private nonprofit institution. Patients have come to it for treatment from throughout the United States and Canada. Its site overlooks the Heart River Valley.

OHIO

Lakeland Institute of Lorain Community Hospital

3500 Kolbe Rd.
Lorain, OH 44053
216-282-7106
Toll-free (in Ohio only): 1-800-362-1039

Note: See immediately following listings for information on Lakeland Institute treatment sites in addition to the central site (sites in four other Ohio cities).

Headed by: Aaron Billowitz, M.D., Medical Director.
Direct inquiries to: Tom Stuber, In-Patient Manager.
Capacity (no. of patients): 50 residential; 15 detoxification.
Types of patients admitted: Men and women; specialized programs for adults and adolescents.
Detoxification program offered?: Usual duration, 3 days; provided only if medically necessary.
Inpatient treatment program—usual duration: Range, 1 to 4 weeks, depending on the individual case.
Inpatient treatment program—main features: "Total abstinence model; mandatory family involvement; individual, couples, family, and group therapy; involvement in AA, NA, Al-Anon."
Outpatient treatment program: Duration varies. "Availability of partial hospitalization program (evening treatment program for adults, day treatment program for adolescents), as well as outpatient and continuing care." Offers specialized programs for adolescents, women, men, cocaine, and relapse treatment. Also offers an Adult Children of Alcoholics Program (with 1½-hour weekly meetings) and an outpatient Children's Program for children ages 3 to 13 who live in an alcoholic home.
Family program or services—main features: "Extensive family programming in residential and partial hospitalization programs, with family charges included in patient per diem charges."
Charges for treatment: Inpatient, adults $380/day, adolescents $420/day. Partial hospitalization program, $84/day.
Can health-care insurance pay for charges?: Yes. Approved for payment by Medicare, Medicaid.
Accredited by: JCAH; State of Ohio Department of Health.
Aftercare programs: Group therapy in 1½-hour weekly sessions

for adults, adolescents, women only, couples, family members; individual sessions also available. Cost, $36.75/group.

Multiply addicted among entering patients: 97 percent; substances include cocaine, marijuana (patients in all nineteen types of programs offered by Lakeland).

Recovery rates: "Currently involved in extensive outcome research program with Case Western Reserve University."

Comments: Lakeland has provided treatment since 1973, and its offerings have been approved by the State of Ohio as a model program for northeastern Ohio. A group of four twelve-person residence units at its central site were architecturally honored by the 1981 Honor Award for Excellence in Architecture of the Wisconsin Society of Architects.

Lakeland Institute of Lorain Community Hospital—Other Treatment Locations Offering "Partial Hospitalization Programs" and Outpatient Programs

Direct inquiries to:

Beachwood, Ohio: Sandra Nichols, Team Leader; 3789B South Green Rd., Beachwood, OH 44122; phone 216-464-9633.

Fairlawn, Ohio: William Boswell, Team Leader; 2725 Abbington Rd., Suite 103; Fairlawn, OH 44313; phone 216-864-2782.

Parma Heights, Ohio: Dana Harlow, Team Leader; Southland Plaza, Suite 501; 6929 W. 130th St.; Parma Heights, OH 44130; phone 216-845-7780.

Sandusky, Ohio: Mark Sikora, Team Leader; 1801 E. Perkins Ave., Sandusky, OH 44870; phone 419-625-7106.

Capacity (no. of patients, each location): Partial hospitalization program: twelve adults, evening treatment; twelve adolescents, day treatment. Outpatient program, unlimited.

Types of patients admitted: Men and women ages 13 and up; specialized programs offered for women only, children of alcoholics, cocaine treatment, relapse treatment.

Detoxification program offered?: Yes.

Outpatient treatment program: Duration varies. "Availability of partial hospitalization program (evening treatment program for adults, day treatment program for adolescents), as well as outpatient and continuing care."

Family program or services—main features: "Extensive family program in partial hospitalization programs, and individualized couples and family therapy."

Charges for treatment: Partial hospitalization, $84/day inclusive. Outpatient group therapy program, $36.75/1½ hour session on a weekly basis.

Can health-care insurance pay for charges?: Yes. Approved for payment by Medicare and Medicaid.

Acredited by: JCAH; State of Ohio, Department of Health.

After care programs: Weekly group sessions, 1½ hours/session. Special groups available for women, adolescents, children. Also individual, couples, and family therapy. Cost, $36.75/session.

Parkside Lodge of Columbus
349 Ridenour Rd.
Colombus, OH 43230
614-417-2552

Headed by: Chris Gerber, Executive Director.
Direct inquiries to: Chris Gerber.
Capacity (no. of patients): 50.
Types of patients admitted: Men and women over age 17.
Detoxification program offered?: Usual duration, 3 to 10 days.
Inpatient treatment program—usual duration: 30 to 45 days.
Inpatient treatment program—main features: "(1) Standard alcoholism/substance abuse program; (2) cocaine program; (3) older adult program."

Outpatient treatment program: Primary treatment duration 6 weeks with three meetings/week and 4 hours/evening meeting.

Family program or services—main features: Family week in inpatient program, family sessions in outpatient primary program.

Charges for treatment: Inpatient, total approximately $7,500 for 28 days; outpatient primary program, total $2,500. Inpatient program, $250/family member for one-week residential family program.

Can health-care insurance pay for the charges?: Yes.

Accredited by: JCAH; State of Ohio, Departments of Health and Mental Health.

Aftercare programs: Continuing care, 2 years; no charge. Attendance at Level I for 3 months posttreatment, 80 percent; attendance at Level II at 1 year posttreatment, 40 percent (others by then do not need continuing care program).

OKLAHOMA

Brookhaven Hospital
201 S. Garnett Rd.

Tulsa, OK 74128
918-438-4257

Headed by: Marilyn Fowler, Administrator.
Direct inquiries to: Marilyn Fowler.
Capacity (no. of patients): 40.
Types of patients admitted: Men and women ages 13 and up.
Detoxification program offered?: Usual duration, approximately 5 days.
Inpatient treatment program—usual duration: Varies by individual needs.
Inpatient treatment program—main features: Treatment for drug and alcohol abuse, dual-diagnosis patients including dual addiction and addiction plus mental health problems.
Outpatient treatment program: Usual duration, 12 weeks.
Family program or services—main features: Family member sessions every other week for 3 days.
Charges for treatment: Inpatient, $240/day; outpatient, total $1,800. No charge for family program.
Can health-care insurance pay for charges?: Yes. Approved for payment by Medicare, and by Medicaid for patients under age 21.
Accredited by: JCAH; State of Oklahoma Departments of Health, Mental Health.
Aftercare programs: Group sessions 2 nights/week; cost included in inpatient fees.
Multiply addicted among entering patients: 90 percent; substances include alcohol, cocaine, prescription drugs; multiply addicted are concentrated among patients ages 17 to 40.
Recovery rates: 85 percent, 6 months; 70 percent, one year.

OREGON

TurnAround at Forest Grove Residential Treatment Center
Forest Grove Community Hospital
1809 Maple St.
Forest Grove, OR 97116
503-357-0774

TurnAround Hillsboro Out-Patient Treatment Center
427 S.E. 8th St.
Hillsboro, OR 97123

503-681-1766

Headed by: Carl E. Jacobs, Program Director.
Direct inquiries to: Carl E. Jacobs.
Capacity (no. of patients): 24.
Types of patients admitted: Men and women adults, and adolescents by exception in special cases.
Detoxification program offered?: Yes, in hospital.
Residential treatment program—usual duration: 28 to 35 days.
Residential treatment program—main features: "12-step-based; individual and group counseling; education; 4-day Family Program is integral part of treatment."
Outpatient treatment program: Minimum 15 weeks in length; first 5 weeks, structured activities for 2½ to 3 hours each weekday; next ten sessions held one night session/week with 1½ hours/session, and one-to-one counseling as needed. "12-step-based; individual and group counseling; education; weekly family program."
Family program or services—main features: "Education and treatment."
Charges for treatment: Residential, $145/day, total $4,600. Outpatient, $62/day, total $1,850. Family program for families of residential patients, $350/family member for 4-day program.
Can health-care insurance pay for charges?: Yes.
Accredited by: State of Oregon Department of Human Resources.
Aftercare programs: 10-week minimum duration; no charge on completion of residential program; $150 charge on completion of outpatient program.
Multiply addicted among entering patients: Residential program entrants, more than 75 percent (estimate); substances abused include alcohol, cocaine, marijuana, and/or other combinations.
Recovery rates: For residential program patients, 91 percent, 6 months; 80 percent, one year. "Program has just completed 3 years; other data too minimal."
Comments: Other TurnAround treatment centers are located in Salem and Astoria.

PENNSYLVANIA

Chit Chat Farm; Caron Hospital; Caron Family Services
Caron Foundation

Galen Hall Rd., Box A
Wernersville, PA 19565
215-678-2332

Headed by: Chit Chat Farm, Jeb Bird, Executive Director; Caron Hospital, Jan Heist, Executive Director; Caron Family Services, Ann Smith, Executive Director.

Direct inquiries to: Executive Director of the respective division.

Capacity (no. of patients): 63, inpatient rehabilitation treatment, Chit Chat Farm; 20, inpatient detoxification treatment, Caron Hospital; 50, Caron Family Services.

Types of patients admitted: Men and women adults (over age 19); admissions accepted 24 hours/day, 7 days/week, after arrangements have been made by phone.

Detoxification program offered?: In Caron Hospital; average length of stay, 3 to 9 days; will detoxify from all drugs; offers "Change" program to assist patients to identify themselves as an addicted individuals and to develop motivation for further treatment.

Inpatient rehabilitation treatment program—usual duration: 28 days approximate.

Inpatient rehabilitation treatment program—main features: "The concepts, philosophy, and steps of Alcoholics Anonymous, combined with lectures, films, and group therapy, help educate and motivate [the patient] to examine and accept the disease and the effects it has had on [his or her] life. Additionally, work therapy, an integral part of the program, [makes the patient] feel a part of the recovering community." Chit Chat experience is meant to provide the basis for the patient's involvement in the long-term recovery program of AA or NA. Unique "monitor system" of case management with three-staff-member treatment team for each patient headed by the patient's "monitor" serving as a guide to treatment and recovery plans.

Outpatient treatment programs: Offered through two outpatient treatment centers at other Pennsylvania locations as follows:

Philadelphia: Caron Counseling Services/Chit Chat-Philadelphia, Ten Penn Center, Suite 1000, Philadelphia, PA 19601; phone 215-568-6718, 215-557-0929.

West Reading: Caron Counseling Services, 529 Reading Ave., Suite D, West Reading, PA 19611; phone 215-373-5447.

Services at each center include intervention services; a variety of evaluation, diagnostic, and treatment services for chemically dependent individuals and their families whose conditions indicate they may be treated effectively as outpatients. Intensive outpatient treatment is based on the Chit Chat inpatient model, runs for 26 weeks, and requires participants to be chemical-free starting 7 days prior to treatment. Also offer Women's Group, for women only; codependency services for children of alcoholics ages 5 to 12, for adolescent children of alcoholics ages 12 to 19, for adult children of alcoholics, and for adult codependents.

Family program or services—main features: Primary program is a 5½-day residential treatment experience followed by weekly aftercare sessions at Caron or by referral. Open to anyone who has lived with a chemically dependent person (and not only anyone related to a person in Chit Chat rehabilitation treatment). Also offered: Adult Children of Alcoholics treatment for persons over age 16 (in a pioneering program); Parent and Child Program for child age groups 6 to 12, 12 to 14, and 14 to 16; adolescent program; and couples program.

Charges for treatment: Inpatient rehabilitation program, $195/day. Detoxification, $260/day (approved for payment by Medicare). Family program, total $750.

Can health-care insurance pay for charges?: Yes.

Accredited by: JCAH, Caron Hospital, Chit Chat Rehabilitation Centers; Commonwealth of Pennsylvania, Office of Drug and Alcohol Programs.

Aftercare programs: For all programs, aftercare planned before treatment ends to include aftercare group meetings and ongoing attendance/participation at local AA, NA, Al-Anon, and/or ACOA meetings. Caron Foundation also operates an eleven-bed aftercare facility for women 10 miles from Chit Chat Farm, the *Rosie Kearney House*, 225 E. Wyomissing Ave., Mohnton, PA 19540, phone 215-777-1869.

Multiply addicted among entering patients: 50 percent; substances include prescribed medications, cocaine. The multiply addicted tend to be "younger than ten years ago," in the 25-to-40 age group.

Comments: Chit Chat Foundation (now the Caron Foundation) was established in 1957 by the late Richard J. Caron (a Reading, Pennsylvania, industrialist and recovering alcoholic who died in 1975) and in 1959 purchased a resort hotel and started operating it as Chit Chat Farms. Chit Chat has since treated more than 20,000 patients and has become known worldwide. For professionals in chemical dependency treatment, it offers a variety of accredited "training experiences" in rehabilitation treatment, detoxification treatment, and family services.

Chit Chat West

Caron Foundation
27 W. Freeman St.
Robesonia, PA 19551
215-693-5861

Headed by: Richard Miller, Executive Director.
Direct inquiries to: Richard Miller.
Capacity (no. of patients): 48.
Types of patients admitted: Men and women over age 19.
Detoxification program offered?: Yes.
Inpatient treatment program—usual duration: 28 days approximately.
Inpatient treatment program—main features: See Chit Chat Farm listing.
Charges for treatment: Inpatient rehabilitation, $195/day.
For other features: See Chit Chat Farm listing.

Chit Chat Westfield

Caron Foundation
355 Church St.
Westfield, PA 16950
814-367-5901

Headed by: John Flannery, Executive Director.
Direct inquuiries to: John Flannery.
Capacity (no. of patients): 48.
Types of patients admitted: Men and women over age 19.
Detoxification program offered?: Yes (at Soldiers and Sailors Hospital, Wellsboro, Pa.).
Inpatient treatment program—usual duration: 28 days approximately.
Inpatient treatment program—main features: See Chit Chat Farm listing.
Charges for treatment: Inpatient rehabilitation, $195/day.
For other features: See Chit Chat Farm listing.

Livengrin Foundation
4833 Hulmeville Rd.
Bensalem, PA 19020
215-638-5200

Headed by: Richard M. Pine, Executive Director.
Direct inquiries to: Debra Moses.
Capacity (no. of patients): 72 beds.
Types of patients admitted: Inpatient program, men and women ages 18 and up; outpatient programs, minimum age 7.
Detoxification program offered?: Usual duration 3 to 5 days.
Inpatient treatment program—usual duration: 21 to 28 days; average, 24 days.
Inpatient treatment program—main features: "Based on 12 steps of AA, using group and individual counseling, work/recreational therapy, spiritual counseling, special interest groups, psychodrama, aftercare counseling."
Outpatient treatment program: Usual duration, 3 to 6 months. Main features include "evaluations; individual, group, and family counseling; education; 12-week intensive outpatient program."
Family program or services—main features: "5-day residential family program, Saturday Family Program, Children's Program (ages 7 to 12), family sessions/conjoint, outpatient family therapy."
Charges for treatment: Inpatient: rehabilitation, $175/day; detoxification, $205/day. Outpatient: individual counseling, $50/hour; family counseling, $50/hour; group sessions, $25/1½ hours; family program, $35/first family member, $15/each additional member. Residential family program: $550/5 days; Children's Program, $15/day.
Can health-care insurance pay for charges?: Yes.
Accredited by: JCAH; Commonwealth of Pennsylvania, Office of Drug and Alcohol Programs.
Aftercare programs: "Referrals to outpatient counseling, halfway houses, support groups (AA, NA, CA, Al-Anon), Livengrin Alumni Association." Provided without charge.
Multiply addicted among entering patients: 51 percent, average; substances include cocaine, marijuana, amphetamines.
Comments: Has been providing alcoholism/addiction treatment since 1966. Sponsors annual conferences for physicians, nurses, and social workers and conducts industrial training and community service seminars. Located on a 45-acre site in Bucks County, Pennsylvania.

Marworth
Marworth/Waverly
Lily Lake Rd.
Waverly, PA 18471
717-563-1112

Marworth/Shawnee
P.O. Box 98
Shawnee-on-Delaware, PA 18356
717-424-8065

Headed by: Marworth/Waverly, Nicholas Colangelo, Ph.D., President; Marworth/Shawnee, John Leadem, Executive Director.

Direct Inquiries to: Respective location (Waverly; Shawnee).

Capacity (no. of patients): Waverly, seventy-two-bed facility; Shawneee, fifty-six-bed facility.

Types of patients admitted: Men and women, ages 18 and up; Shawnee also admits adolescents ages 14 and up.

Detoxification program offered?: Usual duration, 3 to 5 days.

Inpatient treatment program—usual duration: Adults, 28 to 42 days (depending on whether alcohol-addicted or chemically cross-addicted); Shawnee adolescent program, 42 days.

Inpatient treatment program—main features: "The core of treatment philosophy at Marworth is that the power to stay sober resides in a group rather than in an individual, and patients are therefore encouraged to maintain a strong AA commitment. The treatment program is made up of five tracks: detox, overcoming denial, interaction with peers, aftercare planning, and a family program."

Family program or service—main features: 5-day residential family program. To participate, a family member not need have a relative in treatment at Marworth.

Charges for treatment: Inpatient, $225/day, total $6,300 (28 days) to $9,450 (42 days). Family program (for 5-day program): Waverly, $500/first family member, $250/each additional member; Shawnee $600/first family member, $100/each additional member.

Can health-care insurance pay for charges?: Yes.

Accredited by: JCAH; Commonwealth of Pennsylvania.

Aftercare programs: 12 weeks minimum.

Multiply addicted among entering patients: Substances abused include prescription and street drugs.

Recovery rates: Waverly, 75 percent to 80 percent, 1 year (1988 study; for Shawnee, no outcome study conducted).

RHODE ISLAND

Edgehill Newport
200 Harrison Ave.
Newport, RI 02840
401-849-5700

Headed by: Frank Fanella, President.
Direct inquiries to: John Wallace, Ph.D., Director of Treatment.
Capacity (no. of patients): 160.
Types of patients admitted: Men and women adults ages 18 and up who are alcohol-, polydrug-, and/or chemical-dependent.
Detoxification program offered?: 3 days' average duration; duration variable.
Inpatient treatment program—usual duration: Average 28 days rehabilitation; variable.
Inpatient treatment program—main features: "Emphasis upon a biopsychosocial disease model; emphasis upon group and peer interactional work; consistent with all aspects of the philosophy of Alcoholics Anonymous."
Outpatient treatment program: Usual duration, 30 days. Main features include "group therapy, individual therapy, family therapy, Adult Children of Alcoholics group therapy; adolescent assessment and treatment."
Family program or services—main features: Intensive 3-weekend outpatient program involving considerable amounts of couples therapy.
Charges for treatment: Inpatient, $253/day, rehabilitation, $330/day detoxification, total $8,074. Outpatient, $58/day, total $1,740. Family program, $329/family member (6-day program).
Can health-care insurance pay for charges?: Yes.
Accredited by: JCAH; State of Rhode Island, Department of Mental Health, Retardation, and Hospitals, Division of Substance Abuse Services.
Aftercare programs: Outpatient care in home communities for out-of-area residents; transition group meeting weekly for 12

weeks for local residents; transition group costs, $276 for 12 sessions of 1½ hours each.

Multiply addicted among entering patients: 50 percent; substances include cocaine, marijuana, tranquilizers mainly; small number addicted to opiates. (Data are for inpatient and outpatient entrants; multiply addicted patients are typically "adults, socially stable persons.")

Recovery rates: 68 percent to 70 percent, 6 months; 63 to 65 percent, 1 year. ("Our outcome statistics vary considerably depending upon which patient-population and survey we are considering. We are still compiling vigorously obtained data for periods longer than 1 year.")

SOUTH CAROLINA

Chaps Baker Treatment Center
Baker Hospital
2750 Speissegger Dr.
N. Charleston, SC 29405
803-744-2110, ext. 2931

Headed by: Terry Jorgensen, C.A.D.C., Program Director.
Direct inquiries to: Terry Jorgensen.
Capacity (no. of patients): 44.
Types of patients admitted: Men and women adults.
Detoxification program offered?: Usual duration, 5 days.
Inpatient treatment program—usual duration: 23 days; average total, 28 days.
Inpatient treatment program—main features: "Groups, lectures, films, AA, NA, family program."
Outpatient treatment program: Usual duration, 42 days; main features same as with inpatient program.
Family program or services—main features: Therapy addresses all family issues.
Charges for treatment: Inpatient, $221/day, total $6,200 plus $1,075 physician fee. Outpatient, $96/day, total $3,500. Family program, charge included in patient fees.
Can health-care insurance pay for charges?: Yes. Approved for payment by Medicare.
Accredited by: JCAH.

Aftercare programs: Offered for patient and family members without additional charge.

Multiply addicted among entering patients: 60 percent.

TENNESSEE

Cumberland Heights Alcohol and Drug Treatment Center

P.O. Box 90727, Route 2, River Rd.
Nashville, TN 37209
615-352-1757

Headed by: J. K. Albright, Executive Director.

Direct inquiries to: Mary Ann Quirk, Supervisor, Aftercare/Public Relations.

Capacity (no. of patients): 71.

Types of patients admitted: Men and women adults and adolescents, ages 14 and up.

Detoxification program offered?: Yes; duration varies; offered only as first phase of 30-day program.

Inpatient treatment program—usual duration: 30 days, including detoxification.

Inpatient treatment program—main features: "AA/NA philosophy; group therapy."

Outpatient treatment program: Usual duration, 20 days. Main features: "patient can work and receive treatment in the evening."

Family program or services—main features: 5-day program.

Charges for treatment: Inpatient: adult, $155/day, total $5,000; adolescent, $155/day, total $7,500. Family program, no additional charge.

Can health-care insurance pay for charges?: Yes.

Accredited by: JCAH.

Aftercare programs: Group sessions facilitated by alumni group leaders; available at no additional charge.

Recovery rates: 82 percent, 6 months; 78 percent, 1 year. ("We do not keep aftercare statistics after one year.")

TEXAS

Austin State Hospital, Alcohol and Drug Abuse Treatment Center

4110 Guadalupe
Austin, TX 78751

512-452-0381, ext. 4362

Headed by: Frank Karass, Ph.D., Unit Director.
Direct inquiries to: Juanita Maxfield, Administrative Technician.
Capacity (no. of patients): 48.
Types of patients admitted: Admission only by court commitment; serves 40 Texas counties; admits men and women ages 18 and up.
Detoxification program offered?: No.
Inpatient treatment program—usual duration: 28 days, 7 days evaluation plus 21 days rehabilitation.
Inpatient treatment program—main features: "Group therapy, AA 12-step program, drug/alcohol education, AIDS education, some family counseling."
Charges for treatment: Based on sliding scale; inpatient, $130/day.
Can health-care insurance pay for charges?: Yes. Approved for payment by Medicare, Medicaid.
Accredited by: JCAH.
Aftercare programs: Through State of Texas Department of Mental Health and Retardation, outpatient counseling and some suport groups in patients' home counties.
Multiply addicted among entering patients: 85 percent; substances include alcohol, pot, speed, cocaine, heroin, tranquilizers, barbiturates.

Starlite Village Hospital
P.O. Box 317, Elm Pass Rd.
Center Point, TX 778010
512-634-2212

Headed by: F. E. Searle, M.D., Medical Director.
Direct inquiries to: Annabelle Lindner, Administrator.
Capacity (no. of patients): 37.
Types of patients admitted: Men and women adults and adolescents with alcohol or drug abuse problems and possibly also with psychiatric problems.
Detoxification program offered?: Usual duration, 7 days.
Inpatient treatment program—usual duration: 21 days, alcohol; drugs, 6 weeks including detoxification.
Inpatient treatment program—main features: "The treatment

program is based on the 12 steps of the AA program and the AA 'Big Book.' "

Outpatient treatment program: Usual duration, 30 days. Same features as those of inpatient program.

Family program or services—main features: "Identifying the roles the family members play; breaking through the denial; opening communication between family members."

Charges for treatment: Inpatient, $430/day; outpatient, $105/day.

Can health-care insurance pay for charges?: Yes. Approved for payment by Medicare, Medicaid.

Accredited by: JCAH, Texas Department of Health.

Aftercare programs: "one-year follow-up, and five locations for group meetings; presently, no charge for aftercare."

Multiply addicted among entering patients: 80 percent; substances include alcohol, minor tranquilizers, street drugs.

Comments: Located on a wooded hilltop overlooking the Guadalupe River 50 miles northwest of San Antonio.

UTAH

University of Utah Health Science Center, Alcohol and Drug Abuse Clinic

50 N. Medical Dr.
Salt Lake City, UT 84132
801-581-6228

Headed by: Gary Jorgenson, Ph.D., Psychologist and Clinic Director.

Direct inquiries to: Gary Jorgenson.

Capacity (no. of patients): 130.

Types of patients admitted: For outpatient treatment only, men and women ages 15 and up.

Detoxification program offered?: No.

Outpatient treatment program: Usual duration, 365 days. Main features include: "Psychological workup and individualized treatment plans based on the psychological evaluation."

Family program or services—main features: "Work with families on an as-needed basis."

Charges for treatment: $60/individual session, $30/group session, $350 for evaluation.

Can health-care insurance pay for charges?: Yes.
Accredited by: State of Utah, Division of Alcoholism and Drugs.
Multiply addicted among entering patients: 85 percent; substances include alcohol, drugs of all types.
Recovery rates: 50 to 60 percent, 5 years.

VERMONT

Brattleboro Retreat
75 Linden St.
Brattleboro, VT 05301
801-257-7785

Adult Addictions Division: Ripley Center for Addictions;
Osgood I/II

Headed by: Dr. Valerie Yandow, Division Director.
Direct inquiries to: Glenna Annis, Director of Admissions.
Capacity (no. of patients): Ripley, 24; Osgood, 26.
Types of patients admitted: Men and women ages 18 and up.
Ripley, patients having problems with alcohol and/or other drugs
("no opioids or intravenous drug use"). Osgood, "dual-diagnosis"
patients having alcohol/drug problems and possibly psychiatric
problems.
Detoxification program offered?: Ripley, average duration, 3
days (varies individually). Osgood, average duration, 5 days ("very
individual; can extend greatly, depending on drug").
Inpatient treatment program—usual duration: Ripley, average
20 to 25 days (varies individually). Osgood, average 30 to 34 days
("very individualized").
Inpatient treatment program—main features: Ripley, "Rehab
emphases with complete psychiatric hospital program back-up
and consultation if necessary; AA/NA." Osgood, "Structured, inpatient psychiatric hospital treatment, AA/NA core, three psychiatrists, certified chemical dependency counselors, R.N.s, social
workers, other specialists."
Outpatient treatment program: Ripley, offered through outpatient division of Brattleboro Retreat. Osgood, "individual therapy."
Family program or services—main features: Ripley, "Family
weekend biweekly, didactic/counseling focus, family therapy on

request." Osgood, "Bi-weekly family education weekends, family therapy."

Charges for treatment: Ripley, inpatient, $225/day plus ancillary fees. Osgood, inpatient, $435/day plus ancillary fees.

Can health-care insurance pay for charges?: Yes. Osgood, approved for payment by Medicare.

Accredited by: JCAH. Ripley, State of Vermont Agency of Human Services, Department of Social and Rehabilitation Services. Ripley, State of Vermont hospital program licensure.

Aftercare programs: Ripley, "biweekly aftercare group." Osgood, "referred to home community."

Multiply addicted among entering patients: Ripley, 95 percent; substances include all other than opioids. Osgood, 100 percent.

Adolescent Alcohol and Drug Treatment Program—hospital unit; residential unit (at 104 Linden St.)

Headed by: Stuart Copans, M.D., Medical Director.

Direct inquiries to: Andrew MacFarland.

Capacity (no. of patients): Hospital unit, 14. Residential unit, 8.

Types of patients admitted: Men and women. Hospital unit, ages 13 to 19. Residential unit, ages 12 to 19.

Detoxification program offered?: Hospital unit, yes; duration varies. Residential unit, no.

Inpatient treatment program—usual duration: Varies according to the individual case.

Inpatient treatment program—main features: Hospital unit: "dual-diagnosis focus with strong psychiatric and substance-abuse emphasis; strong family program; strong group, AA, NA, Al-Anon involvement." Residential unit: "Residential dual-diagnosis treatment. Interdisciplinary treatment team headed by psychiatrist; individual, group, and family therapy; strong AA, NA, Al-Anon involvement; family weekend program."

Outpatient treatment program: Hospital unit: "outpatient program provides individual, group, and family therapy."

Family program or services—main features: "Regular family therapy sessions, family weekend program, included in per-day rate."

Charges for treatment: Hospital unit, $475/day; residential unit, $210/day.

Can health-care insurance pay for charges?: Yes.

Accredited by: JCAH. Hospital unit, State of Vermont Department of Health. Residential unit, State of Vermont Department of Social and Rehabilitation Services.

Aftercare programs: Family weekend program.

Multiply addicted among entering patients: 100 percent; wide range of substances abused.

VIRGINIA

Note: See also "DISTRICT OF COLUMBIA METROPOLITAN AREA."

Chit Chat Winchester
Caron Foundation
315 E. Cork St.
Winchester, VA 22601
703-662-8865

Headed by: Bud Stalter, Executive Director.

Direct inquiries to: Bud Stalter.

Capacity (no. of patients): 22.

Types of patients admitted: Men and women adults over age 19.

Detoxification program offered?: Yes.

Inpatient treatment program—usual duration: Approximately 28 days.

Inpatient treatment program—main features: Rehabilitation treatment for chemical dependency.

Charges for treatment: $185/day.

Can health-care insurance pay for charges?: Yes.

Accredited by: JCAH; State of Virginia.

Aftercare programs: "Arranged and determined by patient needs and available resources in patient's home locale."

Comments: For further details concerning treatment and background, see Chit Chat Farm listing in "PENNSYLVANIA" section.

St. John's Hospital
12617 River Rd.
Richmond, VA 23233
804-784-3501

Headed by: Cecelia Burton, Chief Executive Officer.

Direct inquiries to: Admissions Department.

Capacity (no. of patients): 70 beds.

Types of patients admitted: Men and women ages 13 and up.

Detoxification program offered?: Yes; duration varies by individual case.

In-patient treatment program—usual duration: Varies; "patient stays till completion of treatment."

In-patient treatment program—main features: Sole purpose of St. John's Hospital is treatment of alcoholism and chemical dependency; "commitment to spiritual principles contained in the 12 steps of Alcoholics Anonymous." Recovery Services program includes: Phase I (3 to 5 days), physical stabilization, assessment; Phase II (5 to 21 in-patient days), residential treatment; Phase III (3 weeks), intensive outpatient treatment, with family-members participation highly recommended; Phase IV (23 months), once-a-week aftercare group meetings.

Out-patient treatment program: Usual duration, 20 days. Same features as inpatient program; spouse or "concerned person" also attends.

Family program or services—main features: "Concerned persons" learn how "to express feelings in relation to the chemically dependent person—how affected; education group; follow-up program."

Charges for treatment: Inpatient, $350/day. Outpatient, $110/day, total $2,200. Family program, no additional charge.

Can health-care insurance pay for charges?: Yes.

Accredited by: JCAH; State of Virginia Department of Mental Health and Mental Retardation.

Aftercare programs: 16 weeks; groups, counseling; no additional charge.

Multiply-addicted among entering patients: 80 percent; substances include alcohol, narcotics, barbiturates, hallucinogens.

Recovery rates: 85 percent, 6 months. Those who continue their recovery program as the hospital stresses probably maintain the same 85 percent recovery rate 1 year and on after treatment.

Comments: A private, nonprofit facility of the Sisters of Bon Secours, St. John's Hospital is situated on 40 acres of wooded land overlooking the James River 10 miles from Richmond, VA. Patients have access to walking trails, an outdoor exercise course, a gymnasium, and picnic areas by the lake on the grounds.

WASHINGTON

Milam Recovery Centers
14500 Juanita Dr., NE
Bothell, WA 98011
206-823-3116

Headed by: Charles H. Kester, President.
Direct inquiries to: Susan Nichols, Public Relations.
Capacity (no. of patients): 140.
Types of patients admitted: Men and women ages 12 and up (one-third of the patients are women).
Detoxification program offered?: Usual duration, 1 to 5 days (six detoxification beds).
Inpatient treatment program—usual duration: 28 to 35 days (includes detoxification).
Inpatient treatment program—main features: "Disease concept of alcoholism/addiction. AA."
Outpatient treatment program: Three Milam outpatient treatment centers in Washington (see listings). Also three Milam outpatient treatment centers in Alaska. "Most offer 72 hours of intensive treatment and two years of aftercare."
Family program or services—main features: "Complements inpatient treatment. Family Recovery Week offered for "any person whose life has been affected by another person's alcohol and/or drug problems . . . spouses, parents, adolescents, and adult children of alcoholics"; program runs from 5 P.M. Sunday to 12 noon the next Sunday.
Charges for treatment: Inpatient, total $4,872 for 28 days. Outpatient, total $2,160. Family Recovery Week (7 days), $975/family member including lodging and meals.
Can health-care insurance pay for charges?: Yes.
Accredited by: State of Washington, as an alcoholism and drug treatment facility.
Aftercare programs: 22 weeks (cost included in inpatient charges).
Multiply addicted among entering patients: 90 percent; substances include alcohol, cocaine, marijuana, prescription drugs, heroin.
Recovery rates: "77 percent completely abstinent after 4 years."
Comments: Located 20 miles from downtown Seattle on a 50-

acre site of wooded hills northeast of Lake Washington. The Milam Recovery Centers' treatment sequence is based on the findings of Dr. James R. Milam, as set forth in his widely known books (see Appendix 1).

Milam Counseling Centers (offering out-patient treatment programs) in Washington State:

Angle Lake: 19530 Pacific Highway South, Seattle, WA 98188; phone 206-824-9780.

Eastlake: Linbrook Office Park, 10422 N.E. 37th Circle, Suite B, Kirkland, WA 98033; phone 206-822-5095.

Northlake: 17962 Midvale Ave. N., Seattle, WA 98133; phone 206-542-6106.

Residence XII

14506 Juanita Dr., N.E.
Bothell, WA 98011
206-823-8844

Headed by: Chandra Smith, Executive Director.

Direct inquiries to: Val Roney.

Capacity (no. of patients): 24 women.

Types of patients admitted: Women only, ages 19 and up, ambulatory, in early through late stages of chemical dependency.

Detoxification program offered?: Usual duration, 1 to 3 days (in hospital).

Inpatient treatment program—usual duration: 30 to 42 days (6 weeks, polydrug abuse).

Inpatient treatment program—main features: "Spirituality; assertiveness; gender-specific; sexuality; anger management; empowerment of gender."

Outpatient treatment program: Sessions 1½ hours per week for 16 weeks, usual duration; "gender-specific."

Family program or services—main features: "Lectures, group therapy, discussion, films, Al-Anon."

Charges for treatment: Inpatient, $130/day, total $3,900 for 30 days. Outpatient and family programs included in inpatient treatment costs.

Can health-care insurance pay for charges?: Yes.

Accredited by: State of Washington, Bureau of Alcohol and Substance Abuse.

Aftercare programs: "Referred out" after treatment to sources in patient's home locale.

Multiply addicted among entering patients: 75 percent; substances include cocaine, marijuana, prescription drugs. (Data are for patients who are typically women in their late twenties and early thirties.)

Recovery rates: 80 percent, 6 months; 70 percent, one year; 60 percent, 3 years; 60 percent, 5 years.

Comments: Residence XII functions as a "healing center" where "sober living skills are taught."

WEST VIRGINIA

Charleston Area Medical Center (CAMC), Adult Care Unit, Adolescent CareUnit

CAMC General Division
Morris and Washington Streets
Charleston, WV 25301
304-348-6060, Adult CareUnit
304-348-6066, Adolescent CareUnit

Headed by: Andrea S. Wilson, Program Manager.
Direct inquiries to: Andrea S. Wilson.
Capacity (no. of patients): Adult Unit, 25; Adolescent Unit, 20.
Types of patients admitted: Men and women; Adult Unit, ages 18 and up; Adolescent Unit, ages 13 to 17.
Detoxification program offered?: 3 to 5 days (varies by individual case).
Inpatient treatment program—usual duration: Adult Unit, 28 days. Adolescent Unit, 6 to 8 weeks.
Inpatient treatment program—main features: Adult Unit: "Special relapse offerings; Adult Children of Alcoholics groups; aftercare; extensive family program." Adolescent Unit: "Disease concept; AA/NA principles and philosophy; highly structured program; individual and group therapy; level system."
Outpatient treatment program: None.
Family program or services—main feature: Adult and Adolescent Units: "All-day workshops every Saturday; individual family sessions weekly; family discharge planning workshop; two full-time family therapists."
Charges for treatment: Adult Unit, $275/day, $7,420 total. Ado-

lescent Unit, $296/day, $12,432 total. Family program cost included in inpatient charges.

Can health-care insurance pay for charges?: Yes. Adult Unit approved for payment by Medicare.

Accredited by: JCAH; State of West Virginia Department of Health.

Aftercare programs: "Patient aftercare, family aftercare, relapse patient aftercare" provided at no additional cost.

Multiply addicted among entering patients: Adult Unit: 40 percent; substances include alcohol, marijuana, prescription medications. Adolescent Unit: 90 percent; substances primarily alcohol and marijuana.

Recovery rates: Data from *CareUnit Evaluation of Treatment Outcome* (Irvine, Calif.: Comprehensive Care Corp., 1988; 18551 Von Karman Ave., Irvine, CA 92715). The booklet reports on the recovery status of 723 adult CareUnit patients who had remained in treatment at least 5 days and were discharged from a total of fifty CareUnit facilities between January 1 and March 31, 1986. Among significant findings of the research: "61 percent of the sample were categorized as recovering, 43 percent reported total abstinence in the year following discharge and another 18 percent experienced a limited relapse following treatment, but also had at least 6 months' continuous abstinence."

Comments: The CareUnit program is a nationwide network of both freestanding hospitals and contract units in general acute care hospitals that together provide inpatient chemical dependency treatment for some 46,000 adults and adolescents a year. CompCare (Comprehensive Care Corp.) is the program's parent organization.

WISCONSIN

Hazelden Wisconsin Adolescent Program
Clarence Snyder Hall
Route 2, Box 193
Turtle Lake, WI 54889
715-986-4520

Note: Provisions of this program are similar to those of the Hazelden Pioneer House in Minnesota; see entry for "Hazelden

Foundation," segment on "Hazelden Pioneer House," in the "MIN-NESOTA" section.

Meriter Madison General Hospital, NewStart
202 S. Park St.
Madison, WI 53715
608-267-6291

Headed by: Brian Boegel, A.C.S.W., Director.
Direct inquiries to: Brian Boegel.
Capacity (no. of patients): 38.
Types of patients admitted: Men and women ages 18 and up.
Detoxification program offered?: Usual duration, 2 to 10 days.
Inpatient treatment program—usual duration: 21 days (both inpatient hospital and residential).
Inpatient treatment program—main features: "Education; professional, individual, and group therapy; introduction to AA."
Outpatient treatment program: Duration, as needed; typical program runs 4 weeks, with sessions 4 days/week and 4 hours/session.
Family program or services—main features: "Group and individual therapy, and a one-day educational seminar."
Charges for treatment: $230/day hospital, $120/day residential.
Can health-care insurance pay for charges?: Yes. Approved for payment by Medicare, Medicaid.
Accredited by: JCAH; State of Wisconsin Department of Health and Social Services.
Aftercare programs: Weekly group therapy.
Multiply addicted among entering patients: 85 percent; substances abused include "all, except heroin."

WYOMING

DePaul Hospital, Chemical Dependency Center
2600 E. 18th St.
Cheyenne, WY 82001
307-632-6411, ext. 264

Headed by: Victor J. Lisek, Director.
Direct inquiries to: Victor J. Lisek.
Capacity (no. of patients): Seventeen-bed facility.

Types of patients admitted: Men and women ages 19 and up with alcohol and/or drug problems.

Detoxification program offered?: Yes.

Inpatient treatment program—usual duration: 28 days, detoxification and rehabilitation. Relapse program, 10 to 14 days.

Inpatient treatment program—main features: "Alcohol/substance abuser alone has no control (disease); effective treatment must focus on self-worth and program of growth; AA and the 12 steps; love the person—hate the behavior; help, don't fix."

Outpatient treatment program: "Only for former patients. 12 weeks of 2-hour group sessions."

Family program or services—main features: "(1) Involvement at admission; (2) two full-day (16-hour) intensive program; (3) involved in aftercare."

Charges for treatment: $210/day, total $5,880; all-inclusive.

Can health-care insurance pay for charges?: Yes. Approved for payment by Medicare, Medicaid.

Accredited by: JCAH; State of Wyoming Department of Health and Social Services.

Aftercare programs: "12-week, 2-hour group sessions" provided at no additional charge.

Multiply addicted among entering patients: 35 percent; substances include cocaine, marijuana, tranquilizers. (Multiply addicted patients are typically ages 25 to 35; 80 percent men, 20 percent women.)

Recovery rates: 65 percent, 6 months; 50 percent, 2 years (based on Center statistics for the years 1986–1987, 1987–1988).

Directory of Leading Treatment Centers in Canada

ALBERTA

Henwood Treatment Centre
Box 100, RR 6
Edmonton, Alberta T5B 4K3
403-472-6033

Headed by: Betty Roline, Director.

Direct inquiries to: Betty Roline or Bob Hunter, Assistant Director.

Capacity (no. of patients): 76 (64 for primary clients and 12 for family members).

Types of patients admitted: Men and women adults.

Detoxification program offered?: No.

Inpatient treatment program—usual duration: 21 days, rehabilitation.

Outpatient treatment program: None.

Family program or services—main feature: 1-week residential family program.

Charges for treatment: Inpatient program, total $20 user fee. Family program, no charge.

Can health-care insurance pay for charges?: No.

Accredited by: Operated by the Alberta Alcohol and Drug Abuse Commission.

Aftercare programs: 1-week follow-up program occurs 3 months after discharge.

Multiple-addicted among entering patients: 30 percent; substances include alcohol, prescription drugs, cocaine, marijuana.

Lander Treatment Centre
221-42 Avenue West, Box 1330
Claresholm, Alberta T0L 0T0
403-625-3311

Headed by: Robert Hale-Matthews, Manager.

Direct inquiries to: Ruth Towill, Program Manager.

Capacity (no. of patients): 48.

Types of patients admitted: All people over age 14 "experiencing problems with alcohol and/or other drugs, including significant others affected by the problem."

Detoxification program offered?: No.

Inpatient treatment program—usual duration: 21 days, extending over a 3-month period in a unique 3-phase sequence of 2 weeks in residence at Lander (Phase 1), 8 weeks at home with contact maintained by the Lander staff (Phase 2), and 1 week follow-up back at Lander in a residential structured program (Phase 3).

Inpatient treatment program—main features: "Client-centered treatment. Counselors work from an instructional counseling model with expected learning outcomes. Treatment focuses on cognitive restructuring, experiential learning, family involvement, and community support such as AA." Also offered is the "Relapse Prevention Program," a 12-day residential program for clients who have been unable to find success through inpatient treatment programs. Inpatient programs include recreation therapy in which clients are encouraged to attempt new leisure activities in sports, arts, and crafts that could be continued and developed in their home communities.

Family program or services—main features: "Family program for 1 week concurrent with first 2 weeks of inpatient program; complementary to Al-Anon." Participants in family program may or may not have a family member in treatment, but should come from a family that has an active, or recovering, substance abuser.

Charges for treatment: Inpatient program, total $20 (under revision). Family program, total $20/family member.

Can health-care insurance pay for charges?: Yes.

Accredited by: Operated by the Alberta Alcohol and Drug Abuse Commission.

Aftercare programs: "Beyond Sobriety" program offered as a 5-day residential workshop for persons having 18 months or more of continuous abstinence, but who are experiencing some dissatisfaction with the quality of their lives.

Multiple-addicted among entering patients: 30 percent; substances include alcohol, marijuana, cocaine, benzodiazepenes.

Recovery rates: "Abstinence is only one of many goals used to measure success. 33 percent of clients show a substantial reduction in the use of alcohol or drugs, as well as improvement in health, productivity, relationships, etc."

Comments: Lander also provides "practicum" programs of residential training for professionals and addiction workers, and programs of supervised student training for students in nursing, social work, or related educational programs. It is situated "in a scenic, tranquil location . . . where the prairies meet the mountains."

BRITISH COLUMBIA

Pacifica
811 Royal Ave.
New Westminster, British Columbia V3M 1K1
604-525-7461

Headed by: Pauline M. Grey, Ph.D., Executive Director.

Direct inquiries to: Dr. Grey or Intake Worker.

Capacity (no. of patients): 30.

Types of patients admitted: Men and women age 19 and over who have no acute psychiatric disturbance and who have completed physical withdrawal from substance abuse (detoxification) and are physically stabilized.

Detoxification program offered?: No.

Inpatient treatment program—usual duration: 28 days.

Inpatient treatment program—main features: "Group therapy aimed at reducing denial and increasing self-awareness. Family involvement required on 2 specific days . . . The goal of treatment is total abstinence accompanied by a satisfying lifestyle." Treatment components include: a variety of therapeutic techniques; family involvement; introduction to AA; good nutrition and encouragement of regular exercise; and medical care by the program's consulting physician.

Family program or services—main features: Spouses and children over age 5 invited to attend two "family days."

Charges for treatment: Inpatient program, $85/day, total $2,295. Family program, no charge.

Accredited by: Administered by the Fraser Valley Alcoholism Society; funded by the British Columbia Ministry of Health.

Aftercare programs: Referral is made to outpatient facilities.

Multiple-addicted among entering patients: 40 percent.

Recovery rates: In two recent analyses of former patients, it was found that 72 percent and 66.7 percent respectively were alcohol/drug-free 6 months after treatment at Pacifica.

Comments: "The program is suited to those addicted individuals whose lifestyle shows a degree of social stability, usually indicated by current or recent employment."

ONTARIO

Addiction Research Foundation, Clinical Institute
33 Russell St.
Toronto, Ontario M5S 2S1
416-595-6000

Headed by: Mr. E. F. Watson, Director.

Direct inquiries to: Ms. Laura Kue, Intake Coordinator, phone 416-595-6021.

Capacity (no. of patients): Program for the Employed, 16 persons; Detoxification Unit, 20 beds; Medical Ward, 20 beds. Open capacity in: Outpatient and Primary Care Services; Assessment and Follow-Up Unit; Youth Clinic including Young Drug Users Program; Abstinent Lifestyle Treatment Program; Drug Therapy Program; Family and Community Medicine and Ambulatory Services; and Emergency and Walk-In Department.

Types of patients admitted: Inpatients—men and women age 16 or older. Outpatients—males and females of any ages.

Detoxification program offered?: 3–7 days usual duration; spent either in the nonmedical Detoxification Unit or the Medical Ward.

Inpatient treatment programs—usual duration: 21–28 days, in either the Program for the Employed or the Young Drug Users Program.

Treatment programs—main features: Program for the Employed: Open to men and women over age 20; Phase One runs 3 weeks and includes sessions held Monday–Friday 9 a.m.–5 p.m. and attended on a nonresidential basis by those who can commute from home (and on a residential or inpatient basis by others), participation by family members on two family days; Phase Two provides aftercare for one year with monthly evening group meetings and optional additional therapist sessions.

Youth Clinic: Open to individuals ages 16–24 with primary complaint of drug use, or of alcohol if under age 19; includes Young Drug Abusers Program (4-week day or residential treatment with sessions Monday–Friday 8:30 a.m.–5 p.m.), 6-month aftercare with weekly therapist sessions.

Abstinent Lifestyle Treatment Program: Open to individuals of ages 25 and older; includes 3-week day or residential program with sessions Monday–Friday 9 a.m.–5 p.m.

Drug Therapy Program: for patients who report abuse of alcohol, opiate-type narcotics, or prescription drugs and for whom both pharmacologicial and sociobehavioral treatment may be indicated; drug-treatment options include disulfiram (Antabuse), calcium carbimide, methadone, and others as appropriate; average stay in program 6–12 months.

Charges for treatment: Services are free to Ontario residents.

Accredited by: The Foundation is an agency of the Province of Ontario government, and is funded by the Ontario Ministry of Health.

Multiple-addicted among entering patients: 75 percent or more. Percentages of the multiple-addicted by their primary substance of abuse: 60 percent, alcohol; 15 percent, cocaine; 10 percent, cannabis; and 10 percent, opiates.

Comments: The Clinical Institute of the Foundation is a research and teaching hospital affiliated with the University of Toronto. It provides research-based treatment programs for people suffering from physical, social, and psychological problems associated with the use of alcohol or other drugs.

QUEBEC

Domrémy-Montréal
15,693, boul. Gouin
Ste-Genevieve, Quebec H9H 1C3
514-626-7750

Headed by: Mr. Pierre Lamarche, General Director.
Direct inquiries to: Mr. Michel Landry or Mr. Jean Boislard.
Capacity (no. of patients): Inpatients, 85; outpatients, open.
Types of patients admitted: Men and women age 18 and up; functionally francophone.
Detoxification program offered?: No.
Inpatient treatment program—usual duration: 29 days (varies in individual cases from 8 to 32 days).
Inpatient treatment program—main features: "Psycho-sociosanitary approach; under professional care; individual and group therapy."
Outpatient treatment program: Usual duration 6 months; same basic features as inpatient program.
Family program or services—main features: "Services offered to patient's relatives when needed and/or asked for."
Charges for treatment: None.
Accredited by: Quebec Ministry of Social Affairs.
Multiply-addicted among entering patients: 50 percent; substances include alcohol and drugs, illegal or prescription; multiple-addicted are ages 18–65, and 75 percent of them are men.

The Portage Program for Drug Dependencies, Lac Echo Centre
3418 Drummond Street
Montreal, Quebec H3G 1Y1

514-282-0404

Headed by: Dr. Peter Vamos, Executive Director.
Direct inquiries to: Sonia Quimet, Executive Assistant.
Capacity (no. of patients): 100.
Types of patients admitted: Men and women from adolescent ages and up. "Portage residents come from a wide variety of backgrounds. The average age is 26 and most have been on drugs for several years."
Detoxification program offered?: No.
Inpatient treatment program—usual duration: between 8 and 11 months.
Inpatient treatment program—main features: "At Portage, the residents undergo an intensive, highly structured series of therapy sessions and work routines centered around honesty and responsibility, the two fundamental values of the community. Therapeutic techniques include social learning and role modeling, a system of upward mobility, group therapy, and individual counseling." The Lac Echo residential facility is located in a quiet country setting just outside Montreal. It is based on the "therapeutic community" concept of treatment of drug abuse.
Family program or services—main features: "Information/orientation sessions, discussion groups, family groups."
Charges for treatment:"Portage is a public program; the cost is assumed by the Quebec government for all persons living in Quebec. Private clients are charged a fee."
Accredited by: Funded by the Province of Quebec.
Aftercare programs: Group and individual counseling on a regular basis provided by Portage for approximately 1 year as part of its aftercare program.
Multiply-addicted among entering patients: 98 percent; substances include downers, alcohol, cannabis, cocaine, heroin, hallucinogens, and speed. The multiply-addicted are 20 percent women and generally single, and have been abusing drugs for about 7 or 8 years.
Recovery rates: 85 percent, 6 months and 1 year after completing treatment.
Comments: Portage was founded in 1972, and its first staff members received training at the Daytop Village program for drug abuse treatment in New York. With its head office on Drummond Street in Montreal and its original therapeutic community at Lac Echo, Portage also operates: Ste-Famille House, a 16-bed transition

and re-entry facility in Montreal; a 10-bed transition and re-entry house in Toronto; a day-care assessment and re-entry facility in Quebec City; Donnaconna-Portage, the first therapeutic community in a federal maximum-security penitentiary, with 80 beds; the Elora facility, a therapeutic community for male offenders ages 16 and 17, with 50 beds; and Portage Italy, admission and re-entry facilities in Varese and Milan.

Index

319